# The Best of
# Clean Eating2

*Improving your life one meal at a time.*

Mexican Pozole with Roasted Corn & Feta, p. 86

# The Best of
# Clean Eating 2

*Improving your life one meal at a time.*

FROM THE EDITORS OF **Clean Eating** MAGAZINE

**RKP** ROBERT KENNEDY PUBLISHING

Published by Robert Kennedy Publishing
400 Matheson Blvd. West
Mississauga, ON
L5R 3M1 Canada
Visit us at www.rkpubs.com
and www.cleaneating.com

Library and Archives Canada Cataloguing in Publication


    The best of Clean eating 2 : over 200 recipes, with cleaned-up comfort
foods & fast family dinners / editor in chief Alicia Rewega, and editors of
Clean Eating magazine. -- 2nd ed.


Includes index.
ISBN 978-1-55210-097-4


    1. Cooking (Natural foods).  2. Cooking.  3. Reducing diets--Recipes.
I. Rewega, Alicia.  II. Title.  III. Title: Clean eating.


TX741.B48 2011          641.5'63          C2011-903044-6


10 9 8 7 6 5 4 3 2 1

Distributed in Canada by
NBN (National Book Network)
67 Mowat Avenue, Suite 241
Toronto, ON
M6K 3E3

Distributed in USA by
NBN (National Book Network)
15200 NBN Way
Blue Ridge Summit, PA
17214


Printed in Canada

## Robert Kennedy Publishing
# BOOK DEPARTMENT

**MANAGING DIRECTOR**
**Wendy Morley**

**SENIOR EDITOR**
**Amy Land**

**EDITOR, ONLINE AND PRINT**
**Meredith Barrett**

**ASSOCIATE EDITOR**
**Rachel Corradetti**

**ONLINE EDITOR**
**Kiersten Corradetti**

**EDITORIAL ASSISTANTS**
**Sharlene Liladhar, Brittany Seki,
Chelsea Kennedy**

**ART DIRECTOR**
**Gabriella Caruso Marques**

**ASSISTANT ART DIRECTOR**
**Jessica Pensabene Hearn**

**EDITORIAL DESIGNERS**
**Brian Ross, Ellie Jeon**

**PROP/WARDROBE STYLIST**
**Kelsey-Lynn Corradetti**

**MARKETING COORDINATOR**
**Patricia D'Amato**

**INDEXING**
**James De Medeiros**

# Table of Contents

We've made it our goal to gear our recipes to you and your loved ones, and I can assure you that there's something in this book for every palate.

# Introduction

## The Best of the Best!

It's hard to believe a year has gone by since we published our first *Best of Clean Eating* cookbook and even harder to believe it's been four fantastic years of publishing the magazine.

We've learned a lot about our readers in this time, and thanks to the relaunch of our website last year and our social media pages, we've been positively (and pleasantly) bombarded with requests and feedback from you. This has helped tremendously in deciding what to include in this "Best of" cookbook.

One thing you made crystal clear is that you wanted more quick, easy and budget-friendly meals that your entire family will rave about. You reminded us that clean eating is not something you do alone; food is the social glue that bonds your families and brings good friends closer together. Because of that, we've made it our goal to gear our recipes to you and your loved ones, and I can assure you that there's something in this book for every palate – even your picky little eaters.

Inside, you'll find clean twists on exotic meals from around the globe (for the adventurous eater) as well as classic favorites reinvented to suit your clean-eating lifestyle. We were also careful to include a wide variety of options that incorporate a diverse selection of lean proteins to choose from, including meatless and gluten-free fare.

This time around, we categorized your recipes according to meals: breakfasts, lunches, mains, sides, holidays, desserts and more. This way, if you're looking for something specific, you'll spend less time leafing through the pages and more time enjoying a lip-smacking meal at the table with your family.

Another thing we've learned about you is that while you do enjoy the occasional light salad or wrap, you also crave hearty, comforting fare that looks and tastes sinful but is all the while kind to your waistline. You'll find the majority of these handpicked recipes fall within this category. So curl up with a satisfying bowl of comfort tonight and throw the usual post-indulgence guilt to the wind – you won't need it here!

And if there's one thing we know very well about you, it's that you can't get enough of Resident Chef Joanne Lusted's culinary creations. Throughout the table of contents and the pages of this cookbook, look out for the "New!" tag to easily locate the 23 brand-new recipes Chef Jo created exclusively for this book – you will not find them anywhere else! *(Psst: We tried the Baked Lobster & Brie Dip with Lemon Rosemary Crackers (p. 115) and the Chocolate Chip Cookie Dough Chocolate Cake (p. 245) on set during the making of this book and simply couldn't get enough!)*

Every single one of our creations is tested by our wonderful recipe developers, and then put through the wringer again by our dedicated team of reader recipe testers – all to ensure you get the very best results in your own kitchen. Beyond the pure pleasure you get from seeing your family enjoy recipes that they'll never know are healthy (unless you let the secret slip!), I sincerely hope that you enjoy preparing them as much as we did testing and selecting them.

To good food and great health!

Alicia Rewega
Editor in Chief

# Breakfast & Brunch

Breakfast Casserole with Turkey
Sausage & Romano Cheese, p. 16

Breakfast should be nutritious, but it doesn't have to be boring! *Clean Eating* is here to help you by offering nutrient-dense, low-fat, figure-friendly foods without sacrificing taste. From Pecan-Maple Oatmeal to Mango Spice Muffins, we've selected our very best to keep you satisfied until your next clean meal. And don't worry, your kids won't turn their noses up at yummy options like Breakfast Banana Splits and Tex-Mex Morning Pizzas. Get the whole family off to a good morning start.

## Breakfast Banana Splits

*Serves* 4. ***Hands-on time:*** *5 minutes.* ***Total time:*** *5 minutes.*

**It's not just for kids! Perfect for time-pressed adults, this super-quick fruit-and-dairy combo can be tinkered with to suit any taste: Simply swap in a different variety of all-fruit jam (apricot and cherry are must-tries!) or nut (such as toasted unsalted almonds or cashews).**

INGREDIENTS:

- 4 medium bananas
- 2 cups 1% cottage cheese, divided
- 6 Tbsp all-fruit strawberry jam, divided
- ¼ cup roasted peanuts, chopped, divided
- ⅛ tsp sea salt, divided

INSTRUCTIONS:

Peel and cut each banana in half lengthwise. Place 2 banana halves in a shallow dish or bowl (or a deep traveling container if you're off to work). Using an ice-cream scooper, place ½ cup cottage cheese over center of banana and top with 1½ Tbsp jam, 1 Tbsp peanuts and 1 pinch salt. Repeat with remaining ingredients to assemble three more Breakfast Banana Splits. Serve immediately.

*Nutrients per banana split: Calories: 255, Total Fat: 6 g, Sat. Fat: 1.5 g, Monounsaturated Fat: 2.5 g, Polyunsaturated Fat: 1.5 g, Carbs: 44 g, Fiber: 4 g, Sugars: 25 g, Protein: 17 g, Sodium: 460 mg, Cholesterol: 4.5 mg*

NUTRITIONAL BONUS: **Weighing in at only 81 calories, a ½-cup serving of low-fat cottage cheese contains 14 g of muscle-building and -mending protein, along with plenty of vitamin B12, selenium, phosphorus and riboflavin, which also aids in tissue repair and growth.**

# Easy Make-Ahead Breakfast Quiche

*Serves* 4.

This easy morning meal option is versatile enough to allow you to pop in your own favorite produce.

## INGREDIENTS:

- 2 cups chopped mushrooms
- ¾ cup chopped roasted red peppers (from jar), squeezed of liquid
- ½ cup chopped artichoke hearts (in water, not marinated), squeezed of liquid
- ½ cup finely chopped green onions
- 1 Tbsp olive oil
- Liberal sprinkling herbes de Provence
- Olive oil cooking spray
- 6 eggs, lightly beaten (or equivalent egg substitute)
- 1½ oz goat cheese
- ½ oz grated Parmesan

## INSTRUCTIONS:

ONE: Preheat oven to 350°F.

TWO: In a large skillet on medium to medium-high, sauté mushrooms, red peppers, artichoke hearts and onions in olive oil and herbes de Provence until softened and warmed through. Place mixture in a round cake pan, or divide among four large ramekins, either option misted lightly with cooking spray. Cover with eggs and add goat cheese in small drops before sprinkling with Parmesan.

THREE: Cook in oven for 25 minutes or until set. Enjoy or let cool to room temperature, cover and store in fridge. Serve warmed or cold.

*Nutrients per serving (¼ quiche and ½ cup vegetables): Calories: 168, Total Fat: 8 g, Sat. Fat: 3 g, Carbs: 7 g, Fiber: 3 g, Sugars: 2 g, Protein: 17 g, Sodium: 367 mg, Cholesterol: 8 mg*

**Raspberry Jam Omelettes**

**Pear-Cheese Quesadillas**

# Pear-Cheese Quesadillas

*Serves* 4. *Hands-on time:* 8 minutes. *Total time:* 10 minutes.

**Quesadillas are often filled with beans, peppers, chicken and a host of other savory ingredients, making them ideal options for lunch and dinner. Well, we've turned the convention on its head by bringing your favorite south-of-the-border-style sandwich into the early morning hours and filling it with sweeter options to rev up your day.**

## INGREDIENTS:

• 4 whole-grain tortillas (each 10 inches in diameter)

• 2 Tbsp raw honey

• 5 oz low-fat mozzarella cheese, grated (1¼ cups)

• ¼ cup dried currants

• 1 small ripe pear, cored and very thinly sliced

## INSTRUCTIONS:

ONE: Place tortillas on a clean work surface and spread ½ Tbsp honey on each.

TWO: Heat 2 large nonstick skillets on medium. Place 1 tortilla, honey side up, in each skillet and evenly sprinkle each surface with ⅓ cup cheese and then 2 Tbsp currants. Arrange pear slices over top, dividing between 2 tortillas evenly, before sprinkling both tortillas with another ⅓-cup layer of cheese.

THREE: Place remaining 2 tortillas, honey-side down, over each layered tortilla in skillets and gently press with a spatula to "seal." Gently flip quesadillas and cook other side until lightly browned, about 2 minutes. Transfer quesadillas to a cutting board and slice into quarters. Place 2 wedges on each of 4 plates.

Nutrients per 2 wedges (1 quesadilla half): *Calories: 318, Total Fat: 8 g, Sat. Fat: 2.5 g, Carbs: 44 g, Fiber: 4 g, Sugars: 19 g, Protein: 14 g, Sodium: 420 mg, Cholesterol: 12.5 mg*

# Raspberry Jam Omelettes
## WITH CINNAMON YOGURT

*Serves* 4. *Hands-on time:* 10 minutes. *Total time:* 10 minutes.

**If adding fresh orange juice to your omelette is uncharted territory, don't hesitate to give it a try. The addition will infuse your morning meal with a soft citrus flavor – an ideal pick-you-up.**

**OPTION: You can also divide the omelette mixture in half and cook it in two small nonstick skillets.**

## INGREDIENTS:

• ½ cup nonfat plain Greek yogurt

• ⅛ tsp ground cinnamon

• Olive oil cooking spray

• 2 whole large eggs

• 6 large egg whites

• ¼ cup fresh orange juice

• Pinch sea salt

• ⅓ cup all-fruit raspberry jam

## INSTRUCTIONS:

ONE: In a small bowl, blend yogurt and cinnamon; set aside.

TWO: Mist bottom and sides of a medium nonstick skillet with cooking spray and heat on medium.

THREE: In a medium bowl, whisk together whole eggs, egg whites, orange juice and salt. Pour egg mixture into hot pan. Cook, occasionally lifting omelette around edges with a rubber spatula to allow uncooked egg to flow underneath, until egg is no longer runny on surface and bottom is golden, about 6 minutes. Spread jam across surface and gently loosen omelette from pan bottom and sides in order to fold omelette in half. Slide omelette onto a platter and cut into 4 portions. Transfer each portion to a plate and garnish with a dollop of yogurt-cinnamon mixture.

Nutrients per serving (¼ omelette and 2 Tbsp Cinnamon Yogurt): *Calories: 97, Total Fat: 3 g, Sat. Fat: 1 g, Carbs: 35 g, Fiber: 0 g, Sugars: 2 g, Protein: 11 g, Sodium: 156 mg, Cholesterol: 105 mg*

**NUTRITIONAL BONUS: Here's a reason to rethink your "egg whites only" rule: Egg yolks are rich sources of choline, folate, lutein, zeaxanthin and vitamin D, which translate to not only a healthy heart but also to improved sleep and memory, red blood cell production, eye health and blood pressure regulation. Plus, almost half of the high-quality protein found in eggs comes from their yellow core.**

# Breakfast Casserole
## WITH TURKEY SAUSAGE & ROMANO CHEESE

*Serves 6. Hands-on time: 15 minutes. Total time: 1 hour.*

After a quick assembly, this dish can be baked right away or stored tightly sealed in the refrigerator and baked in the morning for a no-fuss breakfast. Or you can be daring and serve it for dinner!

### INGREDIENTS:

- Olive oil cooking spray
- 5 cups cubed (½-inch) whole-grain flax bread
- 1 Tbsp olive oil
- ½ lb all-natural low-fat turkey sausage, meat removed from casing (TIP: Simply omit sausage for a vegetarian option.)
- ¼ cup finely diced sweet onion
- 1½ cups skim milk, divided
- 1 dried chipotle pepper, rehydrated in hot water for 10 minutes, seeded and diced (about 1 Tbsp)
- 6 large egg whites (¾ cup)
- 1 oz Pecorino Romano cheese, finely grated (about ¼ cup), divided
- 2 Tbsp finely chopped fresh parsley
- 2 large plum tomatoes, cut crosswise into 15 slices

**TIP: Dried chipotle peppers can be found in the spice aisle of larger grocery stores and specialty food markets.**

### INSTRUCTIONS:

**ONE:** Preheat oven to 375°F. Lightly mist an 11-cup (2.6 L) casserole dish with cooking spray and line bottom with bread cubes in an even layer; set aside.

**TWO:** Heat oil in a nonstick skillet over medium heat. Add turkey and onion and cook, breaking meat into small pieces with a wooden spoon and stirring until meat is cooked through, about 5 minutes.

**THREE:** Meanwhile, add ¼ cup milk and chipotle to a blender and mix until chipotle is finely chopped. Add remaining 1¼ cups milk and blend. Add egg whites, half of cheese and parsley and pulse until combined. Pour mixture over bread in casserole dish and spoon turkey mixture evenly over top. Finish with an even layer of tomatoes. Using your hands or a rubber spatula, lightly press tomatoes into egg mixture to moisten. Sprinkle with remaining half of cheese and bake until puffed and golden brown on top, about 40 minutes. Serve hot from the oven or at room temperature.

**MAKE AHEAD: This casserole can be assembled completely until ready to bake, covered with plastic wrap and refrigerated for up to 12 hours. Baking time will increase by about 10 minutes when cooking straight from the refrigerator and casserole should be covered with aluminum foil during cooking.**

*Nutrients per 4-oz serving: Calories: 226, Total Fat: 7 g, Sat. Fat: 3 g, Carbs: 23 g, Fiber: 7 g, Sugars: 5 g, Protein: 17 g, Sodium: 483 mg, Cholesterol: 34 mg*

**For a photo of this recipe, see page 10.**

# French Toast
## WITH DARK CHERRY-CITRUS TOPPING

*Serves 4. Hands-on time: 11 minutes. Total time: 17 minutes.*

While the thought of French toast may make your mouth water, traditional recipes often call for the bread to be cooked in oil and slathered with butter. And, if over-dipped, the bread can become fragile and fall apart (especially if you opt for low-cal breads). So, we've come up with an easy way to coat and cook your French toast while controlling calories significantly.

### INGREDIENTS:

**TOPPING**

- 4 oz frozen dark sweet cherries, thawed and quartered
- 4 dried apricot halves, diced
- 1 tsp orange zest
- ½ tsp pure vanilla extract
- 1 to 2 packets stevia
- ½ cup nonfat plain Greek yogurt
- Pinch ground cinnamon

**TOAST**

- 1 Tbsp safflower oil
- 3 large eggs
- 2 egg whites
- 1 tsp orange zest
- 4 1-oz slices reduced-calorie whole-grain bread

### INSTRUCTIONS:

**ONE:** Prepare topping: In a small saucepan, combine ¼ cup water, cherries and apricots and bring to boil on medium-high heat. Boil for 20 to 30 seconds to reduce mixture slightly. Remove from heat, stir in orange zest, vanilla and stevia; cover and set aside.

**TWO:** Prepare toast: Heat oil in a large nonstick skillet over medium. In a shallow pan, such as a pie pan, whisk eggs, egg whites and orange zest. Working quickly, dip each slice of bread into egg mixture and place on a plate until all slices have been coated. Slide bread slices (instead of lifting off the plate) into skillet and cook for 3 minutes per side or until golden.

**THREE:** To serve, divide cherry mixture evenly among bread slices, then top with yogurt and cinnamon.

*Nutrients per serving (1 slice toast, 2 Tbsp topping, 2 Tbsp yogurt): Calories: 210, Total Fat: 8 g, Sat. Fat: 1.5 g, Monounsaturated Fat: 4 g, Polyunsaturated Fat: 1 g, Carbs: 23 g, Fiber: 4 g, Sugars: 5 g, Protein: 12 g, Sodium: 89 mg, Cholesterol: 158 mg*

French Toast with Dark Cherry-Citrus Topping

Baby
Spinach
Goat Cheese
Omelettes

# Pecan-Maple Oatmeal
## WITH BANANAS & CINNAMON

*Serves 4.* ***Hands-on time:*** *5 minutes.* ***Total time:*** *8 minutes.*

**Thanks to the addition of ripe bananas in this recipe, a drizzle of pure maple syrup and a bit of sweet nuttiness from toasted pecans are enough to flavor this warm bowl of comfort.**

### INGREDIENTS:

- ⅛ tsp sea salt
- 2 cups quick-cooking oats
- 2 medium ripe bananas, sliced, divided
- 1 tsp ground cinnamon, plus additional to taste
- 2 tsp pure vanilla extract
- 2 to 3 packets stevia
- ¼ cup chopped unsalted pecan pieces, toasted
- 4 tsp pure maple syrup

### INSTRUCTIONS:

ONE: In a large saucepan, bring 3¾ cups water and salt to a boil. Stir in oats and half of bananas, reduce heat to low to maintain a low simmer, and cook for 3 minutes, uncovered, stirring occasionally.

TWO: When water has been absorbed and oats are thick, remove from heat and stir in remaining bananas, cinnamon, vanilla and stevia. Serve topped with pecans and maple syrup, dividing both evenly. If desired, sprinkle lightly with additional cinnamon.

*Nutrients per 1-cup serving: Calories: 298, Total Fat: 8 g, Sat. Fat: 0.5 g, Monounsaturated Fat: 3 g, Polyunsaturated Fat: 1.5 g, Carbs: 49 g, Fiber: 7 g, Sugars: 13 g, Protein: 7 g, Sodium: 61 mg, Cholesterol: 0 mg*

# Baby Spinach Goat Cheese Omelettes
## WITH HONEY TOAST

*Serves 4.* ***Hands-on time:*** *6 minutes.* ***Total time:*** *16 minutes.*

**With the creamy rich taste of goat cheese and the pop of color from the spinach, "doable upscale" is a term that perfectly describes this sophisticated yet easy to prepare dish.**

### INGREDIENTS:

- 4 1-oz slices reduced-calorie whole-grain bread
- Fresh ground black pepper, to taste, optional
- 4 tsp raw honey

**OMELETTES**

- 3 large eggs
- 4 egg whites
- ¼ cup skim milk
- 2 tsp safflower oil, divided

**FILLING**

- 2 cups baby spinach, divided
- 4 scallions, bulbs removed, white and green parts finely chopped, divided
- ½ tsp dried rosemary, divided
- ¼ tsp red pepper flakes, divided
- 2 oz goat cheese, crumbled, divided
- ¼ tsp sea salt, divided

### INSTRUCTIONS:

ONE: Preheat oven to 200°F. Prepare omelettes: In a medium bowl, whisk together eggs, egg whites and milk. In a small nonstick skillet on medium, heat 1 tsp oil, tilting skillet to coat bottom lightly. Add half of egg mixture to skillet, tilting to cover bottom of skillet evenly. Cook eggs for 5 to 6 minutes. As eggs begin to set, gently lift edge of omelette with a spatula and tilt skillet so uncooked portion flows underneath.

TWO: Once egg mixture is set, remove from heat and spoon half of each of the filling ingredients over half of omelette: spinach, scallions, rosemary, pepper flakes, cheese and salt. Loosen omelette with spatula and fold half over filling ingredients. Slide omelette onto serving plate and place in oven to keep warm. Repeat with remaining half of egg mixture, 1 tsp oil and filling ingredients. (NOTE: You may need to reduce heat to medium-low for second batch if bottom begins to brown too quickly.)

THREE: Toast bread. To serve, cut each omelette in half and divide among 4 plates. Season each with pepper, if desired. Drizzle 1 tsp honey over each piece of toast.

*Nutrients per serving (½ omelette, 1 slice toast, 1 tsp honey): Calories: 257, Total Fat: 11 g, Sat. Fat: 4 g, Monounsaturated Fat: 4 g, Polyunsaturated Fat: 2 g, Carbs: 22 g, Fiber: 3 g, Sugars: 9 g, Protein: 17 g, Sodium: 447 mg, Cholesterol: 218 mg*

# Mango Spice Muffins

*Serves 12. **Hands-on time:** 20 minutes. **Total time:** 40 minutes.*

No need to worry about white whole-wheat flour: It's not bleached but, rather, made from naturally pale spring wheat. It also has a finer grind than traditional whole-wheat flour, resulting in a lighter texture and milder flavor in baked goods.

## INGREDIENTS:

- 2 cups white whole-wheat flour
  (TRY: King Arthur 100% Organic White Whole Wheat Flour)
- ½ cup organic evaporated cane juice
- 2 tsp baking powder
- ½ tsp baking soda
- 1 tsp ground ginger
- ¼ tsp ground cloves
- ½ tsp sea salt
- 1 large egg
- ¼ cup safflower oil
- 8 oz nonfat plain Greek yogurt
- ¼ cup plus 2 Tbsp low-fat milk
- 1 tsp pure vanilla extract
- 1 large semi-firm mango, peeled and
  cut into ¼-inch dice (1¼ cups)
- ¼ cup unsweetened golden raisins
- 2 Tbsp unsweetened shredded or flaked coconut

## INSTRUCTIONS:

ONE: Ensure that a rack is positioned in the center of the oven and preheat to 375°F. Line a standard 12-cup muffin pan with paper liners (or coat with olive oil cooking spray). In a large bowl, whisk together flour, cane juice, baking powder, baking soda, ginger, cloves and salt. In a separate large bowl, beat egg. Add oil, yogurt, milk and vanilla to bowl with egg and whisk to combine.

TWO: Add wet ingredients to dry ingredients and stir gently until flour is moistened. Fold in mango and raisins until evenly distributed (do not over mix; batter will be thick). Spoon batter evenly into prepared muffin cups and sprinkle with coconut, dividing evenly.

THREE: Bake until edges are light golden brown and a tester comes out clean when inserted in the center of a muffin, 16 to 18 minutes. Let cool in pan for 5 minutes, then remove muffins and transfer to a cooling rack. Serve warm or at room temperature. Muffins are best the day they are made.

*Nutrients per muffin: Calories: 200, Total Fat: 6 g, Sat. Fat: 1 g, Monounsaturated Fat: 1 g, Polyunsaturated Fat: 4 g, Carbs: 31 g, Fiber: 3 g, Sugars: 12 g, Protein: 6 g, Sodium: 104 mg, Cholesterol: 18 mg*

# Peachy Dutch Pancake

*Serves 6. **Hands-on time:** 15 minutes. **Total time:** 30 minutes.*

Baked in a skillet, this simple dish looks like a giant popover and tastes more like a crêpe than a heavy American pancake.

## INGREDIENTS:

- 3 large eggs
- ¾ cup low-fat milk
- 2 Tbsp organic evaporated cane juice
- ½ tsp pure vanilla extract
- ¼ tsp plus a pinch sea salt
- Large pinch ground nutmeg
- ½ cup whole-wheat pastry flour
- 2 Tbsp natural buttery spread (TRY: Earth Balance Buttery
  Spread with Olive Oil), cut into 4 chunks
- 1 cup frozen peach slices, thawed and patted dry
- 2 Tbsp sliced unsalted almonds
- Juice ½ lemon

## INSTRUCTIONS:

ONE: Place a heavy, 12-inch ovenproof or cast-iron skillet in oven and preheat to 425°F.

TWO: In a large bowl, lightly beat eggs. Add milk, cane juice, vanilla, salt and nutmeg; whisk to combine. Add flour and whisk just until blended (a few lumps are fine). Open oven door and carefully add buttery spread to skillet. Close oven while spread melts, 1 to 2 minutes. Wearing a heat-proof glove or oven mitt, remove skillet from oven and pour melted spread into batter; whisk just until blended (do not over mix).

THREE: Pour batter into hot skillet and arrange peach slices over top. Carefully return skillet to oven and bake until edges are puffed and golden brown, 17 to 19 minutes.

FOUR: Meanwhile, heat another skillet on medium. Add almonds and cook until golden brown, stirring often to prevent burning, 4 to 5 minutes. When pancake is done, sprinkle with almonds and drizzle with lemon juice. Bring pancake to table right away (so everyone can admire it before it deflates); slice and serve.

*Nutrients per serving (⅙ of pancake): Calories: 159, Total Fat: 8 g, Sat. Fat: 2 g, Monounsaturated Fat: 3 g, Polyunsaturated Fat: 2 g, Carbs: 17 g, Fiber: 2 g, Sugars: 8 g, Protein: 6 g, Sodium: 174 mg, Cholesterol: 108 mg*

Peachy Dutch Pancake

Cocoa Spiced Lattes p. 261

Mango Spice Muffins

22

Tex-Mex
Morning
Pizzas

# Tex-Mex Morning Pizzas

**Serves** 4. **Hands-on time:** 12 minutes. **Total time:** 15 minutes.

**Making your own spicy bean mixture means you won't have to rely on prepared refried beans, which often contain whopping amounts of sodium and even lard. If you want to make this breakfast even heartier (and you have a few more minutes to spare), dish up a poached egg alongside each two-pizza serving.**

## INGREDIENTS:

- 4 whole-grain English muffins, each split in half
- 1½ cups cooked or low-sodium canned pinto beans, drained and rinsed (NOTE: Always opt for BPA-free cans.)
- ¾ cup fresh low-sodium tomato salsa (medium or hot, depending on your tastes), divided
- 2 Tbsp chopped fresh cilantro
- ½ tsp ground cumin
- ½ tsp ground chile powder
- 4 oz low-fat cheddar cheese, shredded (1 cup)

## INSTRUCTIONS:

ONE: Arrange broiler rack on highest position in oven and preheat broiler to high.

TWO: Lightly toast English muffins in toaster or toaster oven.

THREE: In a medium bowl, combine beans, ¼ cup salsa, cilantro, cumin and chile powder. Gently mash mixture with a potato masher or fork until it is chunky but sticks together. Divide mixture into 4 equal portions.

FOUR: Spread half of each portion of bean mixture over craggy side (interior) of each English muffin half. Place halves, bean side up, on a foil-lined baking sheet and top with cheese, dividing evenly. Broil for 3 to 4 minutes or until cheese bubbles. Serve each pizza half with 1 Tbsp salsa.

*Nutrients per 2 pizzas (2 topped English muffin halves): Calories: 297, Total Fat: 4 g, Sat. Fat: 1 g, Carbs: 48 g, Fiber: 9 g, Sugars: 3 g, Protein: 19.5 g, Sodium: 542 mg, Cholesterol: 6 mg*

# The Mack Muffin

**Serves** 1. **Hands-on time:** 10 minutes. **Total time:** 20 minutes.

**Our Associate Art Director Jennifer MacKenzie simply *had* to create this *Clean Eating* twist on the popular fast-food breakfast sandwich (she definitely has the right name for it!). You'll love the way the spicy kick will rev up your metabolism and taste buds.**

## INGREDIENTS:

- White vinegar, as needed
- 1 large egg
- Olive oil cooking spray
- 1 cup spinach
- 1 whole-wheat English muffin
- 1 Tbsp light cream cheese
- 1 slice tomato
- Sea salt and fresh ground black pepper, to taste
- 1 tsp hot sauce, optional (TRY: Sriracha chile sauce)

## INSTRUCTIONS:

ONE: Bring a large, deep saucepan with at least 5 or 6 cups of water to a boil. Add about 1 tsp vinegar for every cup of water. (Taste to make sure the amount is correct – vinegar should be barely noticeable.) Lower heat to a slow simmer. Carefully crack egg into a teacup or large ladle. Lower teacup or ladle into water and pour egg out as gently as possible, careful not to break yolk. Egg white will coagulate in water and turn white. Cook until egg white is formed and set and yolk begins to thicken but is not hard, 3 to 4 minutes. Remove egg with a slotted spoon or strainer; set aside.

TWO: Heat a medium nonstick pan over medium heat and mist with cooking spray. Once pan is hot, add spinach and sauté for 1 to 2 minutes, until slightly wilted. Remove spinach from pan and set aside.

THREE: Toast English muffin. To assemble, spread ½ Tbsp cream cheese on each half of English muffin. Place spinach on bottom half of English muffin, then add poached egg and tomato. Season with salt and pepper. Finish with hot sauce, if desired, before topping with other half of English muffin.

*Nutrients per assembled muffin: Calories: 243, Total Fat: 8.5 g, Sat. Fat: 3 g, Carbs: 31 g, Fiber: 5.5 g, Sugars: 8 g, Protein: 14 g, Sodium: 416 mg, Cholesterol: 218 mg*

**NUTRITIONAL BONUS: A superfood must-have, spinach contains impressive amounts of vitamin A for healthy eyesight and the mineral folate for cell reproduction – respectively 56% and 15% of your daily need in just 1 cup of the raw leafy green.**

# Multigrain Pancakes
## WITH RASPBERRIES & RICOTTA SAUCE

*Serves 4.* *Hands-on time:* *10 minutes.* *Total time:* *20 minutes.*

### INGREDIENTS:

- 1¼ cups white whole-wheat flour
- ½ cup spelt flour
- ¼ cup wheat germ
- ½ cup regular oatmeal, ground
- 1 tsp Sucanat
- ⅛ tsp sea salt
- ¼ tsp baking soda
- 1 tsp baking powder
- 1 egg
- 1 egg white
- 1 cup low-fat buttermilk
- 1 cup unsweetened plain soy milk
- Olive oil cooking spray
- 1 cup raspberries

### RICOTTA SAUCE

- ½ cup nonfat plain Greek yogurt
- ½ cup low-fat ricotta cheese
- 2 Tbsp pure maple syrup
- ⅛ tsp ground cinnamon

### INSTRUCTIONS:

ONE: Prepare pancakes: In a medium bowl, mix both flours, wheat germ, oatmeal, Sucanat, salt, baking soda and baking powder. In a smaller bowl, whisk together egg and egg white, buttermilk and soy milk until foamy. Pour wet ingredients into dry and mix until well-blended; let sit for 5 minutes so flours have time to absorb liquid (mixture will thicken).

TWO: Prepare ricotta sauce: In a small bowl, combine yogurt, ricotta, maple syrup and cinnamon with a whisk until smooth and creamy.

THREE: Heat a griddle or large skillet over medium-high (about 350°F) and coat with cooking spray. Pour pancake batter onto griddle in large spoonfuls (4 inches in diameter). Cook until bubbles form around edges, about 3 minutes. Flip and cook for another 2 to 3 minutes.

FOUR: To serve, stack pancakes evenly among plates, drizzle with ¼ cup ricotta sauce and top with ¼ cup raspberries. Serve immediately.

**TIP: If you'd like a thinner sauce, simply add water, 1 Tbsp at a time.**

Nutrients per serving (about 4 pancakes, ¼ cup raspberries, ¼ cup ricotta sauce): *Calories: 408, Total Fat: 6 g, Sat. Fat: 2 g, Monounsaturated Fat: 1 g, Polyunsaturated Fat: 1 g, Carbs: 70 g, Fiber: 10 g, Sugars: 17 g, Protein: 23 g, Sodium: 350 mg, Cholesterol: 13 mg*

# Tomato & Scallion Breakfast Melts

*Serves 4.* *Hands-on time:* *8 minutes.* *Total time:* *11 minutes.*

**These versatile melts can be enjoyed with a knife and fork at your kitchen table or eaten on the go. They're easier to eat than a sandwich and will free up your other hand to jot down the day's to-do list. And this recipe can be easily converted to a lunch or dinner option, making it the poster-melt for multipurpose meals!**

### INGREDIENTS:

- 4 whole-grain English muffins, split
- ¼ cup nonfat plain Greek yogurt
- 1½ Tbsp Dijon mustard
- 1 Tbsp extra-virgin olive oil
- ½ tsp dried oregano
- ⅛ tsp sea salt
- 2 oz low-fat sharp cheddar cheese, grated (about ½ cup)
- ½ cup grape tomatoes, quartered
- 4 scallions, bulbs removed, white and green parts finely chopped

### INSTRUCTIONS:

ONE: Preheat broiler to high. Place muffins, cut side up, on a baking sheet and broil for 2 minutes or until beginning to lightly brown on edges.

TWO: In a small bowl, whisk together yogurt, Dijon, oil, oregano and salt. Spoon equal amounts of mixture (about 1½ tsp) onto each muffin half, spreading evenly to coat. Sprinkle with cheese, tomatoes and scallions, dividing each evenly. Broil for 1 to 1½ minutes or until cheese has melted.

Nutrients per serving (2 topped muffin halves): *Calories: 230, Total Fat: 6 g, Sat. Fat: 1 g, Monounsaturated Fat: 3 g, Polyunsaturated Fat: 1 g, Carbs: 34 g, Fiber: 2 g, Sugars: 2 g, Protein: 11 g, Sodium: 563 mg, Cholesterol: 3 mg*

Tomato &
Scallion
Breakfast
Melts

Stove-Top
Potato &
Apple
Breakfast
Frittata

# Stove-Top Potato & Apple Breakfast Frittata

*Serves* 4. ***Hands-on time:*** *30 minutes.* ***Total time:*** *45 minutes.*

**Adding crunchy and colorful vegetables to a traditional Spanish frittata of potatoes, eggs and onions makes this hearty breakfast even more satisfying – not to mention nutritious.**

### INGREDIENTS:

- ¼ lb Idaho or Yukon gold potatoes, peeled
- 3 tsp olive oil, divided
- 4 eggs
- 4 egg whites
- 2 medium carrots, peeled and grated
- 2 stalks celery, minced, leaves reserved and minced, divided
- ½ tsp sea salt
- ½ cup peeled and grated jicama, placed in a bowl of cold water to prevent it from browning
- 1 large firm Gala or Fuji apple, unpeeled
- ½ Spanish onion, sliced into thin rounds

### INSTRUCTIONS:

ONE: Thinly slice potatoes by cutting them in half, placing them flat side down on a cutting board, and then using a very sharp knife to make thin, even slices. As you finish cutting the potato halves, push the slices back together to prevent them from browning.

TWO: Heat 1 tsp oil in a 10- or 12-inch thick-bottomed nonstick pan on medium-high for 1 minute. Add potatoes in a thin layer, so each slice is touching pan's surface. Cook potatoes undisturbed for 5 minutes, then flip each slice over and cook for another 4 minutes, until edges are brown and centers nearly translucent. Work in batches, placing each round of cooked potatoes on a cool plate and setting them aside.

THREE: Meanwhile, crack eggs and egg whites into a large bowl and break up yolks with a fork. Stir in carrots, celery stalks and salt. Squeeze water out of jicama and stir jicama into egg mixture.

FOUR: While last batch of potatoes is cooking, thinly slice apple. Transfer final batch of potatoes onto a cool plate and set aside. Then add 1 tsp oil, apple and onion to same pan used to cook potatoes. Reduce heat to medium and cook for 5 minutes, stirring occasionally, until apple and onion slices are nearly translucent.

FIVE: Add potatoes to egg mixture then stir in apple and onion. Add remaining 1 tsp oil to same pan, pour in egg mixture and cover. Cook over medium heat for 15 minutes or until edges brown and begin to pull away from pan. During cooking, slip a heatproof spatula around edge of frittata once or twice to make sure it isn't sticking. Invert frittata by removing the pan from the heat, placing a large plate over the pan and flipping frittata onto plate. Slide frittata back into pan, uncooked-side-down, and cook, uncovered, for 5 more minutes. Slide frittata out of pan and onto serving plate. Garnish with reserved celery leaves.

Nutrients per serving (¼ of frittata): *Calories: 246, Total Fat: 8 g, Sat. Fat: 2 g, Monounsaturated Fat: 4 g, Polyunsaturated Fat: 1 g, Carbs: 30 g, Fiber: 5 g, Sugars: 10 g, Protein: 13 g, Sodium: 422 mg, Cholesterol: 211 mg*

# Strawberry-Vanilla Millet Porridge

*Serves* 4. ***Hands-on time:*** *2 minutes.* ***Total time:*** *17 minutes.*

***Clean Eating*** **Graphic Designer Pamela Graver created this recipe as a weekend alternative to the oatmeal she enjoys Monday through Friday. She loves it not only because it's quick to make and can be easily modified using different ingredients, but also because, as she says, "Any breakfast that includes maple syrup and strawberries is a winner with me!"**

### INGREDIENTS:

- Pinch sea salt
- 1 cup dry millet (not millet flour)
- 1 cup strawberries, quartered
- 4 Tbsp pure maple syrup
- 2 to 4 tsp pure vanilla extract
- Skim milk or unsweetened almond milk, as desired

### INSTRUCTIONS:

ONE: In a pot, bring 3 cups water and salt to a boil.

TWO: Stir in millet and reduce heat to low, maintaining a low simmer. Cover and cook for 15 minutes, stirring occasionally. About 5 minutes before millet is finished cooking, stir in strawberries so they can stew and release their juices into the porridge.

THREE: When water has been absorbed and porridge is thick, remove from heat and stir in maple syrup and vanilla. If porridge is still thicker than you'd prefer, add a splash of milk to reach your desired consistency.

**NOTE: Make sure to wait until porridge is quite thick before stirring in maple syrup and vanilla. If not, the mixture will thin out. Only then add milk, if desired.**

**SUBSTITUTIONS: Try apples and cinnamon in place of strawberries and vanilla extract.**

Nutrients per 1-cup serving: *Calories: 265, Total Fat: 2 g, Sat. Fat: 0.25 g, Carbs: 53 g, Fiber: 5 g, Sugars: 15 g, Protein: 6 g, Sodium: 35 mg, Cholesterol: 0 mg*

**NUTRITIONAL BONUS: A seed most commonly used as a cereal in Asia and Africa, millet is rich in iron, potassium, magnesium, calcium, manganese, fiber and the whole vitamin B family. In fact, a single helping of our hearty breakfast porridge fulfills about 10% or more of your daily quotas for thiamine (B1), riboflavin (B2), niacin (B3) and B6.**

Crispy Chicken Sandwich
with Lemon Dill Yogurt, p. 30

# Sandwiches

Sandwiches and clean eating need not be mutually exclusive. Not only are these offerings convenient, portable and downright tasty, they're also super-simple to assemble, making mealtime quick and easy. In the following pages, you'll find 14 gourmet options – including subs, sliders, muffulettas and more – that will be as good to your wallet as they are to your waistline.

# Crispy Chicken Sandwich
## WITH LEMON DILL YOGURT

*Serves* 4. ***Hands-on time:*** *15 minutes.* ***Total time:*** *15 minutes.*

**Knowing what to request at the meat counter will save you loads of sandwich prep time in the kitchen: Ask your butcher for quarter-inch-thick chicken cutlets or scaloppine. Using thin cuts instead of thick, whole chicken breasts can cut your cooking time in half!**

**INGREDIENTS:**
- ⅓ cup nonfat plain Greek yogurt
- 3 Tbsp chopped fresh dill
- 1 Tbsp fresh lemon juice
- ¼ tsp each sea salt and fresh ground black pepper, divided
- 4 egg whites
- 1 tsp Dijon mustard
- 1 cup whole-wheat panko bread crumbs
- ⅓ cup whole-wheat flour
- 4 4-oz boneless, skinless chicken cutlets, pounded ¼ inch thick
- 1 Tbsp olive oil
- 4 thin whole-grain sandwich buns, toasted
- 2 cups watercress, trimmed
- ½ English cucumber, thinly sliced
- 2 jarred roasted red peppers, drained and sliced

**INSTRUCTIONS:**

**ONE:** In a small bowl, whisk together yogurt, dill and lemon juice. Season with ⅛ tsp each salt and pepper; set aside.

**TWO:** In a separate small bowl, whisk together egg whites, Dijon and remaining salt and pepper; set aside. Transfer panko to a shallow pan or plate. Transfer flour to a second shallow pan or plate.

**THREE:** Dredge each chicken cutlet in flour, shaking off excess, then in egg white mixture. Press cutlets gently into panko and transfer to a baking tray or plate.

**FOUR:** Heat oil in a nonstick skillet on medium-high. Working in batches if necessary, sear breaded chicken cutlets for 3 to 4 minutes per side, until golden brown and fully cooked. Transfer to a paper-towel-lined plate.

**FIVE:** Assemble sandwiches: Split buns and spread yogurt-lemon mixture onto cut sides of bread, dividing evenly. Layer bottom half of each bun with 1 chicken cutlet and even amounts of watercress, cucumber and roasted peppers. Cover with top half of each bun and serve immediately.

**Nutrients per sandwich:** *Calories: 348, Total Fat: 7 g, Sat. Fat: 1 g, Monounsaturated Fat: 3.5 g, Polyunsaturated Fat: 2 g, Carbs: 34 g, Fiber: 5 g, Sugars: 4 g, Protein: 37 g, Sodium: 500 mg, Cholesterol: 65 mg*

**For a photo of this recipe, see page 28.**

# Inside-Out Cheese Sliders

*Serves 4.* **Hands-on time:** *15 minutes.* **Total time:** *25 minutes.*

**By using your broiler, you can easily cook up all of these petite patties at once. If you use a skillet, consider cooking the burgers in two batches – a strategy that eliminates overcrowding the pan, which would cause the patties to steam instead of developing a flavorful golden exterior.**

## INGREDIENTS:

- 1 lb 95% lean ground beef
- ¼ tsp each sea salt and fresh ground black pepper
- 1 oz reduced-fat cheddar cheese, cut into ⅓-inch cubes (scant ¼ cup)
- 3 Tbsp whole-grain mustard
- 1 Tbsp raw honey
- 8 small whole-wheat dinner rolls
- ½ cup packed baby spinach leaves

## INSTRUCTIONS:

ONE: Place oven rack 6 to 7 inches from broiler and preheat to high. Cover a baking sheet or broiler pan with foil. In a large bowl, combine beef, salt and pepper. Divide meat into 8 equal balls, about 2 inches in diameter. Divide cheese into 8 equal portions.

TWO: With your thumb, make an indentation in 1 of the meatballs and insert a portion of cheese cubes. Push the edges of the meatball over the indentation to completely cover the cheese (this prevents the cheese from leaking out during cooking), then flatten the meatball into a ½- to ¾-inch-thick patty; place on prepared baking sheet. Repeat with remaining meatballs and portions of cheese.

THREE: Broil until tops of patties are deeply browned, 6 to 7 minutes. Flip and broil until the second side is browned and patties are firm to the touch with no pink remaining in the center, about 5 more minutes (internal temperature should read 160°F on an instant-read thermometer).

FOUR: In a small bowl, stir together mustard and honey. To serve, split open each roll and spread on 1 tsp mustard mixture. Top with 1 patty and spinach leaves, dividing equally among all sliders.

*Nutrients per 2 sliders: Calories: 359, Total Fat: 9.5 g, Sat. Fat: 2.5 g, Monounsaturated Fat: 2 g, Polyunsaturated Fat: 0.5 g, Carbs: 37 g, Fiber: 4 g, Sugars: 8 g, Protein: 32 g, Sodium: 533 mg, Cholesterol: 61 mg*

Mushroom Melts

THE BEST OF CLEAN EATING 2

# Mushroom Melts

*Serves* 4. **Hands-on time:** *15 minutes.* **Total time:** *20 minutes.*

The flavor of melted cheese and savory mushrooms, plus the satisfaction of watching your kids eat their broccoli without complaint: Could you ask for anything more at lunchtime?

## INGREDIENTS:

- ½ lb broccoli florets
- 1 lb portobello mushrooms, cut into ½-inch-thick slices
- ½ Spanish onion, sliced into rounds
- 2 tsp extra-virgin olive oil
- 8 1-oz slices whole-wheat bread
- Sprinkling dried thyme
- Sprinkling dried basil
- 4 oz sliced part-skim mozzarella cheese

## INSTRUCTIONS:

ONE: Fill a medium pot one-third full of water and place over high heat. When water comes to a boil, add broccoli, reduce heat to medium and simmer for 5 minutes; drain and set aside.

TWO: Meanwhile, in a nonstick pan, sauté mushrooms and onion in oil over medium heat for about 5 minutes, until mushrooms are soft and onion is translucent. Remove from heat and set aside.

THREE: Build sandwich: Place a quarter of mushroom mixture onto each of 4 slices of bread. Then add 2 oz broccoli and sprinkle with thyme and basil. Finish each with 1 oz mozzarella and top slice of bread.

FOUR: Toast sandwiches in a toaster oven (or bake at 250°F) for about 3 to 5 minutes, until cheese is melted and bread is golden brown on the bottom. Sandwiches baked in a standard oven will cook for 5 to 7 minutes.

**TIP: If possible, use a toaster oven in lieu of your oven. The cheese will become bubbly and brown even faster.**

*Nutrients per sandwich: Calories: 282, Total Fat: 9 g, Sat. Fat: 3 g, Monounsaturated Fat: 4 g, Polyunsaturated Fat: 1 g, Carbs: 34 g, Fiber: 8 g, Sugars: 6 g, Protein: 19 g, Sodium: 455 mg, Cholesterol: 18 mg*

## Nutritional Bonus:

You may know that broccoli is high in iron, but so are mushrooms. In fact, portobellos are also very good sources of copper, a much-needed mineral and antioxidant that helps you utilize dietary iron and fend off cellular damage.

---

# Almond, Bean & Grain Burgers
## WITH STRAWBERRY SHALLOT SAUCE

*Serves* 4. **Hands-on time:** *20 minutes.* **Total time:** *45 minutes.*

We've loaded these burgers with flavor and texture from crunchy almonds, smooth, chewy bulgur, aromatic shallots and garlic and sweet-peppery strawberry sauce. You won't miss the meat!

## INGREDIENTS:

### SAUCE
- 1 tsp olive oil
- 1 Tbsp minced shallots
- 1 tsp minced garlic
- 1 cup fresh or frozen strawberries, whole and hulled
- ¼ tsp fresh ground black pepper
- ½ tsp raw honey

### BURGERS
- 1½ tsp olive oil, divided
- ¼ cup minced shallots
- 3 large cloves garlic, minced

- ¼ cup bulgur wheat
- 1½ cups cooked black beans
- ¼ cup sliced unsalted almonds, toasted
- ½ tsp sea salt
- ½ tsp fresh ground black pepper
- ¼ cup nonfat plain Greek yogurt
- ¼ cup whole-wheat panko bread crumbs
- 4 whole-wheat, sprouted-grain or multigrain hamburger buns
- Greens, such as arugula or spinach leaves, optional

## INSTRUCTIONS:

ONE: Prepare sauce: Heat oil in a small saucepot on medium-high. Add shallots and garlic and sauté for 1 minute. Add strawberries and ¼ cup water and simmer for 20 minutes, stirring often, until berries break down completely and liquid reduces and thickens. Stir in pepper and honey. Remove from heat and set aside.

TWO: Prepare burgers: Heat 1 tsp oil in a medium saucepot on medium-high. Add shallots and garlic and sauté for 2 minutes, until shallots are soft and translucent. Add ⅓ cup water and bring to a boil. Stir in bulgur, return to a boil, cover and remove from heat. Let sit for 15 minutes.

THREE: Meanwhile, put beans, almonds, salt and pepper in food processor. Pulse mixture 25 times, until a coarse paste begins to form.

FOUR: In a large bowl, combine yogurt and bread crumbs. Add hot bulgur and mix thoroughly. Scrape bean-almond mixture into bowl and work ingredients together. Divide into 4 equal piles and form each into a ½-inch-thick patty. Refrigerate patties for about 15 minutes, uncovered.

FIVE: Remove patties from refrigerator. Heat a large skillet (not nonstick) on high. Brush remaining ½ tsp oil over skillet. When skillet is very hot, add patties and sear for 2 to 3 minutes per side. (**NOTE:** If your skillet is not large enough to hold all 4 patties without crowding, cook in batches.)

SIX: Place 1 patty between each bun with about 1 Tbsp strawberry sauce. Add greens, if desired.

*Nutrients per serving (1 burger and 1 Tbsp sauce): Calories: 388, Total Fat: 10 g, Sat. Fat: 1 g, Monounsaturated Fat: 5 g, Polyunsaturated Fat: 2.5 g, Carbs: 61 g, Fiber: 12 g, Sugars: 9 g, Protein: 16 g, Sodium: 477 mg, Cholesterol: 0 mg*

# Meatball Sub
## WITH ROASTED VEGGIES & TOMATO SAUCE

*Serves 4. **Hands-on time:** 20 minutes. **Total time:** 40 minutes.*

Bursting with meaty goodness and doused in tasty red sauce, you'll need two napkins and a fork for this one! Buy the leanest ground beef or bison you can find, preferably grass fed and free range for maximum beefy flavor.

### INGREDIENTS:

- 1 lb 95% lean ground beef
- ¼ cup rolled oats
- 1 large egg white
- 1 Tbsp tomato paste
- 1 tsp dried thyme
- 1 tsp dried oregano, divided
- ½ tsp ground black pepper
- 2 cloves garlic, chopped, divided
- Olive oil cooking spray
- ½ medium zucchini, cut into ½-inch-wide strips (4 oz)
- ½ medium red bell pepper, cut into ½-inch-wide strips (4 oz)
- ½ medium yellow onion, cut into ¼-inch-wide strips (3 oz)
- 1 tsp extra-virgin olive oil
- 1 cup fresh tomatoes, seeded, chopped and squeezed to release juices; seeds and juices discarded
- 1 tsp dried basil
- 14 oz whole-wheat baguette (18 inches long; widest baguette you can find)

### INSTRUCTIONS:

**ONE:** Preheat oven to 400°F. In a large bowl, combine beef, oats, egg white, tomato paste, thyme, ½ tsp oregano, black pepper and 1 clove garlic. Line a sheet pan with foil and spray lightly with cooking spray. Form beef mixture into about 50 1-inch balls. Place balls on pan, not allowing them to touch. On another sheet pan, toss zucchini, bell pepper and onion with oil. Put both pans in oven and set timer for 5 minutes.

**TWO:** In a small bowl, stir together tomatoes, basil, remaining ½ tsp oregano and remaining 1 clove garlic. When timer goes off, remove meatballs from oven and pour tomato mixture over them. Turn meatballs to coat with tomato mixture. Place back in oven for another 10 minutes, again setting timer. When timer goes off again, remove meatballs and set aside. Stir vegetables, return to oven and roast for another 10 minutes.

**THREE:** Slice baguette into 4 sections, then slice each section in half horizontally so it opens like a book. Spread open each section and tear out a bit of bread from the middle to make room for the meatballs. Toast bread in toaster or under a hot broiler for 1 minute to crisp.

**FOUR:** To assemble sandwiches, open up each piece of toasted bread, pile on a quarter of meatball mixture and top with a quarter of roasted vegetables. Close sandwich and serve with a fork for any stray meatballs and sauce.

**NOTE: If you miss the cheese, simply divide 2 oz shredded part-skim mozzarella among the subs for only an additional 36 calories, 2 g of fat and 88 mg of sodium per serving.**

*Nutrients per sandwich: Calories: 452, Total Fat: 10 g, Sat. Fat: 3 g, Monounsaturated Fat: 3 g, Polyunsaturated Fat: 1 g, Carbs: 59 g, Fiber: 8 g, Sugars: 5 g, Protein: 25 g, Sodium: 552 mg, Cholesterol: 60 mg*

# Chicken Cheesesteak Wrap Panini

*Serves 4. **Hands-on time:** 20 minutes. **Total time:** 1 hour.*

**Philly cheesesteak fans won't be disappointed by our clean chicken version of the classic.**

### INGREDIENTS:

- 1 large yellow onion, very thinly sliced (about 4 cups)
- 2 Tbsp malt vinegar
- 1 large red bell pepper, sliced into ¼-inch strips
- 8 oz cremini mushrooms, stemmed and thinly sliced (about 2 cups)
- 2 4-oz boneless, skinless chicken breasts, sliced into about ⅛- to ¼-inch pieces
- ¼ tsp fresh ground black pepper
- 2 oz low-fat cheddar cheese, grated (½ cup)
- ¼ cup 1% milk
- 4 large whole-wheat or multigrain wraps (about 12 inches)

### INSTRUCTIONS:

**ONE:** Heat a large sauté pan on high. When skillet is hot, add onion and stir constantly for 2 minutes, until onion begins to soften. Reduce heat to medium-high and cook onion for 2 more minutes without stirring.

**TWO:** Add vinegar and ¼ cup water, a bit at a time, stirring and scraping any brown bits from bottom of skillet. Reduce heat to low and let onion simmer for 30 minutes, stirring occasionally, until very soft and golden.

**THREE:** Meanwhile, heat a separate large sauté pan on high. Add red pepper and mushrooms to hot, dry pan and sauté for 2 minutes, stirring constantly. Reduce heat to medium-low and let vegetables simmer for 5 more minutes, until very soft and until most of liquid has evaporated.

**FOUR:** Increase heat to high and add chicken to pan. Sauté for 5 to 7 minutes, stirring often, until chicken is cooked all the way through. Season with black pepper, cover pan and keep warm (very low heat).

**FIVE:** When onions are very soft, add cheese and milk to skillet, stirring as cheese melts into onion.

**SIX:** Place a quarter of chicken mixture and a quarter of onions in a line on bottom third of each wrap, leaving about 2 inches empty on each end. Roll the bottom end over mixture, squeezing gently around filling. Continue to roll up the rest of the wrap.

**SEVEN:** Place wrap on a hot panini press and press wrap for 2 minutes to toast. Don't have a panini press? No problem! See p. 49.

**EIGHT:** To cut pressed wrap, start 2 inches from end and cut diagonally toward other end, creating a triangular piece. Reposition knife and cut again, starting at the top of the last cut and down toward the other end of the wrap. Continue until you are left with 4 or 5 triangles.

*Nutrients per wrap: Calories: 273, Total Fat: 5 g, Sat. Fat: 1 g, Carbs: 31 g, Fiber: 4 g, Sugars: 5 g, Protein: 23 g, Sodium: 307 mg, Cholesterol: 38 mg*

Chicken
Cheesesteak
Wrap
Panini

Pulled Pork
Sandwiches

**Try This:**
If you've got a jar of pickles
lining your fridge door
(see p. 38 for our Quick-Pickled
Vegetables recipe), try them
alongside this open-faced
dinner for a satisfying bite and
tang (plus, it's budget friendly!).

# Pulled Pork Sandwiches
## WITH APPLE CIDER VINEGAR & TOASTED MUSTARD SEED DRESSING

*Serves 4. **Hands-on time:** 25 minutes. **Total time:** 35 minutes.*

**Traditional pulled pork is typically made with fattier cuts of meat, such as the shoulder or Boston butt. Instead, we've opted for lean pork tenderloin, briefly simmering it in water to keep the meat moist and pull-able. Tossing the lean shreds with their deglazed pan juices adds another layer of flavor to normally mild-mannered pork.**

### INGREDIENTS:

- 1 tsp mustard seeds
- 2 Tbsp apple cider vinegar, divided
- 1 Tbsp extra-virgin olive oil
- ¼ head cabbage, thinly sliced
- 1 large carrot, peeled and grated
- 1 small yellow onion, thinly sliced
- ¾ lb pork tenderloin, trimmed of visible fat, cut into 2-inch pieces
- 4 1-oz slices reduced-fat Provolone cheese
- 4 slices whole-grain bread

### INSTRUCTIONS:

ONE: Heat a small nonstick pan on medium-low for 1 minute. Add seeds and toast, shaking pan often, for 5 minutes. In a small bowl, combine toasted seeds with 1 Tbsp vinegar and oil; set aside. In a medium bowl, combine cabbage, carrot and onion; set aside.

TWO: Fill a large, shallow saucepan with ½ cup water. Bring water to a boil, then reduce heat to medium-low and add pork. Flip each piece once and move them around to make sure pieces don't stick to pan. Cover pan and simmer for 5 minutes. Flip pieces over and continue cooking for 5 more minutes. Cut into a piece to see if meat is cooked through. If not, continue cooking for an additional 2 minutes and check again.

THREE: Transfer pork to a plate, allowing cooking liquid to remain in pan. Heat on high for 3 minutes or until cooking liquid has reduced to a thick glaze on the bottom of the pan. Remove pan from heat and deglaze with remaining 1 Tbsp vinegar, scraping pan with a spatula to pull up thickened cooking liquid.

FOUR: Using 2 forks, shred pork. With pan still off of heat, place pork back into pan and stir well, thoroughly combining deglazing liquid with pork.

FIVE: Build each sandwich by placing 1 slice of Provolone on each slice of bread. Top with 3 oz pulled pork, about ¾ cup cabbage mixture and 1½ tsp mustard seed dressing.

*Nutrients per open-faced sandwich: Calories: 303, Total Fat: 12 g, Sat. Fat: 4 g, Monounsaturated Fat: 4 g, Polyunsaturated Fat: 1 g, Carbs: 19 g, Fiber: 4 g, Sugars: 3 g, Protein: 30 g, Sodium: 386 mg, Cholesterol: 70 mg*

# Salsa Burgers

*Serves 4. **Hands-on time:** 20 minutes. **Total time:** 20 minutes.*

**Pico de gallo is a fresh salsa made with diced tomatoes, onions, jalapeños and cilantro. Mixed with beef, the Mexican staple adds moisture and mild flavor to these burgers. Look for it near the produce aisle or in the deli section of your supermarket. You can substitute jarred chunky salsa in a pinch, but be sure to drain it thoroughly to remove as much liquid as possible.**

### INGREDIENTS:

- 1 lb 95% lean ground beef
- ⅓ cup fresh pico de gallo or tomato salsa, drained well
- ¼ tsp plus a pinch sea salt, divided
- ¼ tsp fresh ground black pepper, plus additional to taste, divided
- 1 small avocado, peeled, pitted and roughly chopped
- ¼ red bell pepper, finely chopped (about ¼ cup)
- 3 Tbsp cilantro, chopped
- 2 tsp fresh lime juice
- ¼ tsp garlic powder
- ½ cup nonfat plain Greek yogurt, optional
- 4 multigrain hamburger buns
- 4 to 8 radicchio leaves, ribs removed, optional

### INSTRUCTIONS:

ONE: Place oven rack 6 to 7 inches from broiler and preheat to high. Line a baking sheet or broiler pan with foil. In a large bowl, combine beef, pico de gallo, ¼ tsp salt and ¼ tsp pepper. Shape mixture into 4 equal patties, each ½ inch thick, and place on prepared baking sheet. Broil for 6 to 7 minutes or until burgers are browned. Flip and repeat on second side until burgers are firm to the touch and no longer pink in the center, 5 to 6 more minutes (internal temperature should read 160°F on an instant-read thermometer).

TWO: Place avocado in a small bowl and mash to a chunky consistency with a fork or potato masher. Add red pepper, cilantro, lime juice, garlic powder, pinch salt and pepper, to taste; stir to combine.

THREE: To serve, spread 2 Tbsp yogurt on bottom half of each bun and top with 1 to 2 radicchio leaves, if desired. Then add patty and 3 Tbsp avocado mixture to each before finishing with top halves of buns. Garnish burger with additional cilantro, if desired.

**OPTION: Alternatively, you can cook the patties in a large skillet misted with olive oil cooking spray over medium heat for 5 to 6 minutes per side.**

*Nutrients per burger: Calories: 336, Total Fat: 14 g, Sat. Fat: 3 g, Monounsaturated Fat: 7 g, Polyunsaturated Fat: 2 g, Carbs: 28 g, Fiber: 7 g, Sugars: 5 g, Protein: 27 g, Sodium: 488 mg, Cholesterol: 60 mg*

# Do-It-Yourself Pickles

Transform seasonal produce into sweet and sour pickles in your very own kitchen.

## Quick-Pickled Fall Vegetables

*Serves 24. **Makes** 8 cups. **Hands-on time:** 30 minutes.*
*Total time: 3 hours, 30 minutes (including refrigeration time).*

Unlike typical fermented pickles, which can take weeks or months to be ready to eat, these delicious little pickles are ready in minutes! "How can that be?" you ask. They're marinated in a vinegar solution, whereas fermented pickles have to be soaked in brine for weeks to allow lactic acid bacteria to grow and break down the vegetables.

Get creative with your end-of-summer, early-fall produce! We've offered this basic recipe to get you started, but feel free to make swaps with the help of our substitution charts for different pickles every time!

### INGREDIENTS:

- 2 cups white wine vinegar
- 2½ cups cold water
- 6 sprigs fresh thyme
- ¼ cup raw honey
- 2 bay leaves
- 1 tsp whole coriander seeds
- 2 cloves garlic
- 1 tsp sea salt
- ¼ tsp whole black peppercorns
- ½ tsp red chile flakes, optional
- 2 cups cauliflower, cut into ½-inch pieces
- 2 cups carrots, peeled and cut into ½-inch pieces
- 4 cups green beans, ends trimmed

### INSTRUCTIONS:

**ONE:** Combine the first 10 ingredients in a large saucepan and bring to a boil over high heat. Reduce heat to medium-high and let simmer for 1 to 2 minutes.

**TWO:** Starting with cauliflower, immerse vegetable pieces into simmering brine and blanch until al dente – cooked but still crisp – about 3 minutes. Remove cauliflower with a slotted spoon and let rest on a parchment- or paper-towel-lined tray. Repeat steps with remaining vegetables, cooking 1 variety at a time, according to time in the Vegetable Substitution Guide, at right.

**THREE:** Remove brine from heat and let cool to room temperature. Transfer vegetables to resealable containers (you can either place veggies in same container or store separately at this point) and pour cooled brine over top, ensuring that vegetables are completely covered in brine. Cover and refrigerate vegetables for a minimum of 3 hours. To serve, remove vegetables from brine and enjoy! Pickles will last, covered and refrigerated, for up to 1 week.

**Nutrients per ¼-cup serving:** *Calories: 33, Total Fat: 0 g, Sat. Fat: 0 g, Carbs: 7 g, Fiber: 2 g, Sugars: 4 g, Protein: 1 g, Sodium: 99 mg, Cholesterol: 0 mg*

# Spice It Up

Change up the flavor of your brine by including any of these spicy additions.

| Spice | Works Best With | Vinegar |
|---|---|---|
| 1 sliced jalapeño or 1 whole habanero pepper | Green or yellow beans, cauliflower, corn | Coconut |
| Pinch saffron | Turnips, cauliflower | White balsamic |
| 6 sprigs fresh dill (do not add thyme) | Beets, carrots | Apple cider |
| 6 sprigs fresh cilantro (do not add thyme) | Corn, green beans | Rice wine |
| 2 whole cinnamon sticks | Beets, carrots, parsnips | Red wine |
| 2 whole star anise pods | Beets, cauliflower | Coconut |
| 1 tsp allspice or whole cloves (do not add coriander) | Parsnips, green beans | Apple cider |

**TIP:** Pickle and store beets and colored carrots on their own, as their pigments can stain other veggies.

# Vegetable Substitution Guide

Pick a few pieces of produce from the following list to quick-pickle or experiment with your favorite crunchy vegetables.

**CAULIFLOWER**
cut into ½-inch pieces
3 minutes blanching time

**BEETS**
peeled and cut into
1-inch wedges
3 minutes blanching time

**GREEN AND YELLOW BEANS**
trim ends and leave whole
2½ minutes blanching time

**CORN**
cut into ½-inch round disks
3 to 4 minutes blanching time

**SMALL TURNIPS**
about 2 to 3 inches
in diameter, peel and
cut into wedges
2 minutes blanching time

**CARROTS**
peeled and diced
into ½-inch pieces
3 minutes blanching time

**PARSNIPS**
peeled and sliced into
½-inch pieces
2 minutes blanching time

# Gyro

*Serves 4. **Hands-on time:** 15 minutes. **Total time:** 1 hour (includes marinating).*

Gyros (pronounced yeer-oh) are Greek sandwiches typically made with cuts of lamb or beef, which are ground, spiced and then molded into large pieces called cones and cooked on a rotisserie. Slow cooking meat for hours on a spit may be essentially unrealistic for the typical home cook, so we've opted for broiled and thinly sliced lean steak.

## INGREDIENTS:

- 1 Tbsp fresh oregano leaves, finely chopped, or 1 tsp dried oregano
- ¼ tsp cumin, ground
- ½ tsp paprika
- ¼ tsp fresh ground black pepper
- 1 clove garlic, crushed
- 1 Tbsp fresh lemon juice
- 2 tsp olive oil, divided
- 1 lb eye round beef steak, trimmed of visible fat and sliced into 4 4-oz lean beef tenderloins
- Olive oil cooking spray (optional)
- 1 large red onion, thinly sliced
- 2 medium sweet peppers (red, green or a combination), thinly sliced
- 4 whole-wheat pitas (6½-inch diameter)
- 2 medium tomatoes, coarsely chopped
- 1 cup tzatziki (see recipe, p. 110)

## INSTRUCTIONS:

**ONE:** In a small bowl, mix together oregano, cumin, paprika, pepper, garlic, lemon juice and 1 tsp oil. Rub mixture onto steaks, place in a zip-top bag and let marinate for 30 minutes or overnight in refrigerator.

**TWO:** Preheat broiler to high. Place steaks on a foil-lined baking sheet misted with cooking spray, or stoneware, and broil for 7 to 10 minutes. When done, remove from oven and let sit for 5 minutes; slice thinly.

**THREE:** Meanwhile, heat remaining 1 tsp oil in a small sauté pan over medium-high. Add onion and sweet peppers and cook until soft, about 7 to 10 minutes. Set aside.

**FOUR:** To assemble, cut pitas in half, open pocket and place 2 oz steak, ½ cup sweet pepper-onion mixture and ½ cup tomatoes in each pita half. Top each with 2 Tbsp tzatziki.

*Nutrients per 2 pita halves: Calories: 440, Total Fat: 9 g, Sat. Fat: 2.5 g, Carbs: 47 g, Fiber: 8 g, Sugars: 7 g, Protein: 43 g, Sodium: 420 mg, Cholesterol: 85 mg*

# Steakhouse Wrap Panini

*Serves 4. **Hands-on time:** 15 minutes. **Total time:** 45 minutes.*

**Thin slices of lean flank steak coated with punchy black pepper and smoky paprika get a steakhouse-inspired treatment with a vibrant spinach-blue cheese sauce.**

## INGREDIENTS:

- 2 medium sweet potatoes, peeled
- 1 tsp olive oil
- 2 cups baby spinach
- 2 large green onions, trimmed and cut into 1-inch pieces
- 1 Tbsp crumbled blue cheese
- ¼ cup low-fat buttermilk
- 8 oz flank steak
- ½ tsp fresh ground black pepper
- ¼ tsp smoked paprika
- 4 large whole-wheat or multi-grain wraps (about 12 inches in diameter)

## INSTRUCTIONS:

**ONE:** Preheat oven to 425°F. Place a sheet pan in oven as it warms. Quarter sweet potatoes, cutting each in half lengthwise and then in half lengthwise again. Cut each quarter into 4 thin wedges. Remove hot pan from oven and brush with oil. Lay potato wedges in an even layer across pan. Transfer potatoes to oven and bake for 25 minutes, flipping them over halfway through, until both sides start to brown. Remove potatoes from oven and set aside.

**TWO:** Meanwhile, in a blender, add spinach, onions, blue cheese and buttermilk. Blend until completely smooth, pulsing, scraping the sides and stirring as needed. Set aside or refrigerate until ready to use.

**THREE:** Sprinkle both sides of flank steak with pepper and paprika and rub spices all over surface of meat. Place steak on a broiler pan. Turn on broiler and place broiler pan on highest rack in oven, beneath broiler, for 5 minutes. Flip meat over and broil for 5 more minutes, until cooked to medium. Let steak rest for 5 minutes before slicing it very thinly against the grain.

**FOUR:** Place 8 potato wedges in the center of each wrap. Top with quarter of steak, then drizzle 3 Tbsp spinach-blue cheese sauce over top.

**FIVE:** Pull bottom third of wrap over filling and then fold ends in. Continue to roll the wrap forward onto itself, like a burrito, until the filling is entirely enveloped in the wrap.

**SIX:** Place wrap on a hot panini press, seam side down. Press wrap for 2 minutes to toast. Don't have a panini press? No problem! See p. 49.

*Nutrients per wrap: Calories: 304, Total Fat: 8 g, Sat. Fat: 2 g, Monounsaturated Fat: 2 g, Polyunsaturated Fat: 0.5 g, Carbs: 37 g, Fiber: 5 g, Sugars: 5 g, Protein: 19 g, Sodium: 303 mg, Cholesterol: 21 mg*

**Nutritional Bonus:**
You'll love our Steakhouse Wrap Panini for more than just its rich taste: It provides 15% of your daily requirement of zinc, an essential mineral that supports fertility and cell production. Plus, the sweet potatoes and spinach contain vitamin C, which helps your body absorb the flank steak's iron offering.

Steakhouse Wrap Panini

THE BEST OF CLEAN EATING 2

Crispy Almond-Coated Fish

# Crispy Almond-Coated Fish
WITH ARTICHOKE SPREAD ON RYE

*Serves 2. **Hands-on time:** 10 minutes. **Total time:** 30 minutes.*

**Here, a mild white fish is enveloped in crunchy textures and savory flavors for a satisfying and energizing meal. Jarred artichoke hearts and roasted peppers make this a snap to prepare, but you can also roast your own peppers at home. Simply broil a red bell pepper until blackened, turning every few minutes. Immediately place the pepper in a small saucepan with a lid or under an inverted glass bowl for five minutes, then peel and seed.**

## INGREDIENTS:

- 2 whole artichoke hearts, jarred in water
- ¼ cup roasted red peppers
- 2 tsp balsamic vinegar
- ½ tsp extra-virgin olive oil
- 2 Tbsp slivered unsalted almonds
- 2 Tbsp cornmeal
- ½ tsp dried thyme
- Olive oil cooking spray
- 8 oz white fish fillet (tilapia, cod or catfish), cut into 2 portions (or 2 4-oz fillets)
- 4 slices light rye bread
- 1 cup frisée or romaine lettuce, washed, dried and torn

## INSTRUCTIONS:

ONE: Preheat oven to 400°F. In a food processor, combine artichoke hearts, peppers, vinegar and oil and process to a coarse paste. Scrape out and set paste aside. Wash and dry food processor bowl. Add almonds, cornmeal and thyme to food processor and grind to a chunky powder. Scrape out onto a plate or pie pan.

TWO: Mist a baking sheet with cooking spray. Roll fish fillets in cornmeal mixture to coat and place on baking sheet. Press any leftover cornmeal mixture onto tops of fillets and mist lightly with cooking spray. Bake for 12 to 15 minutes, depending on thickness of fillets.

THREE: Meanwhile, toast bread and divide evenly between 2 plates. Divide artichoke-pepper paste in half and spread each half onto 1 slice of bread on each plate. When fish is done, flaking easily when pierced with a fork, place each fillet on top of artichoke-pepper paste. Cover each with frisée, dividing evenly, and top with remaining slice of bread. Serve hot.

*Nutrients per sandwich: Calories: 349, Total Fat: 10 g, Sat. Fat: 2 g, Monounsaturated Fat: 5 g, Polyunsaturated Fat: 2 g, Omega-3s: 240 mg, Omega-6s: 1,940 mg, Carbs: 35 g, Fiber: 5 g, Sugars: 4 g, Protein: 30 g, Sodium: 480 mg, Cholesterol: 56 mg*

# Grilled Portobello & Onion Burgers
WITH BLUE CHEESE & CREAMY DIJON SAUCE

*Serves 4. **Hands-on time:** 5 minutes. **Total time:** 14 minutes.*

**With their meaty texture, portobellos make ideal vegetarian burgers and sandwich fillers. You may be surprised to learn that portobellos (*cappellone*, or "big hats," as they're known in Italy) are actually oversized cremini mushrooms (aka baby bellas). Both portobellos and creminis share the same family, *Agaricus bisporus*, with a mushroom that you're probably all too familiar with – the common white variety.**

## INGREDIENTS:

**BURGER**

- 4 large portobello mushroom caps, wiped clean with damp cloth
- 4 slices red onion, each round about ¼ inch thick (about 1 medium onion)
- 1½ Tbsp extra-virgin olive oil
- 4 whole-wheat hamburger buns
- 2 oz blue cheese, crumbled (½ cup)
- 4 romaine lettuce leaves

**SAUCE**

- 2 Tbsp nonfat plain Greek yogurt
- 1 Tbsp extra-virgin olive oil
- 2 tsp Dijon mustard
- 2 cloves garlic, minced
- 2 tsp dried basil
- 1 Tbsp finely chopped parsley
- ⅛ tsp sea salt

## INSTRUCTIONS:

ONE: Heat a grill pan on medium-high. Lightly brush mushroom caps and onion with oil. Grill mushroom caps and onion for 4 to 5 minutes per side or until mushrooms are tender. (**NOTE:** Mushrooms will begin to release their juices when they are tender.) Set aside on a separate plate. Grill buns, cut sides down, for 1 to 2 minutes per side or until toasted.

TWO: Meanwhile, prepare sauce: Combine all sauce ingredients in a small bowl. Spread sauce on bottom half of each bun, dividing evenly. Top with onion, mushroom caps (smooth side down), cheese and lettuce, dividing each evenly. Top with other bun halves.

**Nutrients per serving (1 burger and 1 Tbsp sauce):** *Calories: 253, Total Fat: 11 g, Sat. Fat: 3 g, Monounsaturated Fat: 5 g, Polyunsaturated Fat: 1.5 g, Carbs: 31 g, Fiber: 5 g, Sugars: 7 g, Protein: 10 g, Sodium: 487 mg, Cholesterol: 10 mg*

# Turkey & Roasted Zucchini Muffuletta

*Serves 10. **Hands-on time:** 1 hour. **Total time:** 1 hour, 30 minutes (plus 1½ hours to chill).*

**In 1906, workers from the neighboring farmers' market would frequent the Central Grocery in New Orleans to pick up meat, cheese, olive salad and bread for a typical four-course lunch. Seeing them try to balance little plates on their laps, the proprietor of the store decided to simply hollow out the bread and stuff it with the other three courses; thus the muffuletta was born! Traditionally made with salami, lots of olive oil and loaded with cheese, our *CE* version features roasted turkey breast and is packed with vegetables!**

## INGREDIENTS:

- 2½ lb bone-in turkey breast, skin and visible fat removed
- 4 tsp olive oil, divided
- ¼ tsp fresh ground black pepper, divided
- 4 cloves garlic, minced, divided
- 2 zucchini, trimmed and sliced ¼-inch thick lengthwise
- ¼ cup each pimento-stuffed green olives and pitted Kalamata olives
- 2 stalks celery, diced
- 2 medium jarred roasted red peppers, finely diced (about 1 cup)
- ½ small sweet onion, finely diced (about ¾ cup)
- 2 Tbsp red wine vinegar
- 1 Tbsp each chopped fresh oregano and parsley
- 1 round whole-grain sourdough or pumpernickel loaf (about 10 inches in diameter)
- 6 oz low-fat mozzarella or provolone cheese, sliced

## INSTRUCTIONS:

**ONE:** Preheat oven to 350°F and ensure one rack is in top third of oven and one in bottom third.

**TWO:** Brush turkey breast all over with 1 tsp oil and season with ⅛ tsp pepper and half of garlic. Place turkey breast onto a parchment-lined baking sheet and roast on bottom rack in oven for about 1 hour, until juices run clear when pierced with a knife or a thermometer inserted into thickest part of breast reads 160°F. Remove from oven and set aside to cool.

**THREE:** Meanwhile, brush zucchini strips with 1 tsp oil and season with remaining pepper. Arrange zucchini in a single layer on a separate parchment-lined baking sheet and roast on top rack for about 25 minutes, turning once, until lightly charred and golden. Remove from oven and set aside to cool.

**FOUR:** While turkey and zucchini roast, prepare olive salad: Coarsely chop olives and transfer to a medium bowl. Add remaining garlic and 2 tsp oil, celery, roasted peppers, onion, vinegar, oregano and parsley. Set aside.

**MAKE AHEAD: Turkey, zucchini and olive salad can be prepared up to this point up to 48 hours in advance. However, purchase fresh bread the day of or day before serving.**

**FIVE:** With serrated knife parallel to cutting board, slice loaf in half horizontally. Remove center of loaf by pulling out small chunks with your fingertips, leaving a ¾-inch border around edges. Reserve removed bread pieces for future use (bread crumbs, stuffing, etc).

**SIX:** Once turkey is cool enough to handle, remove and discard bone and shred turkey into small pieces.

**SEVEN:** To assemble sandwich, spread half of olive salad onto bottom half of loaf. Layer with zucchini, cheese and turkey, then top with remaining olive salad. Sandwich together with top half of loaf and wrap tightly in plastic wrap. Place onto a tray and weigh down with a cast-iron skillet over top, or another tray with a brick or heavy cans on top. Place into fridge and allow to press and set for 1 to 2 hours.

**EIGHT:** Remove weight and plastic wrap and cut sandwich into 10 wedges with a serrated knife.

**TIP: This sandwich is a great way to use up leftover holiday turkey. Also, the center of the bread that was pulled out may be stored in a sealable freezer-safe container until ready to use. It will last up to 3 months in your freezer.**

**Nutrients per 3-inch-wide wedge:** *Calories: 343, Total Fat: 9 g, Sat. Fat: 2.5 g, Monounsaturated Fat: 4 g, Polyunsaturated Fat: 1 g, Carbs: 24.5 g, Fiber: 4 g, Sugars: 5 g, Protein: 37 g, Sodium: 658 mg, Cholesterol: 81 mg*

**Nutritional Bonus:**
Every 100 g of olives, about ¾ cup, contains 11 g of monounsaturated fats and 19% of your recommended daily intake of vitamin E. Monounsaturated fats are stronger and more stable than other fats, and are great for cell protection. Combined with the antioxidant properties of vitamin E, these fats protect your cells and lower the risk of inflammation and damage from free radicals.

**Eggplant Parmesan Wrap Panini**

**Nutritional Bonus:**
While calcium may be best known for its bone-building abilities, it is capable of much more: It aids in blood clotting, muscle contraction and the maintenance of low blood pressure. So, you'll be happy to learn that this health-boosting vegetarian sandwich packs 25% of your daily need.

# Eggplant Parmesan Wrap Panini

*Serves 4. **Hands-on time:** 20 minutes. **Total time:** 30 minutes.*

**This *CE* iteration of an Italian-American favorite honors the beloved flavors of complex marinara sauce, soft, earthy eggplant and decadent melted cheese without all the frying fuss.**

INGREDIENTS:

- 1 medium eggplant (about 1 lb), cut into ½-inch cubes
- 2 medium tomatoes, cut into ½-inch cubes (about 2 cups)
- 2 large cloves garlic, halved
- ½ tsp dried parsley
- ½ tsp dried oregano
- ½ tsp dried basil
- ¼ cup part-skim ricotta cheese
- 2 oz part-skim mozzarella, grated (½ cup)
- 3 Tbsp grated Parmesan cheese
- 4 large whole-wheat or multigrain wraps (about 12 inches in diameter)

INSTRUCTIONS:

ONE: Heat a large sauté pan on medium-high. When pan is hot, add eggplant and tomatoes and sauté for 2 minutes, stirring constantly, until eggplant begins to soften and both vegetables release liquids. Add garlic and herbs and sauté for 5 more minutes, stirring regularly. Reduce heat to medium and cover pan, allowing vegetables to simmer for 5 minutes. Remove from heat, uncover, stir and let cool slightly.

TWO: Meanwhile, in a medium bowl, stir together ricotta, mozzarella and Parmesan.

THREE: Spread 2 Tbsp cheese mixture in center of 1 wrap, then place quarter of eggplant mixture (about ½ cup) in a pile on top of cheeses. Pull bottom of wrap up over filling. Fold both sides inward so creases form at the ends of the filling, creating a pouch. Fold down top 2 corners, as with wrapping paper on the side of a gift box. Finally, hold the remaining top edge of the wrap and pull it down toward the center of the pouch, like an envelope flap. Repeat steps with remaining wraps, cheese spread and eggplant filling.

FOUR: Place wrap on a hot panini press, flap side down. Press wrap for 2 minutes or according to manufacturer directions to toast. Don't have a panini press? No problem! See p. 49.

Nutrients per wrap: *Calories: 362, Total Fat: 8 g, Sat. Fat: 3 g, Monounsaturated Fat: 1.5 g, Polyunsaturated Fat: 0.25 g, Carbs: 33 g, Fiber: 6 g, Sugars: 5 g, Protein: 13 g, Sodium: 384 mg, Cholesterol: 17 mg*

## How to Assemble the Eggplant Parmesan Wrap Panini

ONE: Spread 2 Tbsp cheese mixture in center of 1 wrap, then place quarter of eggplant mixture (about ½ cup) in a pile over top of cheeses. Pull bottom of wrap up over filling.

TWO: Fold both sides inward so creases form at the ends of the filling, creating a pouch.

THREE: Fold down top 2 corners, as with wrapping paper on the side of a gift box.

FOUR: Finally, hold the remaining top edge of the wrap and pull it down toward the center of the pouch, like the top of an envelope flap.

# Slice, Press, Wrap & Roll

"The foundation of a good sandwich is always the bread."

## Breaking Down Bread

The foundation of a good sandwich is always the bread. To make your mile-high meals a source of slow-burning complex carbohydrates (translation: maximum energy for a longer period of time), always seek out whole-grain breads, rolls and wraps. In the last few years, the options for eating whole grains have expanded at bakeries and many more low-salt, EFA-enhanced, low-carb and gluten-free labels are popping up on the bread shelves. If you haven't already, perhaps it's time you get out of your sliced white bread rut and take a walk on the baked-goods wild side, reaching for one of these deliciously versatile options instead:

**Rye loaf**

**Multigrain baguette, roll or English muffin**

**Flaxseed wrap**

**Whole-grain tortilla or naan**

**Whole-wheat focaccia or ciabatta**

If you're pessimistic about how great an impact simply swapping your bread can make, consider this: One slice, or one ounce, of your average store-bought white bread offers 0.6 grams of dietary fiber, while the same amount of a 100 percent whole-wheat loaf contains more than double that amount of fiber – two grams. This difference can be attributed to the fact that, unlike refined white flour, whole grains have not had their fiber-rich bran and germ removed by milling. And if that weren't enough, less-processed grains are also an impressive source of a host of minerals, such as selenium, potassium and magnesium.

# How to Pack Your Wrap for Lunch

**ONE:** Place a 12-inch piece of wax or parchment paper on your counter in a diamond position. Place filled tortilla in the center. Fold bottom edge of paper toward the center.

**TWO:** Fold right edge of paper across the wrap.

**THREE:** Fold left edge of paper over and continue to roll it around the wrap completely

**FOUR:** Twist top of paper, enclosing wrap, but be careful not to crush tortilla or filling. When you're ready to eat, simply untwist and tear away top end and use the paper to keep the wrap rolled together.

## YOUR SIMPLE PANINI

While a countertop press is a great investment for hot-sandwich lovers, you won't have to run out and buy one to create the signature crispness of our panini. A grill pan or skillet coupled with another heavy pan or dish to weigh down the sandwich will mimic the work of a machine. The kitchen supply store can wait – nourishing ingredients and a little imagination are all you need to start rolling out grilled wraps of your own.

# Salads
# & Sides

Top: Hot & Sour Swiss Chard, p.68
Right: Bulgur Waldorf Salad, p. 52

Salads and sides are the accoutrements to your main dish that serve to liven up your meal as well as infuse it with nutrition. We've selected our most flavorful and interesting options for you to enjoy. You'll love our cleaned-up version of the classic Buffalo Chicken Salad, and we've put a unique twist on greens with our Hot & Sour Swiss Chard. We've got a side to please every palate and suit any main. Best of all, these choices are as simple to create as they are savory.

# Bulgur Waldorf Salad

*Serves 4. **Hands-on time:** 15 minutes.*
***Total time:** 1 hour, 15 minutes (includes chilling time).*

Consisting of apples, mayonnaise, celery and walnuts, the Waldorf Salad was created in the late 1800s at New York's Waldorf-Astoria Hotel. Countless versions have popped up since, but our *Clean Eating* spin includes nontraditional bulgur for added nutrition and fiber, and is lightened with low-fat yogurt in place of the traditional mayo. Need a quick fix for breakfast? A bowl of this hearty salad will do the trick. Simply add a few egg whites for increased protein and you're ready to start your day.

## INGREDIENTS:

- 1 cup prepared bulgur (soaked as per package directions)
- 1 Granny Smith apple, cored and cut into ½-inch pieces
- 1 Tbsp fresh lemon juice
- 1 cup celery, thinly sliced
- 1 cup red seedless grapes, halved lengthwise
- ½ cup low-fat plain yogurt
- 6 to 8 sprigs fresh mint, chopped (about 2 Tbsp)
- Pinch fresh ground black pepper
- 2 Tbsp unsalted walnut pieces, toasted and chopped

## INSTRUCTIONS:

ONE: Place bulgur in a large bowl. Add apple and lemon juice and stir to combine. Add celery, grapes, yogurt and mint, mixing thoroughly. Season with pepper.

TWO: Cover and refrigerate for a minimum of 1 hour or overnight to allow flavors to meld. To serve, sprinkle each serving with ½ Tbsp walnuts.

MAIN-DISH PAIRING: **Make our salad ahead of time to speed up lunch or dinner prep. Try serving it with a broth-based vegetable soup for a flavor-packed meatless (and wallet friendly!) soup and salad combo. Or, for a complete one-dish meal, add about 4 oz cooked, chilled and diced chicken breast to each cup of salad and serve over baby spinach.**

FOOD FACT: **Cracked wheat and bulgur are often confused. The primary difference is that cracked wheat is not precooked, while bulgur is. As a result, bulgur requires very little preparation and can be enjoyed simply by soaking it for 30 minutes in equal parts water.**

Nutrients per 1-cup serving: *Calories: 210, Total Fat: 4.5 g, Sat. Fat: 1 g, Carbs: 38 g, Fiber: 8 g, Sugars: 10 g, Protein: 7 g, Sodium: 50 mg, Cholesterol: 0 mg*

For a photo of this recipe, see page 50.

# Buffalo Chicken Salad

**Serves** 4. **Hands-on time:** *20 minutes.* **Total time:** *25 minutes.*

**Creamy dressing, real blue cheese and tons of crunch make this entrée super satisfying – and it's fewer than 260 calories!**

## INGREDIENTS:

- 1 lb boneless, skinless chicken breasts
- Olive oil cooking spray
- 1 tsp smoked paprika
- 1 tsp chile powder
- ⅛ tsp sea salt
- ½ sweet onion, chopped (about ½ cup)
- ½ cup nonfat plain Greek yogurt
- 5 Tbsp low-fat buttermilk
- 1 to 1½ Tbsp all-natural hot sauce
- 1 head romaine lettuce, thick spines removed, chopped
- 1 head red leaf lettuce, thick spines removed, chopped
- 1 yellow bell pepper, thinly sliced
- 1 pint grape tomatoes, halved
- 1 cup peeled and shredded carrots
- 2 oz blue cheese, crumbled (about ½ cup)

## INSTRUCTIONS:

**ONE:** Preheat broiler to high. Place chicken on a baking sheet coated with cooking spray. Lightly mist chicken with cooking spray and sprinkle evenly on both sides with paprika, chile powder and salt. Broil 6 to 8 inches from heat until center of chicken is no longer pink, about 6 minutes per side. Transfer chicken to a cutting board and let rest for 3 to 5 minutes before cutting into bite-sized chunks.

**TWO:** In a blender, purée onion, yogurt, buttermilk and 1 Tbsp hot sauce. Taste and add remaining hot sauce if you want more heat. Divide romaine and red leaf lettuces among 4 plates and top with bell pepper, tomatoes, carrots and chicken, dividing each evenly. Serve yogurt mixture on the side or drizzle evenly over each plate. Sprinkle with blue cheese and serve immediately.

Nutrients per serving (2½ cups vegetables, ⅔ cup chicken, ¼ cup dressing, 2 Tbsp blue cheese): *Calories: 258, Total Fat: 6 g, Sat. Fat: 3 g, Carbs: 13 g, Fiber: 4 g, Sugars: 6 g, Protein: 35 g, Sodium: 416 mg, Cholesterol: 76 mg*

**TIP:**
You can also cook the chicken on an outdoor or countertop grill. While the cooking time should be about the same, always check doneness by making sure the thickest part of the meat is no longer pink in the center.

# Steak Salad
## WITH BLACK PEPPERCORN YOGURT DRESSING

*Serves 4. **Hands-on time:** 20 minutes. **Total time:** 30 minutes.*

**With sizzling steak, velvety avocado and creamy dressing, this protein-packed salad may sound decadent but, in fact, it comes in at only 187 calories per serving!**

## INGREDIENTS:

### SALAD

- 4 cups chopped iceberg lettuce
- 4 cups chopped arugula
- 4 cups chopped romaine lettuce
- 2 cups thinly sliced mushrooms
- 1 medium red bell pepper, sliced into thin strips
- 1 cucumber, peeled and thinly sliced
- ½ medium red onion, thinly sliced
- Olive oil cooking spray
- 10 oz beef tenderloin, trimmed of visible fat and cut into 3-inch-long strips, (⅛ inch thick and ½ inch wide)
- 4 Tbsp peeled and chopped avocado

### DRESSING

- ½ cup nonfat plain Greek yogurt
- ½ cup low-fat buttermilk
- 1 tsp whole black peppercorns, crushed or ground
- 2 cloves garlic, crushed
- 2 tsp apple cider vinegar
- ¼ tsp sea salt

## INSTRUCTIONS:

**ONE:** Set oven to broil on low. In a large bowl, combine iceberg, arugula and romaine lettuces. Divide greens among 4 plates. Arrange ½ cup mushrooms and quarter of each red pepper, cucumber and onion on each plate of greens.

**TWO:** Prepare dressing: In a small bowl, whisk together yogurt, buttermilk, peppercorns, garlic and vinegar until smooth and incorporated. Season with salt and whisk again.

**THREE:** Mist a small baking pan or stone with cooking spray. Place beef strips on pan and broil for 6 minutes, turning once after 3 minutes. Divide beef among salads (about 2½ oz each). Drizzle each salad with ¼ cup dressing and sprinkle 1 Tbsp avocado over top.

*Nutrients per salad: Calories: 187, Total Fat: 5 g, Sat. Fat: 2 g, Monounsaturated Fat: 2 g, Polyunsaturated Fat: 0.5 g, Carbs: 15 g, Fiber: 5 g, Sugars: 8 g, Protein: 22 g, Sodium: 220 mg, Cholesterol: 39 mg*

# Orzo
## WITH CITRUS & FENNEL

*Serves 4. **Hands-on time:** 20 minutes. **Total time:** 25 minutes.*

**Orzo, which gets its name from the Italian word for barley, is a wonderful blank canvas for a variety of flavors and textures. Here, we've added an orange citrus vinaigrette and springy fennel. Besides flavor and crunch, the fennel offers impressive amounts of dietary fiber, vitamin C, folate, potassium and manganese.**

### INGREDIENTS:

- 5 oz whole-wheat orzo
- 1 Tbsp extra-virgin olive oil
- 1 Tbsp white wine vinegar
- ⅛ tsp fine sea salt
- ¼ tsp fresh ground black pepper
- 1 orange
- ¼ medium bulb fennel, cored and thinly sliced, plus 1 Tbsp feathery fennel fronds, chopped
- 2 green onions, thinly sliced
- ¼ cup crumbled low-fat feta

**OPTION: Add shelled edamame beans, use your favorite small whole-wheat pasta in lieu of orzo or swap the feta for goat cheese to change up this citrusy side.**

### INSTRUCTIONS:

ONE: Cook orzo according to package directions.

TWO: Meanwhile, in a large bowl, whisk together oil, vinegar, salt and pepper.

THREE: Zest orange and add zest to bowl with vinaigrette. Peel orange and, working over a separate medium bowl to catch juices, carefully cut sections from orange and add them to same medium bowl. Cut orange sections in half. Squeeze juice from remaining membrane into large bowl with vinaigrette, discarding membrane.

FOUR: Drain orzo, add to large bowl with vinaigrette and toss. Set aside to cool slightly.

FIVE: Add orange sections to orzo. Stir in fennel, fennel fronds and onions. Top with feta and serve at room temperature or chilled.

*Nutrients per serving (about ¾ cup orzo mixture and 1 Tbsp feta): Calories: 210, Total Fat: 5 g, Sat. Fat: 1.5 g, Carbs: 34 g, Fiber: 3 g, Sugars: 5 g, Protein: 7 g, Sodium: 200 mg, Cholesterol: 5 mg*

# Moroccan Chickpea Salad

*Serves 6. **Hands-on time:** 15 minutes. **Total time:** 15 minutes.*

**This simple salad is hearty enough to stand on its own for a no-cook dinner. And if you have any leftovers, simply pack them for work the next day; a marinated dish such as this often tastes even better once the flavors have had more time to meld. For a more classic lunch salad, try it served over a bed of lettuce and drizzled with a bit of extra lemon juice.**

### INGREDIENTS:

- 3 Tbsp olive oil
- 3 Tbsp fresh lemon juice
- 2 tsp ground cumin
- ¼ tsp each sea salt and fresh ground black pepper
- Pinch ground cayenne pepper
- 3 cups BPA-free canned chickpeas (garbanzo beans), drained and rinsed
- 1 large carrot, peeled and julienned
- 3 green onions, thinly sliced
- 2 plum tomatoes, diced
- 1 red bell pepper, diced
- ¼ cup each chopped fresh cilantro and mint
- ⅓ cup crumbled low-fat feta cheese

### INSTRUCTIONS:

ONE: In a small bowl, whisk together oil, lemon juice, cumin, salt, pepper and cayenne; set aside.

TWO: In a large bowl, combine chickpeas, carrot, onions, tomatoes, red pepper, cilantro, mint and feta.

THREE: Pour lemon juice dressing over chickpea mixture and toss to combine. Serve immediately or cover and refrigerate for up to 24 hours.

*Nutrients per 1-cup serving: Calories: 254, Total Fat: 9 g, Sat. Fat: 2 g, Monounsaturated Fat: 5 g, Polyunsaturated Fat: 1 g, Carbs: 34 g, Fiber: 8 g, Sugars: 7 g, Protein: 10 g, Sodium: 203 mg, Cholesterol: 2 mg*

**NUTRITIONAL BONUS: Chickpeas contain the trace mineral molybdenum, which helps detoxify sulfites – a common preservative – from the body. Just 1 cup of chickpeas contains 164% of your recommended daily intake of this essential micronutrient.**

# Edamame & Chickpea Slaw

*Serves 6. **Hands-on time:** 15 minutes. **Total time:** 1 hour.*

Surprise your family with this refreshing and colorful slaw. Not only is it amazingly easy and delicious, it will improve your family's health— and what could be more important than that?

## INGREDIENTS:

- 1½ cups fresh chickpeas
- Olive oil cooking spray
- ¼ tsp sea salt
- 4 tsp olive oil, divided
- 1 head broccoli stalks, shredded
- 1 head cabbage, shredded
- 1 head purple cabbage, shredded
- 1 cup shelled edamame beans
- ¾ cup green or red bell pepper, julienned
- 1½ cups carrots, shredded
- 4 green onions, chopped
- ⅔ cup apple cider vinegar
- 2 Tbsp raw organic honey
- 2 cloves garlic, minced
- ½ tsp whole caraway seeds
- ½ tsp fresh ground black pepper

## INSTRUCTIONS:

ONE: Preheat oven to 450°F. Place chickpeas on a large roasting pan coated with cooking spray, sprinkle with salt and drizzle with 2 tsp oil. Bake for 30 minutes, tossing occasionally. Remove from oven and let cool.

TWO: Combine broccoli, both cabbages, edamame, bell pepper, carrots and onions in a large bowl; set aside.

THREE: In a small bowl, whisk together vinegar, honey, garlic, caraway seeds, black pepper and remaining 2 tsp oil; pour over slaw, tossing gently. Chill for at least 30 minutes. Top with roasted chickpeas.

*Nutrients per 1-cup serving: Calories: 268, Total Fat: 5 g, Sat. Fat: 0.5 g, Carbs: 47.5 g, Fiber: 12 g, Sugars: 17 g, Protein: 12 g, Sodium: 199 mg, Cholesterol: 0 mg*

**NUTRITIONAL BONUS: Chickpeas (aka garbanzo beans) are an excellent source of folate, magnesium and fiber – all contributors to a healthy cardiovascular system. Folate has been found to lower blood levels of homocysteine – an amino acid that can be a risk factor for cardiovascular disease when elevated. Magnesium helps regulate normal heart rhythm and blood pressure, while fiber (especially the soluble variety found in chickpeas) can help reduce "bad" LDL cholesterol.**

# Vegan Caesar Salad

*Serves 6. **Hands-on time:** 15 minutes. **Total time:** 15 minutes.*

Invented in 1924 by Mexican restaurateur Caesar Cardini, the Caesar salad is one of the most popular – not to mention calorie-dense – salads in the world. We did away with the classic egg yolks, Parmesan cheese and greasy croutons for a few surprising yet equally delicious ingredients: Tempeh transforms into protein-packed croutons, while silken tofu gives the dressing a creamy texture.

## INGREDIENTS:

### SALAD

- ¼ cup pine nuts
- 4 oz tempeh, cut into ¼-inch cubes
- 1 Tbsp fresh lemon juice
- ¼ tsp dried basil
- ⅛ tsp smoked paprika
- ¼ tsp each sea salt and fresh ground black pepper
- 8 cups chopped romaine lettuce
- 4 cups each baby spinach and arugula
- 2 plum tomatoes, diced
- ½ English cucumber, diced

### DRESSING

- ½ cup light firm silken tofu
- 1 clove garlic, crushed
- 2 Tbsp olive oil
- 2 Tbsp fresh lemon juice
- 2 Tbsp apple cider vinegar
- 1 tsp Dijon mustard
- ¼ tsp each sea salt and fresh ground black pepper
- Pinch ground cayenne pepper

## INSTRUCTIONS:

ONE: Preheat oven to 400°F. Place pine nuts on a baking sheet and bake for 3 minutes, until light golden brown. Set aside. Leave oven on at same temperature.

TWO: In a medium bowl, toss tempeh with lemon juice, basil, paprika, salt and pepper. Spread tempeh out in a single layer on a parchment-lined baking tray and bake for 10 minutes, flipping over once halfway through cooking. Set aside.

THREE: Meanwhile, prepare dressing: In the bowl of a 4-cup food processor, add all dressing ingredients and purée until smooth.

FOUR: In a large mixing bowl, combine tempeh croutons with romaine, spinach, arugula, tomatoes and cucumber. Toss with dressing. Transfer to serving bowls and sprinkle with toasted pine nuts. Serve immediately.

*Nutrients per 1⅓-cup serving: Calories: 160, Total Fat: 11 g, Sat. Fat: 1 g, Monounsaturated Fat: 5 g, Polyunsaturated Fat: 3 g, Carbs: 7 g, Fiber: 3 g, Sugars: 2 g, Protein: 10 g, Sodium: 208 mg, Cholesterol: 0 mg*

Vegan
Caesar
Salad

**Nutritional Bonus:**
Who doesn't love free stuff?
Some restaurant main-dish
Caesar salads contain more
than 90 mg of cholesterol.
Thanks to the lack of eggs and
cheese, our vegan version is
happily cholesterol free.

# Quinoa-Stuffed Peppers

*Serves 2. **Hands-on time:** 30 minutes. **Total time:** 45 minutes.*

**Superfoods quinoa and spinach deliver a nutrient-packed one-two punch to this hearty yet sophisticated dish.**

## INGREDIENTS:

### STUFFED PEPPERS

- 2 bell peppers (any color), halved and seeded, stems intact
- ½ cup uncooked quinoa
- ½ cup low-sodium vegetable broth
- 7 oz diced tomatoes, no salt added
- 5 oz spinach
- 1 Tbsp pine nuts

### PESTO

- 2 cups basil or spinach
- ½ clove garlic
- 1½ Tbsp Parmesan cheese
- 1 Tbsp pine nuts
- 1½ Tbsp extra-virgin olive oil
- ⅛ tsp sea salt
- 1 pinch fresh ground black pepper

## INSTRUCTIONS:

**ONE:** Prepare peppers: Preheat broiler to high. Place bell peppers, skin side up, on a baking sheet covered in aluminum foil. Broil until bell peppers start to soften, about 10 minutes.

**TWO:** Meanwhile, combine quinoa, broth and tomatoes in a medium pot. Bring to a boil on high, then reduce heat to low and simmer for 10 to 12 minutes, until liquid is absorbed. Add handfuls of spinach to quinoa mixture and stir to combine. Fill bell pepper halves with quinoa-spinach mixture, dividing evenly.

**THREE:** Prepare pesto: Add basil, garlic, Parmesan, pine nuts, oil, salt and pepper to a food processor and pulse until finely chopped. Add 2 to 3 Tbsp water as needed to thin pesto, if desired.

**FOUR:** Top stuffed peppers with pesto, dividing evenly, or serve on the side. Sprinkle remaining pine nuts over stuffed peppers, dividing evenly.

*Nutrients per serving (2 stuffed halves): Calories: 388, Total Fat: 18 g, Sat. Fat: 2 g, Monounsaturated Fat: 10 g, Polyunsaturated Fat: 4 g, Carbs: 43 g, Fiber: 9 g, Sugars: 7 g, Protein: 14 g, Sodium: 327 mg, Cholesterol: 4 mg*

# Roasted Red Pepper & Feta Mashed Yukon Gold Potatoes

*Serves 8. **Hands-on time:** 10 minutes. **Total time:** 45 minutes.*

**Yukon gold potatoes have thin skin, buttery flesh and a lower starch content than Russet or Idaho potatoes, which translates to a naturally richer flavor in need of less added seasoning.**

## INGREDIENTS:

- 1½ lb Yukon gold potatoes (3 medium), quartered
- 2 whole cloves garlic
- ½ tsp sea salt (optional), plus additional, to taste
- ½ cup low-fat plain yogurt
- 1 roasted red bell pepper, diced
- ½ cup low-fat feta cheese, crumbled
- 3 Tbsp fresh lemon juice
- 6 to 8 sprigs flat-leaf parsley, roughly chopped (about 2 Tbsp)
- Fresh ground black pepper, to taste

## INSTRUCTIONS:

ONE: Place potatoes and garlic in a medium pot and cover with cold water. Bring to a boil over high heat, add ½ tsp salt, if desired, and cook until potatoes are tender when pierced with a fork, about 10 minutes.

TWO: Remove from heat, drain water, then return potatoes and garlic to pot and mash until almost smooth. (Potatoes should still be slightly chunky.) Fold in yogurt, red pepper, feta, lemon juice and parsley. Season with salt and pepper and serve immediately.

*Nutrients per ½-cup serving: Calories: 100, Total Fat: 1.5 g, Sat. Fat: 1 g, Carbs: 18 g, Fiber: 1 g, Sugars: 1 g, Protein: 5 g, Sodium: 280 mg, Cholesterol: 5 mg*

### Nutritional Bonus:
Go for gold: The more intense the yellow hue of a gold potato's flesh, the higher its concentration of beta-carotene. Also, by leaving the tender potato skins intact, you'll add even more vitamin C and potassium to your mash.

# How to Roast a Bell Pepper

ONE: Place pepper on a parchment-lined baking sheet in preheated oven set to 400°F. Turn pepper over after 20 minutes and continue to roast for 30 minutes more. To roast over a gas stovetop or grill, place pepper directly over burner or grill set to medium-high. Turning pepper occasionally, carefully char all sides until blackened and pepper is soft.

TWO: Place charred pepper in a glass bowl and cover tightly with plastic wrap. Let steam for 8 to 10 minutes, then remove from bowl. Peel or scrape off and discard charred skins, running pepper under cold water as you work.

THREE: Remove stem and seeds with a knife.

# Summer Vegetable Curry
## WITH CORIANDER KEFIR

*Serves 4. **Hands-on time:** 15 minutes. **Total time:** 1 hour.*

An abundance of colorful vegetables bolstered by the protein of lentils yields a light, filling stew. A smooth, tart drizzle of creamy coriander-spiked kefir – a cultured milk cousin to yogurt – cools the curry. Scoop it up with a spoon or with soft naan, a lightly leavened bread that hails from Indian cuisine.

### INGREDIENTS:

- 1 Tbsp olive oil
- 1 small onion, diced small
- 1 medium eggplant, cut into 1-inch cubes
- 1 medium zucchini, unpeeled and cut into small cubes
- 2 medium carrots, sliced into ½-inch discs
- 1 small bunch Swiss chard, woody stems discarded and leaves torn into big pieces
- ¾ lb fresh plum tomatoes, diced medium
- 4 cloves garlic, minced
- 1 Tbsp curry powder (mild or hot, depending on your preference)
- 1 tsp ground cumin
- 2 tsp ground coriander, divided
- ½ cup dry green lentils
- ¼ tsp each sea salt and fresh ground black pepper
- 1 cup low-fat kefir
- 2 3-oz pieces whole-wheat naan, each sliced into 4-inch pieces and lightly toasted

**TIP: If you have trouble finding prepared whole-wheat naan at your local grocer, try whole-wheat pita or lavash bread in its place.**

### INSTRUCTIONS:

ONE: Heat oil in a large high-sided sauté pan or Dutch oven over medium-high. Add onion, eggplant, zucchini and carrots and sauté for 10 minutes, until vegetables soften, release some liquid and begin to shrink a bit. Add chard, tomatoes and garlic and sauté for 5 minutes. Add curry powder, cumin, 1 tsp coriander, lentils and 3 cups water. Bring mixture to a boil then reduce to a simmer over medium-low. Cover and simmer for 30 minutes, until vegetables are very soft and lentils are just tender. Season with salt and pepper.

TWO: Meanwhile, whisk kefir with remaining 1 tsp coriander in a small bowl. Cover and refrigerate until ready to use.

THREE: Ladle hot vegetable curry into bowls and drizzle with coriander kefir. Serve with warm naan.

**Nutrients per serving (1½ cups curry, ¼ cup coriander kefir, 1½ oz naan):** *Calories: 357, Total Fat: 9 g, Sat. Fat: 2.5 g, Monounsaturated Fat: 3 g, Polyunsaturated Fat: 0.5 g, Carbs: 59 g, Fiber: 15 g, Sugars: 15 g, Protein: 15 g, Sodium: 409 mg, Cholesterol: 0 mg*

**NUTRITIONAL BONUS: Lentils supply an impressive dose of iron, an essential mineral that carries oxygen to the blood. The body most readily absorbs iron from animal proteins, but iron-rich vegetarian fare can get an absorption boost when paired with foods high in vitamin C, such as the variety of veggies in this curry.**

# Slow-Cooked Curried Chickpeas

*Serves 8. **Hands-on time:** 25 minutes.*
*Total time: 5 to 6 or 9 to 10 hours, depending on slow-cooker setting.*

Cooking times can vary quite a bit depending on your slow cooker, so give yourself some extra time, if possible.

### INGREDIENTS:

- 1 lb chickpeas, rinsed and picked over (about 2¼ cups)
- 1 rutabaga (1½ to 2 lb), peeled and cut into ¾-inch dice (4 to 4½ cups)
- ½ large onion, chopped (about ¾ cup)
- 3 cloves garlic, chopped
- 1 bay leaf
- 5 tsp curry powder
- 2 tsp mild chile powder
- 1 lb mustard or collard greens, thick stems removed and leaves chopped (about 8 cups), divided
- 1¼ tsp sea salt, divided
- Fresh ground black pepper, to taste
- 1½ cups uncooked brown rice
- ¾ cup jarred water-packed roasted red peppers, patted dry and sliced
- 1 cup nonfat plain Greek yogurt
- ¼ cup chopped cilantro
- Lime wedges, for garnish, optional

### INSTRUCTIONS:

ONE: Place chickpeas in a large saucepan and add water to cover by about 3 inches. Bring to a boil over high heat and cook for 5 minutes. Reduce heat to medium and simmer, partially covered, for 1 hour. Stir occasionally and add more water, if needed, to cover chickpeas. Drain and rinse.

TWO: Place chickpeas, rutabaga, onion, garlic and bay leaf in a 5- to 7-qt slow cooker, then add 5 cups water. Cover with lid and cook on high for 4 to 5 hours or on low for 8 to 10 hours. (NOTE: Opt for whichever time frame is most convenient; flavor will not be affected.) About 30 to 45 minutes before chickpea mixture is done cooking, stir in curry and chile powders. Add half of greens and replace lid for 5 minutes, until wilted. Then add remaining greens and continue cooking for remaining time or until chickpeas are tender. (The finished dish should be slightly soupy; use a ladle to remove any excess water.) Stir in 1 tsp salt and pepper, to taste.

THREE: Meanwhile, combine rice, remaining ¼ tsp salt and 3 cups water in a small saucepan and bring to a boil over high. Reduce heat to low, cover and simmer for 50 minutes. Remove from heat and keep covered for 10 minutes. Serve chickpeas over rice and top with red peppers, yogurt and cilantro. Garnish with lime wedges on the side, if desired.

**Nutrients per serving (1¾ cups chickpea mixture, ¾ cup rice, 1½ Tbsp red peppers, 2 Tbsp yogurt):** *Calories: 307, Total Fat: 3 g, Sat. Fat: 1 g, Carbs: 59 g, Fiber: 12 g, Sugars: 8 g, Protein: 14 g, Sodium: 460 mg, Cholesterol: 0 mg*

Slow-Cooked Curried Chickpeas

Smashed
Red
Potatoes

**Nutritional Bonus:**
In addition to fiber, the
versatile potato is packed
with vitamins and minerals,
especially potassium and B6,
which help regulate blood
pressure and may lower
the risk of heart disease,
respectively.

# Smashed Red Potatoes
## WITH LEEKS & ROSEMARY

*Serves* 4. ***Hands-on time:*** *15 minutes.* ***Total time:*** *30 minutes.*

**Potatoes are commonly viewed as comfort food, so it might come as a surprise that they are actually low in calories and filled with fiber (especially if you leave the skin on!).**

INGREDIENTS:

- 1 lb small red potatoes, unpeeled and scrubbed
- 1 Tbsp olive oil
- 1 medium leek, white and light green parts only, thinly sliced
- 1 tsp minced fresh rosemary leaves
- ¼ cup low-fat sour cream
- ¼ cup skim milk
- ¼ tsp kosher salt
- Fresh ground black pepper, to taste

INSTRUCTIONS:

ONE: Cut potatoes in half and place in a medium saucepan. Fill pan with enough cold water to cover potatoes by at least 1 inch. Bring water to a boil, reduce heat to medium and cook for 15 minutes or until fork-tender.

TWO: Meanwhile, heat oil on medium-low in a small skillet. Add leek and cook, stirring occasionally, until very soft, about 8 minutes. Add rosemary and stir for 30 seconds. Remove pan from heat.

THREE: In a small bowl, whisk together sour cream and milk; set aside.

FOUR: When potatoes are tender, drain well and return to pot. Lightly smash potatoes using a potato masher. Add leeks, sour cream mixture, salt and pepper, then stir until creamy but still slightly chunky. Serve immediately.

Nutrients per ½-cup serving: *Calories: 154, Total Fat: 5 g, Sat. Fat: 2 g, Monounsaturated Fat: 3 g, Polyunsaturated Fat: 0.5 g, Carbs: 23 g, Fiber: 2 g, Sugars: 4 g, Protein: 4 g, Sodium: 148 mg, Cholesterol: 8 mg*

# Roasted Yellow Beets
## WITH SALSA VERDE

*Serves* 4. ***Hands-on time:*** *20 minutes.* ***Total time:*** *1 hour, 15 minutes.*

**Literally meaning "green sauce" in Italian, salsa verde can be made with any combination of fresh herbs. Simply utilize the additional basil, cilantro, tarragon or dill you have sitting in your refrigerator by substituting it for all or a portion of the parsley in our sauce.**

INGREDIENTS:

- 2 lb small yellow beets
- 2 cups Italian flat-leaf parsley leaves
- 3 Tbsp capers, drained
- 1 whole clove garlic
- 2 Tbsp olive oil
- ¼ cup fresh lemon juice
- Sea salt and fresh ground black pepper, to taste

INSTRUCTIONS:

ONE: Preheat oven to 400°F. Place beets on a large piece of foil and seal to form a tight package. Place wrapped beets onto a baking sheet and roast in oven for 45 to 55 minutes.

TWO: While beets are roasting, prepare salsa verde: Place parsley, capers, garlic, oil, ¼ cup water and lemon juice into a blender. Blend until puréed, occasionally scraping down sides of blender with a spatula to incorporate all ingredients, adding a little more water if purée is too thick for blender to process. Season with salt and pepper. Scrape sauce into a sealable container with a layer of plastic wrap directly on top of the purée (to avoid discoloration), seal container and refrigerate until needed (chilling not necessary; may be served immediately).

THREE: Once beets are tender when pierced with a knife, remove from oven. Allow beets to cool just enough to handle. Wearing rubber gloves, gently peel skins from beets and trim ends. Cut beets in half. To serve, place beets on a platter and drizzle with 4 Tbsp salsa verde. Remaining salsa verde may be kept sealed and refrigerated for about 3 to 5 days.

**MAIN-DISH PAIRING: The salsa verde makes these beets the perfect accompaniment to roast pork tenderloin. Simply drizzle a little extra sauce over the pork for added flavor.**

Nutrients per serving (3 to 5 beets and 1 Tbsp salsa verde): *Calories: 180, Total Fat: 8 g, Sat. Fat: 1 g, Carbs: 25 g, Fiber: 7 g, Sugars: 16 g, Protein: 5 g, Sodium: 490 mg, Cholesterol: 0 mg*

# Brussels Sprouts
## WITH SPICY ALMOND GLAZE

*Serves 4. **Hands-on time:** 20 minutes. **Total time:** 30 minutes.*

**Brussels sprouts do not appeal to many palates. One reason may be that cooking them for longer than five to seven minutes releases the organic compound sinigrin, the catalyst for Brussels sprouts' famous sulphur scent. So, instead of cooking your sprouts by the popular methods of boiling and steaming, sear them in a hot skillet to keep them crunchy and flavorful. Try this *Brassicaceae* family member again for the first time, *Clean Eating* style!**

### INGREDIENTS:

- 1 lb Brussels sprouts
- 3 Tbsp smooth unsalted almond butter
- 2 tsp low-sodium tamari
- 2 tsp raw organic honey
- 2 tsp fresh lemon juice
- 1 tsp ground cayenne pepper or your favorite hot chile sauce
- 1 tsp olive oil
- 1 clove garlic, minced

**OPTION: For a delicious change of taste, feel free to try your favorite unsalted natural nut butter, such as peanut or cashew, in lieu of the almond variety we've recommended.**

### INSTRUCTIONS:

ONE: Trim about ¼ inch from bottom of each sprout. Separate and remove loose outer leaves of each sprout from the center. Place leaves into a bowl and set aside. Slice each sprout center in half. In a separate small bowl, whisk together almond butter, 1½ Tbsp water, tamari, honey, lemon juice and cayenne. Set aside.

TWO: Heat oil in a medium nonstick sauté pan over medium-high. Add garlic and halved sprout centers and sear for about 1 minute. Add leaves and sauté until light golden brown and wilted, about 4 to 6 minutes.

THREE: Add about 2 Tbsp water to pan and stir once. Reduce heat to medium, pour in almond butter mixture and stir until sprouts are coated. Cook for about 30 to 60 seconds longer, until sauce has thickened slightly. Remove from heat and serve immediately.

**MAIN-DISH PAIRING: Enjoy this scrumptious side with steamed brown rice and sautéed shrimp.**

*Nutrients per ¾-cup serving: Calories: 160, Total Fat: 9 g, Sat. Fat: 1 g, Carbs: 19 g, Fiber: 5 g, Sugars: 8 g, Protein: 6 g, Sodium: 200 mg, Cholesterol: 0 mg*

# How to Prep Brussels Sprouts for Cooking

ONE: Trim about ¼ inch from bottom of each sprout.

TWO: Separate and remove loose outer leaves of each sprout from the center. Set leaves aside.

THREE: Slice each sprout center in half.

Brussels
Sprouts
with Spicy
Almond
Glaze

**Nutritional Bonus:**
Though artichokes are tough and thorny on the outside, the rewards of conquering one are plentiful. The leaves and heart are not only delicious, but also low in calories and high in fiber. They are also a good source of magnesium to boost your immune system and folate to promote healthy brain and cell development during pregnancy.

Steamed Artichokes with Lemon-Herb Sauce

# Steamed Artichokes
## WITH LEMON-HERB SAUCE

*Serves 4. **Hands-on time:** 25 minutes. **Total time:** 45 minutes.*

**This totally indulgent veggie dip will make you completely forget you're eating clean.**

### INGREDIENTS:

- 4 medium artichokes
- ½ lemon
- 2 tsp lemon zest
- 1 Tbsp fresh lemon juice
- ½ cup 2% plain Greek yogurt
- 1 small clove garlic, minced
- ⅓ cup low-fat sour cream
- 2 tsp capers, drained, rinsed and minced
- 2 Tbsp minced fresh dill
- 1 Tbsp minced fresh flat-leaf parsley
- 1 tsp olive oil
- ⅛ tsp sea salt

### INSTRUCTIONS:

ONE: With a sharp knife, slice about 1 inch off the top of each artichoke. If leaves have thorns, snip off tips of leaves with kitchen shears. Cut stems, leaving about 1 inch on each artichoke. Rub cut parts of artichokes with lemon to prevent browning.

TWO: Fill a large pot with 2 to 3 inches of water (water should only come up to the bottom of a steamer basket, not cover it) and heat on high. Insert steamer basket into pot and add artichokes to basket; cover. Bring to a boil, then reduce heat to simmer. Cook for 25 to 35 minutes or until outer leaves of artichokes can be easily pulled off.

THREE: Meanwhile, add remaining ingredients to a medium bowl and whisk to combine. Refrigerate mixture until ready to serve. Serve artichokes warm with lemon-herb sauce for dipping.

Nutrients per serving (1 artichoke and ¼ cup yogurt sauce): *Calories: 126, Total Fat: 4 g, Sat. Fat: 2 g, Carbs: 18 g, Fiber: 7 g, Sugars: 3 g, Protein: 11 g, Sodium: 247 mg, Cholesterol: 10 mg*

# Cleaner Scalloped Potatoes

*Serves 8. **Hands-on time:** 45 minutes. **Total time:** 2 hours, 10 minutes.*

**You'll be making this cleaned-up classic again and again! It can be prepared through Step Three up to one day ahead of time. Just cover potatoes and refrigerate. You can bring potatoes to room temperature before baking or add 5 to 10 minutes to baking time.**

### INGREDIENTS:

- Olive oil cooking spray
- 2 tsp olive oil
- 1 medium onion, halved lengthwise and thinly sliced
- ½ tsp sea salt, divided
- Fresh ground black pepper, to taste
- 2 cloves garlic, finely chopped
- ¾ tsp dried thyme
- 1½ Tbsp white whole-wheat flour
  (TIP: Regular whole-wheat flour or whole-wheat pastry flour may be substituted.)
- 2 cups low-fat milk
- 3 oz low-fat Monterey Jack or white cheddar cheese, grated
- 2½ lb Russet potatoes, peeled and sliced as thin as possible (⅛ inch or less)
- 2 oz Parmigiano-Reggiano cheese, grated
- 2 Tbsp whole-wheat panko bread crumbs

### INSTRUCTIONS:

ONE: Preheat oven to 350°F. Coat a 2-qt baking dish with cooking spray.

TWO: Heat oil in a large skillet over medium-high heat. Add onion, ¼ tsp salt and pepper. Cook, stirring frequently, until lightly browned, about 7 minutes. Reduce heat to low and add garlic, thyme and flour. Cook, stirring constantly, for 1 to 2 minutes or until onions are coated with flour. Add milk and increase heat to medium-high. When liquid begins to simmer, reduce heat to low and cook until mixture thickens slightly, about 4 minutes. Add three-quarters of Monterey Jack and remaining ¼ tsp salt, and stir until melted, about 1 minute. Remove from heat.

THREE: Arrange half of potatoes in an even layer in prepared baking dish. Cover with half of onion mixture. Repeat with remaining potatoes and remaining onion mixture.

FOUR: In a small bowl, combine remaining Monterey Jack, Parmigiano-Reggiano and panko; cover and refrigerate until ready to use.

FIVE: Bake potatoes in center of oven for 70 to 85 minutes or until potatoes in center of dish feel tender when pierced with a fork. When finished baking, remove potatoes from oven and sprinkle evenly with cheese-panko mixture. Preheat broiler to high, return baking dish to oven and broil until cheese is melted, about 2 minutes. Let cool for 10 to 15 minutes before serving.

Nutrients per 1-cup serving: *Calories: 201, Total Fat: 4 g, Sat. Fat: 2 g, Carbs: 33 g, Fiber: 3 g, Sugars: 5 g, Protein: 9 g, Sodium: 248 mg, Cholesterol: 9 mg*

# Hot & Sour Swiss Chard

*Serves* 4. ***Hands-on time:*** *10 minutes.* ***Total time:*** *15 minutes.*

For a colorful alternative to standard Swiss chard, look for rainbow, or Bright Lights, Swiss chard at your local farmers' market or grocery store. Its vibrant yellow, pink and purple hues hold up during cooking, brim with antioxidants and look stunning when plated.

## INGREDIENTS:

- 2 Tbsp apple cider vinegar
- 2 Tbsp raw organic honey
- 1 Tbsp unsalted tomato paste
- ¼ to ½ tsp red chile flakes (adjust to taste)
- 1 tsp olive oil
- 1 medium shallot, finely diced
- 1 bunch Swiss chard, sliced into 1-inch pieces, stems and leaves separated (about 2 to 3 cups stems and 4 to 6 cups leaves)
- Sea salt and fresh ground black pepper, to taste

## INSTRUCTIONS:

ONE: In a small bowl, whisk together vinegar, honey, tomato paste and chile flakes. Set aside.

TWO: Heat a large 10- to 12-inch sauté pan over medium-high. Add oil and shallot and sauté for 1 minute, until translucent. Add chard stems to pan and sauté for about 1 minute. Add chard leaves, stir and continue to cook for another 2 minutes. Season with salt and pepper and pour mixture into a bowl.

THREE: Return pan to heat and pour tomato paste mixture into pan. (Be careful: Vinegar will boil immediately, resulting in strong fumes. Keep your face away from pan.) Stir well and allow liquid to reduce for about 30 to 60 seconds so that it thickens enough to coat the back of a spoon. Remove from heat.

FOUR: Place chard onto a serving platter and drizzle with sauce. Serve immediately.

**MAIN-DISH PAIRING: Try this spicy Asian-inspired dish with chicken, beef or shrimp skewers and some boiled soba noodles.**

Nutrients per ⅔-cup serving: *Calories: 69, Total Fat: 1 g, Sat. Fat: 0 g, Carbs: 14 g, Fiber: 1 g, Sugars: 9.5 g, Protein: 1.5 g, Sodium: 198 mg, Cholesterol: 0 mg*

**NUTRITIONAL BONUS: Cook up both the stems and leaves of your Swiss chard. The stems contain more fiber than the leaves but fewer nutrients. The nutritional value of the stems varies, as the nutrients actually flow through the stem to the leaves during the growing process.**

For a photo of this recipe, see page 50.

# Baked Beans & Pears
## WITH QUICK BROCCOLI SLAW SALAD

*Serves* 4. ***Hands-on time:*** *15 minutes.* ***Total time:*** *55 minutes.*

By baking a pear along with your beans and opting for honey and ginger in place of molasses, your vegetarian baked beans will be left with a fresh chewiness not found in traditional recipes. And, with quick prep times for both the beans and broccoli salad, you can relax while dinner practically cooks itself.

## INGREDIENTS:

- 2 Tbsp extra-virgin olive oil, divided
- ½ Spanish onion, chopped
- 1 15-oz can Eden Organic Navy Beans
- 1 Bosc pear, chopped
- ¾ tsp ground dry mustard
- ¾ tsp ground dried ginger
- 1 Tbsp raw honey
- 1 Tbsp balsamic vinegar
- ½ tsp sea salt, plus additional to taste, divided
- 2 cups cooked barley (cooked according to package directions)
- 4 oz daikon radish, grated
- 4 oz broccoli slaw
- 1½ tsp red wine vinegar

## INSTRUCTIONS:

ONE: Preheat oven to 325°F. Rub a 9-inch glass baking dish with 1 tsp oil and set aside.

TWO: In a medium saucepan, sauté onion and 2 tsp oil over medium heat for 5 minutes or until onion is translucent.

THREE: Drain beans over a bowl to catch the liquid, then combine drained beans with onions in a large bowl. Stir in pear, mustard, ginger, honey, balsamic vinegar, ½ tsp salt and 2 Tbsp reserved bean liquid. Spoon bean mixture into dish and cover with aluminum foil. Bake for 45 minutes.

FOUR: About 5 minutes before beans are done, add barley, daikon, broccoli slaw, red wine vinegar and remaining 1 Tbsp oil to a medium bowl. Toss to combine and season with salt. Serve baked beans alongside broccoli salad.

Nutrients per serving (1 cup baked beans and 1 cup broccoli salad): *Calories: 311, Total Fat: 8 g, Sat. Fat: 1 g, Monounsaturated Fat: 5.5 g, Polyunsaturated Fat: 1 g, Carbs: 53 g, Fiber: 11.5 g, Sugars: 10.5 g, Protein: 9 g, Sodium: 277 mg, Cholesterol: 0 mg*

Baked
Beans &
Pears

Quick
Broccoli
Slaw Salad

## Nutritional Bonus:
By including radishes
(traditionally used to improve
digestion) and barley (a rich
source of insoluble fiber to help
ensure regularity), this quick
salad will please your taste buds
and your digestive system.

# Roasted Fennel
## WITH PARMESAN

**Serves** 4. **Hands-on time:** 10 minutes. **Total time:** 45 minutes.

**Fennel is a delicious and often-underappreciated ingredient. The vegetable's healthy offering of vitamin C, fiber, folate, potassium, phytonutrients and antioxidants makes it worth experimenting with in your cooking. To learn more about picking, prepping and cooking these big white bulbs, see p. 71.**

### INGREDIENTS:

- 2 large fennel bulbs, sliced into 4 to 8 wedges
- Sea salt and fresh ground black pepper, to taste
- 1 Tbsp olive oil
- ⅓ cup grated Parmesan cheese

### INSTRUCTIONS:

ONE: Preheat oven to 400°F.

TWO: Fill a large pot halfway with water and bring to a boil. Add fennel wedges and cook for 5 minutes. Drain well and let cool slightly. Place in a square pan. Sprinkle with salt and pepper, then toss with oil.

THREE: Cook in oven for 30 minutes or until fennel pierces easily with a fork. Sprinkle with Parmesan and roast for another 5 minutes. Serve immediately.

Nutrients per ⅔-cup serving: Calories: 108, Total Fat: 6 g, Sat. Fat: 2 g, Monounsaturated Fat: 3 g, Polyunsaturated Fat: 1 g, Carbs: 8 g, Fiber: 4 g, Sugars: 0.5 g, Protein: 5 g, Sodium: 258 mg, Cholesterol: 7 mg

**Nutritional Bonus:**
Just 1 cup of fennel provides 20% of your daily need for vitamin C, which bolsters your immune system and helps to rid the body of free radicals.

# Fennel

## Curious about those big white bulbs but puzzled about how to cook them? Let fennel's unique flavor mellow for a super-low-fat side dish.

If you tend to breeze past the big white bulbs with green fronds in the grocery store, you're not alone. But before you dismiss fennel, lean in and smell. You'll notice a faint scent similar to licorice and celery, which may explain why chefs love this Mediterranean vegetable.

In its raw state, fennel is superb in salads, and at just 49 calories and zero grams of fat per one-cup serving, you'll wonder why you waited so long. It can also be marinated to layer on antipasto platters or it can be roasted (see p. 70) as a perfect side for fish.

If you're still unsure about trying fennel because you're not a licorice lover, put your mind at ease. You'll taste but a hint of anise, one that is more delicate than overwhelming.

## How to Buy and Store

Fennel is sold year-round in supermarkets but peaks in winter and spring. Use these tips when shopping for and storing fennel:
- Choose a firm bright-white bulb with the stalks and fronds still attached.
- Avoid bulbs that show cracks, bruises or browning on outer leaves or at cut bottoms.
- Stored in a plastic bag in the fridge, fennel will keep for up to one week. Any longer and the bulb will become tough and less flavorful.

## Your Guide to Prepping

ONE: Cut off stalks, close to top of bulb.

TWO: Trim bottom of bulb.

THREE: Slice off any wilted or browned sections of the bulb.

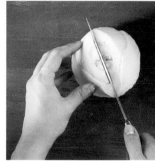

FOUR: Cut bulb in half lengthwise.

FIVE: Lay halves flat and quarter them. Try to keep them attached at the bottom. If pieces are larger than a soup spoon, halve them.

## More Ways to Use Fennel

Use the stalks to flavor stock, dice a few fronds into a green salad for a sweet kick, or stuff the stalks and fronds into the cavity of a chicken ready for roasting.

You won't recognize the background flavor, but you'll love its subtle taste. Or try these other ideas for fennel:

**BRAISE** it with pork chops

**SLICE** it into a slaw

**CHOP** it into a base for soups, along with carrots and onions

**ROAST** it and then chop it into potato salad

**BRUSH** fennel pieces with olive oil and grill them

**SUBSTITUTE** fennel fronds when a recipe calls for dill

**USE** a mandoline to make a salad dressed with olive oil, lemon juice and parsley

**MAKE** a bed out of the fronds for steamed fish

**TOSS** fresh fennel stems onto the coals when grilling meat or fish

# Dressings

Rest assured, the following recipes will definitely catapult your tried-and-true salads straight to the best-dressed list! Whether you're feeling like an oil and vinegar-, a yogurt- or even a tofu-based topper, we've got a dressing to suit your mood and your choice of greens – plus, all nine of these options are brimming with flavor and ready in mere minutes. Bonus: Some of these dressings do double-duty as dipping sauces!

## Creamy Fresh Herb Dressing

*Serves* 4. *Makes* ½ cup. *Hands-on time:* 7 minutes. *Total time:* 7 minutes.

**This herbed dressing can also be transformed into a must-have crudités dip for get-togethers or smart snacking. Simply thicken the mix by increasing the amount of Greek yogurt to ¾ cup.**

INGREDIENTS:

- 6 Tbsp nonfat plain Greek yogurt
- 2 tsp fresh lemon juice
- 1 tsp raw organic honey
- 1 tsp Dijon mustard
- 1 tsp parsley, chopped
- 1 tsp fresh dill, snipped or chopped
- 1 tsp lemon zest
- Fresh ground black pepper, to taste

INSTRUCTIONS:

In a small bowl, whisk together all ingredients until blended. Refrigerate until serving or use immediately. Store in a sealed container in refrigerator for up to 5 days.

*Nutrients per 2-Tbsp serving: Calories: 25, Total Fat: 0 g, Sat. Fat: 0 g, Carbs: 3 g, Fiber: 0 g, Sugars: 1 g, Protein: 2 g, Sodium: 40 mg, Cholesterol: 0 mg*

## Basil Walnut Vinaigrette

*Serves* 4. *Makes* ¼ cup. *Hands-on time:* 10 minutes. *Total time:* 10 minutes.

**Our vinaigrette doesn't just have to be added to a bed of greens to make up a satisfying and wholesome salad. Drizzle it over cooked, cooled rice or whole-wheat pasta with fresh vegetables for an impromptu grain salad.**

INGREDIENTS:

- 10 fresh basil leaves, finely chopped
- ½ clove garlic, minced
- 1 tsp Dijon mustard
- 1 Tbsp wine vinegar
- 1 Tbsp extra-virgin olive oil
- 2 Tbsp low-sodium chicken broth
- Sea salt and fresh ground black pepper, to taste
- 1 Tbsp unsalted walnuts, chopped

INSTRUCTIONS:

In a medium bowl, add basil, garlic, Dijon, vinegar, oil, broth, salt and pepper, whisking to combine thoroughly. Stir in walnuts. Refrigerate until serving or use immediately. Store in a sealed container in refrigerator for up to 2 weeks.

*Nutrients per 1-Tbsp serving: Calories: 45, Total Fat: 4.5 g, Sat. Fat: 0.5 g, Omega-3s: 200 mg, Omega-6s: 990 mg, Carbs: 1 g, Fiber: 0 g, Sugars: 0 g, Protein: 0 g, Sodium: 80 mg, Cholesterol: 0 mg*

# Rice Vinegar & Wasabi Dressing

*Serves 1. **Makes** ¼ cup. **Hands-on time:** / minutes. **Total time:** 7 minutes.*

**For a quick Asian-inspired on-the-go snack, mix this dressing with cooked brown rice and roll it up in a sheet of Nori seaweed.**

### INGREDIENTS:

- 2 Tbsp rice vinegar
- 1 Tbsp extra-virgin olive oil
- ½ tsp wasabi paste (or to taste)
- ½ tsp pure sesame oil
- ¼ tsp toasted unsalted sesame seeds
- Sea salt, to taste

### INSTRUCTIONS:

In a small bowl, whisk together all ingredients until blended. Refrigerate until serving or use immediately. Oil-based dressings last longest in the refrigerator (up to 2 weeks) but should be brought to room temperature before using for best flavor.

*Nutrients per 1-Tbsp serving: Calories: 40, Total Fat: 4 g, Sat. Fat: 0.5 g, Carbs: 0 g, Fiber: 0 g, Sugars: 0 g, Protein: 0 g, Sodium: 75 mg, Cholesterol: 0 mg*

# Honey & White Balsamic Vinaigrette

*Serves 4. **Makes** ¼ cup. **Hands-on time:** 7 minutes. **Total time:** 7 minutes.*

**White balsamic vinegar is milder and less sweet than its dark relative, making it a perfect base for dressings – it won't compete with mild herbs and seasonings.**

### INGREDIENTS:

- 2 Tbsp white balsamic vinegar
- 2 Tbsp extra-virgin olive oil
- 1 Tbsp raw organic honey
- ¼ tsp mustard seeds, ground
- Sea salt and fresh ground black pepper, to taste

### INSTRUCTIONS:

In a small bowl, whisk together all ingredients. Refrigerate until serving or use immediately. Store in a sealed container in refrigerator for up to 2 weeks.

*Nutrients per 1-Tbsp serving: Calories: 90, Total Fat: 7 g, Sat Fat: 1 g, Carbs: 6 g, Fiber: 0 g, Sugars: 5 g, Protein: 0 g, Sodium: 50 mg, Cholesterol: 0 mg*

# Creamy Lemon Dressing

*Serves 4. **Makes** ½ cup. **Hands-on time:** 7 minutes. **Total time:** 7 minutes.*

**Break up last night's cold cooked salmon, mix it with this fresh creamy dressing and serve it alongside rice and greens for a brand-new lunch or dinner that won't have you cringing at the thought of leftovers.**

### INGREDIENTS:

- 4 oz soft tofu, drained
- 1 Tbsp fresh lemon juice
- 1 tsp lemon zest
- ½ Tbsp white wine vinegar or rice vinegar
- 1 Tbsp extra-virgin olive oil
- Sea salt and fresh ground black pepper, to taste
- 1 tsp chives, chopped

### INSTRUCTIONS:

ONE: Place tofu in a blender and process with lemon juice and zest, vinegar and oil, scraping down sides of work bowl as needed.

TWO: Transfer dressing to a small mixing or serving bowl and stir in salt, pepper and chives. Refrigerate until serving or use immediately. Store in a sealed container in refrigerator for 1 to 2 days (dependent on shelf life of tofu).

*Nutrients per 2-Tbsp serving: Calories: 50, Total Fat: 4.5 g, Sat. Fat: 0 g, Carbs: 1 g, Fiber: 0 g, Sugars: 0 g, Protein: 2 g, Sodium: 60 mg, Cholesterol: 0 mg*

# Orange Herb Dressing

*Serves 4. **Makes** ⅓ cup. **Hands-on time:** 7 minutes. **Total time:** 7 minutes.*

**Try this citrus dressing drizzled over fresh fruit and topped with a few sliced and toasted unsalted almonds for an energizing snack.**

### INGREDIENTS:

- 2 Tbsp fresh orange juice
- 2 Tbsp white balsamic vinegar or apple cider vinegar
- 2 Tbsp extra-virgin olive oil
- 1 Tbsp fresh tarragon, minced, or ½ tsp dried tarragon
- ½ Tbsp fresh oregano, minced, or ¼ tsp dried oregano
- ½ tsp orange zest
- Sea salt and fresh ground black pepper, to taste

### INSTRUCTIONS:

In a small bowl, whisk together all ingredients. Refrigerate until serving or use immediately. Store in a sealed container and refrigerate for up to 2 weeks.

*Nutrients per 4-tsp serving: Calories: 80, Total Fat: 7 g, Sat. Fat: 1 g, Carbs: 3 g, Fiber: 0 g, Sugars: 2 g, Protein: 0 g, Sodium: 55 mg, Cholesterol: 0 mg*

# Tarragon Mustard Dressing

*Serves 4.* **Makes** *½ cup.* **Hands-on time:** *7 minutes.* **Total time:** *7 minutes.*

**Try this zesty dressing mixed with cooked cubed chicken and halved grapes for a no-fuss chicken salad.**

INGREDIENTS:

• 4 oz soft tofu, drained

• 1 Tbsp Dijon mustard

• ½ Tbsp fresh lemon juice

• ½ clove garlic, chopped

• 1 Tbsp fresh tarragon, chopped, or ½ tsp dried tarragon

• Sea salt and fresh ground black pepper, to taste

INSTRUCTIONS:

ONE: Place tofu in a blender and process with Dijon, lemon juice and garlic until smooth, scraping down sides of work bowl as needed.

TWO: Transfer dressing to a small mixing or serving bowl and stir in tarragon, salt and pepper. Refrigerate until serving or use immediately. Store in a sealed container in refrigerator for up to 3 days (dependent on shelf life of tofu).

Nutrients per 2-Tbsp serving: *Calories: 25, Total Fat: 1 g, Sat. Fat: 0 g, Carbs: 1 g, Fiber: 0 g, Sugars: 0 g, Protein: 2 g, Sodium: 150 mg, Cholesterol: 0 mg*

# Curry Dressing

*Serves 4.* **Makes** *¼ cup.* **Hands-on time:** *7 minutes.* **Total time:** *7 minutes.*

**Toss this dressing with cooked rice and raisins for a quick curried rice side dish.**

INGREDIENTS:

• 2 Tbsp white balsamic vinegar

• 1 Tbsp apple cider vinegar

• 2 tsp raw organic honey

• ¼ tsp curry powder

• 1 tsp Dijon mustard

• Sea salt and fresh ground black pepper, to taste

INSTRUCTIONS:

In a small bowl, whisk together all ingredients. Refrigerate until serving or use immediately. Store dressing in a sealed container in a cool dark place for up to 6 months.

Nutrients per 1-Tbsp serving: *Calories: 20, Total Fat: 0 g, Sat. Fat: 0 g, Carbs: 5 g, Fiber: 0 g, Sugars: 4 g, Protein: 0 g, Sodium: 80 mg, Cholesterol: 0 mg*

# Buttermilk Ranch Dressing

*Serves 6.* **Makes** *½ cup.* **Hands-on time:** *15 minutes.* **Total time:** *15 minutes.*

**This dressing does double duty as a flavorful vegetable dip. No modifications required!**

INGREDIENTS:

• 5 Tbsp low-fat buttermilk

• 3 Tbsp nonfat plain Greek yogurt

• ¼ tsp onion powder

• 1 tsp fresh dill, chopped

• 1 tsp fresh parsley, chopped

• 1 tsp fresh chives, chopped

• Sea salt and fresh ground black pepper, to taste

INSTRUCTIONS:

In a medium bowl, whisk together all ingredients until blended. Refrigerate until serving or use immediately. Store in a sealed container in refrigerator for up to 5 days.

Nutrients per 1-Tbsp serving: *Calories: 10, Total Fat: 2 g, Sat. Fat: 0 g, Carbs: 1 g, Fiber: 0 g, Sugars: 1 g, Protein: 1 g, Sodium: 55 mg, Cholesterol: 1 mg*

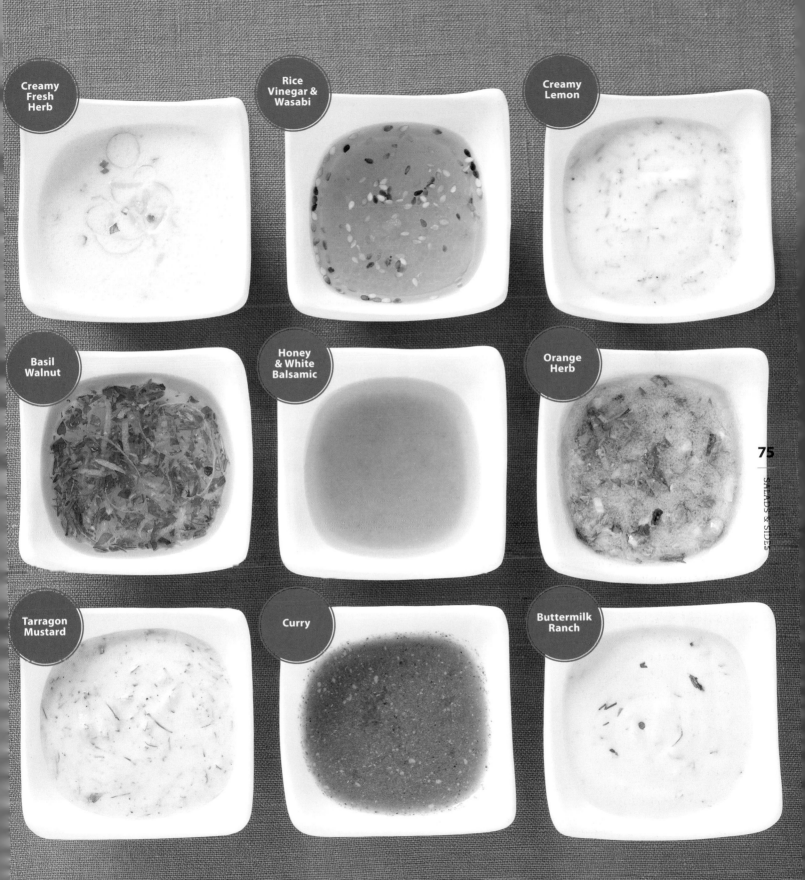

Creamy Fresh Herb

Rice Vinegar & Wasabi

Creamy Lemon

Basil Walnut

Honey & White Balsamic

Orange Herb

Tarragon Mustard

Curry

Buttermilk Ranch

Belgian
Endive

Watercress

Iceberg

Spinach

Loose
Leaf

# Mix 'N'
Match
## Salad Greens

Radicchio

Romaine

Your best first move
when assembling
a salad is to decide
which lettuce or
greens to reach for.
Here you'll find
options for generating
optimum flavor and
health, including what
type of dressing works
best for each green.

Arugula

Boston

## Arugula

**OFFERS:** vitamins A, C and K

**FLAVOR:** peppery

**COMBINE WITH:** milder lettuces (such as Boston or Bibb) and olive oil-based vinaigrettes

**CE DRESSING PICK:** Honey & White Balsamic Vinaigrette (p. 73) and Basil Walnut Vinaigrette (p. 72)

## Belgian Endive

**OFFERS:** antioxidant vitamin E and magnesium

**FLAVOR:** bitter

**COMBINE WITH:** watercress or Boston lettuce and creamy or citrus dressings

**CE DRESSING PICK:** Creamy Lemon Dressing (p. 73) and Orange Herb Dressing (p. 73)

## Boston & Bibb Lettuce

**OFFERS:** B vitamins, calcium and magnesium

**FLAVOR:** subtle, buttery (Boston), sweet (Bibb)

**COMBINE WITH:** spinach, Belgian endive or romaine lettuce and citrus dressings or olive oil-based vinaigrettes

**CE DRESSING PICK:** Orange Herb Dressing (p. 73)

## Iceberg

**OFFERS:** vitamins B1 and B6

**FLAVOR:** crisp, mild

**COMBINE WITH:** arugula, watercress or loose leaf lettuce and creamy dressings

**CE DRESSING PICK:** Creamy Fresh Herb Dressing (p. 72) and Buttermilk Ranch Dressing (p. 74)

## Loose Leaf

**OFFERS:** calcium, magnesium and phosphorous

**FLAVOR:** delicate, sweet

**COMBINE WITH:** Boston, watercress, radicchio, arugula or crisp lettuce varieties (such as iceberg) and wine vinaigrettes

**CE DRESSING PICK:** Honey & White Balsamic Vinaigrette (p. 73)

## Radicchio

**OFFERS:** vitamin B6, iron and zinc

**FLAVOR:** peppery

**COMBINE WITH:** Boston, loose leaf, spinach, Belgian endive or arugula and nut-based vinaigrettes

**CE DRESSING PICK:** Basil Walnut Vinaigrette (p. 72)

## Romaine

**OFFERS:** calcium and vitamins A, C, K and B1

**FLAVOR:** sweet, nutty

**COMBINE WITH:** Bibb lettuce, spinach or arugula and wine vinaigrettes

**CE DRESSING PICK:** Honey & White Balsamic Vinaigrette (p. 73)

## Spinach

**OFFERS:** iron, calcium and folate

**FLAVOR:** mild

**COMBINE WITH:** Boston or Bibb lettuce and citrus vinaigrettes

**CE DRESSING PICK:** Creamy Lemon Dressing (p. 73) and Orange Herb Dressing (p. 73)

## Watercress

**OFFERS:** iron, calcium and folate

**FLAVOR:** spicy

**COMBINE WITH:** Boston or romaine lettuce or Belgian endive and various vinaigrettes

**CE DRESSING PICK:** Basil Walnut Vinaigrette (p. 72)

## The Grand Finale

Try these out-of-the box salad toppers to add variety and vitality to your greens.

**PUMPKIN SEEDS: Pumpkin seeds pump you full of infection-fighting zinc, magnesium to maintain bones and iron for energy.**

TRY: Baby spinach + red lentils + wild rice + cucumbers + pumpkin seeds

**ARTICHOKES: In a United States Department of Agriculture study, artichokes beat out broccoli and spinach to take the top spot as the vegetable with the highest antioxidant content.**

TRY: Fennel + artichoke hearts + shrimp + shredded carrot + parsley

**BEETS: Betalains, the plant pigments responsible for beets' hue, are free-radical-fighting antioxidants, helping to keep you looking and feeling young. Psst: Microwave beets to preserve their antioxidant levels.**

TRY: Romaine + beets + unsweetened dates + roasted peppers + feta

**CITRUS: A University of Western Ontario, Canada, study found that naringenin, a flavonoid found in citrus fruits, may help stave off weight gain by causing the liver to burn up excess fat rather than store it.**

TRY: Mixed greens + grapefruit + avocado + green beans

# Soups,
# Stews & Chilis

Top: Shallot & Fennel Flatbread,
*bestofcleaneating.com/taste/shallot-and-fennel-flatbread/*
Right: Five-Onion Soup with Scallion Crostini, p. 83

Very few things are more satisfying than a comforting bowl of soup, stew or chili. Unfortunately, the canned varieties tend to fall a little short on nutrition and can be a touch high in sodium. The next time you're tempted to crack open a can, try these doable and nutrient-dense *Clean Eating* recipes instead. (P.S. They're very light on salt!) It's easy to create a culinary masterpiece like our Thai Chili or Mexican Pozole – each with a manageable list of figure-friendly ingredients. Even your kids will sip these soups to the very last drop – and probably ask for seconds!

# Thai Chili

*Serves* 4. ***Hands-on time:*** *10 minutes.* ***Total time:*** *27 minutes.*

**Chili is a cherished dish, inspiring state fair cook-offs across the country and culinary-novice husbands to enter the realm of the kitchen. Our version may stray from the traditional, yet it is a delicious combination of vegetarian chili and red curry with a hint of coconut. Meat enthusiasts: Don't be too quick to pass on this beef-free recipe. With its chewy texture, bulgur makes for a satisfying ground-beef substitute, while adding fiber and nixing cholesterol.**

INGREDIENTS:

- 1½ tsp red curry paste
- 1 tsp ground cumin
- 4 cups low-sodium vegetable broth, divided
- ½ cup uncooked bulgur
- ½ medium sweet potato, peeled and cubed (2 cups)
- 1 large green bell pepper, chopped (2 cups)
- 3 cups cooked kidney beans, drained
- ½ cup light coconut milk
- 2 cups jarred or boxed tomato purée/passata
- 2 scallions, chopped
- Fresh ground black pepper, to taste

INSTRUCTIONS:

ONE: In a 4-qt pot, add curry paste, cumin and a bit of broth. Mash mixture and stir until paste is no longer lumpy. Add remaining broth, bulgur, potato and bell pepper. Set over high heat and bring mixture to a boil. Cover tightly, reduce heat to medium-low and cook for 10 minutes.

TWO: Add beans, coconut milk and tomato purée to pot and stir. Cook, uncovered, for 7 minutes, until bulgur is tender and chili is thick. Stir in scallions and black pepper and serve.

*Nutrients per 2½-cup serving: Calories: 341, Total Fat: 5 g, Sat. Fat: 6 g, Carbs: 68 g, Fiber: 17 g, Sugars: 13 g, Protein: 17 g, Sodium: 412 mg, Cholesterol: 0 mg*

**Nutritional Bonus:**
The deep red hue of kidney bean skins is a quick indicator that they contain free-radical-fighting polyphenols. In fact, the beans are ranked with an oxygen radical absorbance capacity score (translation: antioxidant values of foods) of 8,457, while superfood spinach has 1,515.

THE BEST OF CLEAN EATING 2

**Nutritional Bonus:**
The thick, creamy texture is not the only reason this chowder satisfies: It provides 27 grams, or 55%, of your daily protein. Although shrimp and scallops aren't often touted as sources of heart-healthy omega-3 fats, they pack over 4 grams into each serving. You'll also meet 73% of your daily vitamin A requirement, which is important for healthy vision and fending off viral infections.

Seafood Corn Chowder

# Seafood Corn Chowder

*Serves 5.* **Hands-on time:** *20 minutes.* **Total time:** *45 minutes.*

What could be better than curling up with a creamy bowl of this chowder on a chilly night? Bonus: This easy, comforting soup sticks to your ribs, not your hips.

## INGREDIENTS:

- 1 Tbsp extra-virgin olive oil
- 1 white onion, chopped (about 1½ cups)
- 2 large carrots, chopped (about ¾ cup)
- 2 stalks celery, chopped (about ¾ cup)
- Sea salt and fresh ground black pepper, to taste
- 1 jalapeño pepper, chopped (seeded if you'd like to reduce heat)
- 1 tsp smoked paprika
- ¾ tsp dried thyme
- 1 lb Russet potatoes, peeled and chopped (about 2½ cups)
- 3 cups frozen corn kernels
- 1 cup low-fat milk
- ¾ lb sea scallops
- ½ lb medium shrimp, peeled and deveined
- 3 scallions, white and light green parts only, thinly sliced

**TIP:** The chowder can be as mild or spicy as you like. If you enjoy a little heat, add all of the jalapeño seeds.

## INSTRUCTIONS:

**ONE:** Heat oil in a large Dutch oven or stockpot on medium. Add onion, carrots and celery; season with salt and pepper and cook until soft, about 8 minutes. Add jalapeño, paprika and thyme and cook for 1 minute, stirring well. Add 3 cups water, increase heat and bring to a boil. Add potatoes and reduce to a simmer until just tender, 7 to 8 minutes. Add corn and milk; season with salt (¼ tsp minimum) and pepper, and simmer for 3 more minutes. Remove from heat.

**TWO:** Pour 3 cups corn mixture into a blender, covering opening loosely with a kitchen towel to prevent splatters (steam from the hot liquid may cause the blender's lid to pop off) and purée. Transfer purée back to pot, stir to combine and return to medium heat; bring to a simmer.

**THREE:** Add scallops to pot and simmer for 3 minutes (time should begin when liquid returns to simmer). Add shrimp and simmer for 2 minutes or until shellfish are opaque in center. Remove from heat and taste for seasoning. Ladle into bowls, sprinkle with scallions, dividing evenly, and serve.

*Nutrients per serving: Calories: 337, Total Fat: 5 g, Sat. Fat: 1 g, Carbs: 45 g, Fiber: 5 g, Sugars: 7 g, Protein: 28 g, Sodium: 272 mg, Cholesterol: 93 mg*

# Five-Onion Soup
## WITH SCALLION CROSTINI

*Serves 4.* **Hands-on time:** *15 minutes.* **Total time:** *1 hour, 20 minutes.*

The secret to a great onion soup is to slowly sweat and caramelize the onions. (And the secret to not crying while you cook with them can be found on p. 84!)

## INGREDIENTS:

- 1 Tbsp olive oil
- 2 leeks, white and light green parts only, thinly sliced (3 cups) and rinsed in cold water
- 4 shallots, thinly sliced (1½ cups)
- 1 each white and red onion, thinly sliced (3 cups each)
- 2 Tbsp white wine vinegar
- 8 cups low-sodium chicken broth
- 3 sprigs fresh thyme
- 2 bay leaves
- 4 slices whole-grain baguette, about 4 inches long and ¼ inch thick each
- 2 oz goat cheese, softened
- 2 scallions, thinly sliced
- Sea salt and fresh ground black pepper, to taste
- ¼ cup finely sliced chives

## INSTRUCTIONS:

**ONE:** In a large 6-qt saucepan, heat oil on medium-high. Add leeks, shallots and white and red onions. Cook, stirring frequently, for 2 to 3 minutes, until onions have softened slightly. Reduce heat to medium, cover with tight-fitting lid and allow onions to sweat and release water, about 15 to 20 minutes, stirring twice. Remove lid and continue cooking for about 10 minutes. Reduce heat to medium-low and cook for an additional 20 minutes, stirring and scraping bottom of pan with wooden spoon every 10 minutes, allowing onions to caramelize and turn golden brown. (Onions will be very soft and appear almost puréed.)

**TWO:** Increase heat to high, add vinegar and stir until liquid is incorporated. Add broth, thyme and bay leaves and bring mixture to a boil. Reduce heat to medium and simmer for about 30 minutes.

**THREE:** While soup is simmering, prepare crostini: Position oven rack in top third of oven and preheat to broil. Place baguette slices on a baking tray and toast in oven for about 30 seconds to 1 minute per side, until very golden brown. Set aside. In a small bowl, stir together goat cheese and scallions. Season with salt and pepper. Spread about 1½ tsp goat cheese mixture onto each baguette slice and broil for about 1 minute, until cheese is hot and light golden brown.

**FOUR:** Remove bay leaves and thyme from soup. Sprinkle with chives and season with salt and pepper. Ladle soup into bowls, float 1 crostini on top of each bowl and serve immediately.

*Nutrients per serving (about 1¾ cup soup and 1 crostini): Calories: 296, Total Fat: 8 g, Sat. Fat: 3 g, Monounsaturated Fat: 3.5 g, Polyunsaturated Fat: 0.5 g, Carbs: 43 g, Fiber: 7 g, Sugars: 12 g, Protein: 11 g, Sodium: 249 mg, Cholesterol: 17 mg*

**NUTRITIONAL BONUS:** Onions contain flavonoids, powerful antioxidants that are actually more concentrated in the outer layers of the flesh. So, be careful when peeling onions and leave as much of the exterior as possible – over-peeling can cause the flavonoids to dip by more than 20%.

For a photo of this recipe, see page 78.

# All About
# Onions

Because our bulbous little buddies play a role in almost all of the recipes in this chapter, we've put together this handy little guide to the awesome allium. So experiment, have fun and try as many different varieties as you can to find your favorites.

## A Bulbous Potpourri

With over 1,000 different varieties of onions ranging from subtle and sweet to pungent and sharp, which do you use, and when? As a little introductory lesson: There are two categories of dry onions, sweet and storage. Storage onions – possibly better known to you as yellow, white and red – are firm, have a thick papery skin and last for months from harvest. They can hang out in a cool, dark place such as your pantry. Sweet onions – think Vidalia, Walla Walla and Maui – are softer to the touch and best refrigerated. These little gems are mild and tasty even when raw, but will not last as long as your storage onions.

Finally, in a category all their own, are the green onions. Examples include Welsh, scallions and chives, all of which need to be refrigerated.

## Crying Game

Let's address this whole crying thing. When onions are cut, they produce and release a gas called propanethiol S-oxide into the air. The gas combines with fluid on the surface of the eyes to form sulfuric acid, which irritates the eyes and causes them to tear involuntarily. The fact that some onions have higher sulfur contents than others explains why some, such as a yellow cooking onion, have a more pungent flavor and aroma than a sweet Vidalia.

Now, we've heard every trick in the book when it comes to trying to stop the waterworks. The best and simplest advice? Cut faster! That being said, here are a few little tips that may help hold back (or at least ease) the floodgates: Use a sharp chef's knife to help make more precise incisions through the cell walls of the onion and, therefore, reduce the amount of sulfurous gas it releases. Breathe through your mouth, work close to your stove and turn the hood fan on to help suck up some of those gases away from your nose and eyes. If all else fails, strap on a pair of goggles!

### YELLOW

**FLAVOR PROFILE:** strong pungent flavor and aroma; most versatile; best when cooked, very strong when raw; classic onion flavor

**WORKS WELL:** in soups, stocks, stews, braises, stir-frys, diced in stuffings, grated in burgers

### CIPPOLINI

**FLAVOR PROFILE:** similar to shallots, but sweeter

**WORKS WELL:** use whole; caramelize, braise, pickle or roast

## WHITE

**FLAVOR PROFILE:** milder and sweeter than yellow

**WORKS WELL:** use raw or cooked; good in salsas, stir-frys, sandwiches or stews, in spicy dishes due to sweetness, especially Mexican cuisine

## LEEK

**FLAVOR PROFILE:** mild and sweet

**WORKS WELL:** in soups, sauces and with fish

## RED

**FLAVOR PROFILE:** slightly sweet

**WORKS WELL:** use raw or cooked; good on turkey or veggie burgers, salads

## VIDALIA

**FLAVOR PROFILE:** sweet and mild

**WORKS WELL:** use raw or cooked; in salads or sandwiches, grilled and in chutneys or relishes

## PEARL (RED & WHITE)

**FLAVOR PROFILE:** flavor varies by variety; milder and more delicate than mature onion

**WORKS WELL:** on kebabs, for pickling or roasting whole

## SHALLOT

**FLAVOR PROFILE:** delicate, garlicky and sweet

**WORKS WELL:** in sauces and salad dressings

## WELSH

**FLAVOR PROFILE:** bright, sharp, tangy

**WORKS WELL:** when serving raw or adding in the last few minutes of cooking; perfect for finishing and garnish; brushed with olive oil and grilled whole; in Asian cuisine

# Mexican Pozole

## WITH ROASTED CORN & FETA

*Serves 4. **Hands-on time:** 25 minutes. **Total time:** 50 minutes.*

A hearty vegetable-rich stew that dates back to pre-Columbian times, traditional pozole often features pork or chicken. But why not try a lighter, meat-free version that relies on roasted corn, simmered squash and poblano peppers instead?

**PSST:** If you're really hankering for a bit of chicken, pork or steak, you can always add some leftover cooked meat of your choice to the stew during the last few minutes of cooking.

### INGREDIENTS:

- 4 cups frozen corn
- 2 tsp ground cumin, divided
- 2 tsp extra-virgin olive oil, divided
- 1 small yellow onion, chopped
- 2 poblano peppers, ribs and seeds removed, chopped
- 4 cloves garlic, chopped
- 3 cups reduced-sodium, low-fat chicken broth
- 1 2-oz bag sun-dried tomatoes (not packed in oil), chopped
- 1 lb spaghetti squash, skin and seeds removed, flesh cut into 1-inch cubes
- 2 tsp chile powder
- 3 oz low-fat feta cheese
- 1 green onion, trimmed and minced
- ¼ cup fresh cilantro, minced

**TIP:** If poblano peppers aren't available, substitute green bell peppers.

### INSTRUCTIONS:

**ONE:** Preheat oven to 350°F. Cover a baking sheet with parchment paper and place corn on sheet. Sprinkle with 1 tsp cumin and drizzle with 1 tsp oil, then toss corn with fingers to mix. Spread corn out to edges of pan and bake for 35 minutes or until kernels turn golden brown, moving kernels around with a long spoon every 10 minutes to ensure they roast evenly.

**TWO:** Heat remaining 1 tsp oil in a large stockpot on medium for 1 minute. Add onion and poblano pepper and cook for 3 minutes. Stir in garlic and cook for 2 minutes, stirring occasionally. Add broth, 1 cup water, tomatoes, squash, chile powder and remaining 1 tsp cumin, and increase heat to high. When soup comes to a boil, reduce heat to low, cover and simmer for 20 minutes. Stir in roasted corn.

**THREE:** Spoon 2½ cups soup into each of 4 bowls and top each with ¾ oz feta. Garnish with green onion and cilantro.

**Nutrients per serving (2½ cups soup and ¾ oz feta):** *Calories: 362, Total Fat: 9 g, Sat. Fat: 2 g, Monounsaturated Fat: 2.5 g, Polyunsaturated Fat: 1 g, Carbs: 58 g, Fiber: 8 g, Sugars: 7 g, Protein: 18 g, Sodium: 385 mg, Cholesterol: 7.5 mg*

**NUTRITIONAL BONUS:** Thanks in part to the sun-dried tomatoes in this Mexican soup, 1 serving provides you with 27% of your recommended daily intake of both potassium and niacin, plus 32% of your need for manganese. While potassium and niacin play vital roles in maintaining a healthy nervous system, manganese is necessary for bone formation.

# Golden Potato Chowder

## WITH HAM & MUSHROOMS

*Serves 4. **Hands-on time:** 20 minutes. **Total time:** 25 minutes.*

No, your eyes aren't playing tricks on you: When spaghetti squash is cooked, its fibers naturally separate and look like short strands of golden spaghetti. If you'd like to achieve longer "noodles," cut the raw squash into rectangles that are a half-inch in width and thickness but one inch in length, instead of cubing the vegetable.

### INGREDIENTS:

- 1 tsp extra-virgin olive oil
- 1 small yellow onion, chopped
- 2 large carrots, peeled and cut into ½-inch-thick slices
- 8 oz white mushrooms, cut into quarters
- 3 cups reduced-sodium, low-fat chicken broth
- 1 lb spaghetti squash, skin and seeds removed, flesh cut into ½-inch cubes
- 1 lb redskin potatoes, cut into 1-inch cubes
- 2 tsp dried sage
- 6 oz nitrate-free, reduced-sodium, low-fat ham, cut into ½-inch cubes
- ¼ cup skim milk
- 2 oz light cream cheese

### INSTRUCTIONS:

**ONE:** Heat oil in a large stockpot on medium for 1 minute. Add onion, carrots and mushrooms. Cook for 5 minutes, stirring occasionally.

**TWO:** Stir in broth, squash, potatoes and sage. Bring soup to a boil on high, then reduce heat to low, cover and simmer for 10 minutes. Stir in ham and heat through.

**THREE:** Meanwhile, in a small pot, add milk and cream cheese and heat on low. Cook, whisking constantly, for 1 minute or until mixture is smooth. Ladle 1 cup soup into milk mixture and whisk. Pour milk mixture back into stockpot and stir to combine. Serve immediately.

**Nutrients per 2-cup serving:** *Calories: 277, Total Fat: 7 g, Sat. Fat: 2.5 g, Monounsaturated Fat: 2 g, Polyunsaturated Fat: 1 g, Carbs: 38 g, Fiber: 4 g, Sugars: 6g, Protein: 19 g, Sodium: 520 mg, Cholesterol: 34 mg*

**Nutritional Bonus:**
Potatoes have been treated
unfairly over the years, but
the redskins called upon
here provide about half of
this recipe's vitamin C and
potassium – you'll meet
nearly 30% and 33% of
your recommended daily
intake of the two nutrients,
respectively, in a single hearty
serving. While the well known
immunity vitamin is also
necessary for the formation
of collagen and the healing
of wounds, the mineral
potassium may help lower
blood pressure.

# Gingered Chicken Soup

WITH SWEET POTATO DUMPLINGS, CARROTS & GREEN BEANS

*Serves 4. **Hands-on time:** 40 minutes. **Total time:** 45 minutes.*

These fall-apart tender little dumplings give your soup an extra boost of flavor and richness, plus they offer a nutritious way to use up any leftover whole-grain bread by transforming it into fiber-filled bread crumbs.

**TIP:** Leftover homemade bread crumbs can be frozen in an airtight freezer-safe container for up to three months.

## INGREDIENTS:

- 3 slices whole-grain bread
- ½ lb sweet potatoes, peeled and cut into 1-inch cubes
- 4 egg whites
- 1 Tbsp extra-virgin olive oil
- 1 lb boneless, skinless chicken breast, cut into bite-sized pieces
- 28 oz low-sodium chicken broth
- 1 tsp ground ginger
- 2 large carrots, peeled and cut into ½-inch-thick rounds
- ½ lb green beans, trimmed, rinsed and cut into 1-inch pieces
- ¼ head of cabbage, thinly sliced

## INSTRUCTIONS:

ONE: In a food processor, process bread into fine crumbs. Set aside.

TWO: Fill a medium pot halfway with water and bring to a boil on high. Add potatoes, reduce heat to medium-high and simmer for 10 minutes. Drain well and place potatoes in a large mixing bowl. Using a potato masher, mash potatoes with egg whites and 1 cup bread crumbs until mixture is smooth. Set aside.

THREE: In a large stockpot, heat oil on medium for 1 minute. Add chicken and cook, stirring occasionally, for 4 minutes or until chicken is no longer pink.

FOUR: Add broth and 2 cups water, increase heat to high and bring soup to a boil. Stir in ginger, carrots and beans and reduce heat to medium. Simmer, uncovered, for 5 minutes. Stir in cabbage and reduce heat to low.

FIVE: Using a metal tablespoon, slide potato mixture into soup in 1-Tbsp rounds. (Don't worry: They don't have to be perfect spheres!) When final dumpling has been added, continue to lightly simmer soup on low heat for an additional 4 minutes. Serve immediately.

*Nutrients per 2½-cup serving: Calories: 358, Total Fat: 7 g, Sat. Fat: 1.5 g, Monounsaturated Fat: 4 g, Polyunsaturated Fat: 1 g, Carbs: 34 g, Fiber: 8 g, Sugars: 9 g, Protein: 39.5 g, Sodium: 346 mg, Cholesterol: 66 mg*

## Nutritional Bonus:

Adding sweet potatoes to your soup is a great way to infuse the broth with hearty servings of vitamins A, B6 and C, potassium, copper, manganese, iron and fiber. Plus, the orange taters are home to sporamins, unique root storage proteins that possess antioxidant properties and help bolster your immune system.

# "Cream" of Vegetable Soup

*Serves 8. **Hands-on time:** 15 minutes. **Total time:** 55 minutes.*

Use cauliflower, broccoli, asparagus, bell pepper, spinach or another vegetable of your choosing to create this velvety soup, which is enriched with tofu and a sprinkling of Parmesan cheese.

## INGREDIENTS:

- 1 Tbsp olive oil
- ½ cup chopped onion, shallots or leeks
- 4 cups low-sodium vegetable broth
- 1½ lb vegetables, chopped
- 16 oz silken tofu
- 1 Tbsp white wine vinegar
- Sea salt and fresh ground black pepper, to taste
- Dash fresh grated nutmeg
- ⅛ cup grated Parmesan cheese

## INSTRUCTIONS:

ONE: Heat oil in a large heavy-bottomed pot or Dutch oven on medium. Add onion and sauté, stirring occasionally, until tender and translucent, about 5 minutes.

TWO: Add broth and bring to a simmer. Add vegetables and return to a simmer, then reduce heat to maintain simmer. Cover and cook until vegetables are tender when pierced with a fork. (Cooking time will vary depending on types of vegetables. A firmer vegetable such as broccoli can take up to 25 minutes to cook.)

THREE: Working in batches, if necessary, transfer soup to a blender, being careful to not spill the hot soup. Pulse soup, using the purée setting, until it reaches a smooth or desired consistency. Add tofu and vinegar, pulse to combine and purée tofu. Season with salt, pepper and nutmeg.

FOUR: Divide soup evenly among 8 bowls, topping each with 1 tsp Parmesan.

Nutrients per 1-cup serving (using red bell pepper and cauliflower): *Calories: 86, Total Fat: 3.5 g, Sat. Fat: 0.5 g, Monounsaturated Fat: 1 g, Polyunsaturated Fat: 0.25 g, Carbs: 8 g, Fiber: 2 g, Sugars: 3 g, Protein: 5 g, Sodium: 132 mg, Cholesterol: 1 mg*

NOTE: **We used a combination of red bell pepper and cauliflower to achieve this "creamy" soup.**

# Lime Soup
## WITH SOUR CREAM & TORTILLA CRISPS

*Serves 4. **Hands-on time:** 8 minutes. **Total time:** 14 minutes.*

In the city of Merida in the Yucatán Peninsula, you'll find as many varieties of *Sopa de Lima* as restaurants. Our clean version of this soup eliminates the chicken skin more common with traditional recipes, opts for lower-sodium broth and nixes the deep-fried tacos, all without sacrificing classic Mexican taste.

## INGREDIENTS:

- 2 Tbsp extra-virgin olive oil, divided
- 8 oz boneless, skinless chicken breasts, cut into ½-inch cubes
- 1 jalapeño pepper, unseeded and finely chopped
- 1 tsp ground cumin
- 3 cups low-sodium chicken broth
- 1 oz baby spinach leaves
- 1 medium tomato (4 oz), diced
- 4 scallions, bulbs removed, white and green parts finely chopped
- ¼ packed cup chopped cilantro leaves, plus additional for garnish
- ½ tsp sea salt
- 1 whole-grain corn tortilla, very thinly sliced into 2-inch-long pieces (matchsticks)
- 1 lime, quartered
- 4 Tbsp low-fat sour cream

## INSTRUCTIONS:

ONE: Heat 1 tsp oil in a large saucepan on medium-high. Add chicken, jalapeño and cumin and cook for 2 to 3 minutes or until chicken is no longer pink in center, stirring occasionally. Add broth and bring mixture to a boil over high heat. Remove pan from heat, add spinach, tomato, scallions, cilantro, salt and 1 Tbsp oil. Let stand for 5 minutes, covered, to meld flavors and continue cooking vegetables slightly.

TWO: Meanwhile, heat remaining 2 tsp oil in a medium nonstick skillet over medium-high. Add tortilla matchsticks and cook for 1½ to 2 minutes or until golden and crispy.

THREE: Divide soup among 4 bowls and add a squeeze of lime to each. Top with sour cream and sprinkle with tortilla crisps, dividing evenly. If desired, garnish with additional cilantro.

Nutrients per serving (1¼ cups soup, 2 Tbsp sour cream, 2 Tbsp tortilla crisps): *Calories: 234, Total Fat: 11 g, Sat. Fat: 2.5 g, Monounsaturated Fat: 6 g, Polyunsaturated Fat: 1 g, Carbs: 14 g, Fiber: 2 g, Sugars: 4 g, Protein: 18 g, Sodium: 401 mg, Cholesterol: 40 mg*

# Thai Spicy Pork Soup

*Serves 4. **Hands-on time:** 13 minutes. **Total time:** 23 minutes.*

**This Asian soup remains low in sodium while offering heightened flavors thanks to the generous amount of fresh ginger and cilantro.**

## INGREDIENTS:

- 2 Tbsp safflower oil, divided
- 8 oz boneless pork chops, trimmed of visible fat, cut into ½-inch cubes
- 4 oz mushrooms, sliced (1 cup)
- ½ cup finely chopped red onion
- 1 lb tomatoes (about 4 medium), diced
- 2 cups low-sodium chicken broth
- 1 jalapeño pepper, unseeded and finely chopped
- 1 cup light coconut milk
- ½ packed cup chopped cilantro leaves
- 1 Tbsp fresh grated ginger
- 3 stevia packets
- ½ tsp sea salt
- 1 lime, quartered

## INSTRUCTIONS:

**ONE:** Heat 1 Tbsp oil in a large saucepan on medium-high. Add pork and cook for 2 minutes or until almost opaque in center, stirring frequently; set aside on a plate.

**TWO:** Cook mushrooms in remaining 1 Tbsp oil for 2 minutes, then add onion and cook for 2 minutes more or until mushrooms are soft, stirring occasionally. Return pork and any accumulated juices back to pan. Add tomatoes, broth and jalapeño. Bring to a boil over high heat, then reduce heat to a simmer, cover tightly and cook for 10 minutes. Stir in remaining ingredients, except lime, and cook for 5 minutes. Serve soup with lime wedges on the side to squeeze into soup, as desired.

**Nutrients per 1¼-cup serving:** *Calories: 243, Total Fat: 13 g, Sat. Fat: 4 g, Monounsaturated Fat: 6 g, Polyunsaturated Fat: 2 g, Carbs: 14 g, Fiber: 2 g, Sugars: 5 g, Protein: 17 g, Sodium: 344 mg, Cholesterol: 32 mg*

# Creamy Tomato Thyme Soup

*Serves 4. **Hands-on time:** 25 minutes. **Total time:** 45 minutes.*

**This is not your typical tomato soup! Topped with a yogurt swirl and a sprinkling of Parmesan and thyme, this comforting classic has been given a makeover – it doesn't just look sophisticated, but tastes it as well.**

## INGREDIENTS:

- 2 Tbsp olive oil
- 1 medium yellow onion, chopped
- 1 large carrot, peeled and chopped
- 1 stalk celery, chopped
- 2 cloves garlic, minced
- 1 tsp fresh thyme leaves, plus additional for garnish
- Pinch crushed red pepper flakes
- 3½ cups chopped tomatoes including juices (fresh, jarred or boxed)
- 2 cups low-sodium chicken broth
- 1 tsp Sucanat
- 2 Tbsp 2% plain Greek yogurt
- 4 tsp shredded low-fat Parmesan cheese

## INSTRUCTIONS:

**ONE:** Heat oil in a large saucepan on medium-low. Add onion, carrot and celery and cook, stirring occasionally, until vegetables are softened and just starting to brown, about 12 minutes. Add garlic, thyme and pepper flakes and cook, stirring, for 1 more minute. Add tomatoes, including juices, and broth. Increase heat to high and bring mixture to a boil, then reduce heat to low. Simmer, stirring occasionally, for 20 minutes.

**TWO:** Purée soup using an immersion blender or by transferring it, in batches, to a countertop blender (**TIP:** Only fill blender jar half full and leave lid slightly ajar to allow steam to escape when blending hot liquids). If applicable, return soup to pot. Stir in Sucanat, reheating soup if necessary. Serve soup warm, stirring in yogurt and garnishing with Parmesan and thyme leaves.

**Nutrients per serving (1 cup soup and 1 tsp cheese):** *Calories: 151, Total Fat: 8 g, Sat. Fat: 1 g, Monounsaturated Fat: 5 g, Polyunsaturated Fat: 1 g, Carbs: 15 g, Fiber: 3 g, Sugars: 8 g, Protein: 6 g, Sodium: 117 mg, Cholesterol: 1.5 mg*

**Nutritional Bonus:**
Although tomatoes are best fresh off the vine, good-quality jarred or boxed tomatoes are an enjoyable and healthful treat that can be savored throughout the year. Processed tomato products not only retain most of their nutrients, but they also actually contain more bio-available lycopene than their raw, fresh counterparts. Lycopene has been linked to the reduced risk of heart disease and certain cancers.

Creamy Tomato Thyme Soup

Five-Spice
Noodle
Bowls

# Five-Spice Noodle Bowls

*Serves 4. **Hands-on time:** 15 minutes. **Total time:** 15 minutes.*

**Similar to a Vietnamese pho, this aromatic soup can be prepared in a flash. Much of the flavor is owed to the addition of Chinese five-spice powder, a blend that can be found at most markets and large-chain grocery stores. While the spice mixture can often vary, the classic recipe contains fennel, cloves, Szechuan peppercorns, anise and cinnamon.**

INGREDIENTS:

- 2 tsp grape seed oil
- 1 white onion, thinly sliced
- 2 tsp Chinese five-spice powder
- 4 cups low-sodium beef broth
- 3 cups chopped bok choy or whole baby bok choy (about 5 oz)
- 7 oz rice vermicelli noodles, soaked in hot water for 5 minutes
- 8 oz top sirloin beef, trimmed of visible fat and very thinly sliced
- 4 green onions, thinly sliced
- ½ cup cilantro sprigs
- ½ tsp sesame oil
- 2 tsp low-sodium tamari, optional
- 1 tsp sambal oelek or Sriracha hot chile sauce, optional

INSTRUCTIONS:

ONE: In a large pot, heat grape seed oil on medium-high. Add white onion and cook, stirring frequently, until translucent, about 4 to 5 minutes. Add five-spice powder and cook, stirring, until fragrant, about 1 minute. Add broth and bring to a boil. Reduce heat to medium-low and simmer for 5 minutes. Add bok choy.

TWO: Drain vermicelli noodles well and discard water. Divide noodles evenly among 4 large soup bowls. Top each bowl with 2 oz raw beef.

THREE: To serve, ladle broth-bok choy mixture into each bowl over beef, dividing evenly. The heat of the broth will cook the beef to medium-well, about 30 seconds. Garnish each bowl with green onions, cilantro and a few drops of sesame oil. If desired, drizzle ½ tsp tamari and ¼ tsp hot chile sauce over top of each bowl. Serve immediately.

TIME-SAVING TIP: **You'll need very thin slices of beef for your noodle bowl, so enlist the help of your butcher. Or look for sashimi-style thinly sliced beef at your local Asian market.**

*Nutrients per 2-cup serving: Calories: 309, Total Fat: 8 g, Sat. Fat: 2 g, Monounsaturated Fat: 2 g, Polyunsaturated Fat: 2.5 g, Carbs: 40 g, Fiber: 4 g, Sugars: 3 g, Protein: 22 g, Sodium: 328 mg, Cholesterol: 30 mg*

# Pumpkin & Coconut Soup

*Serves 6. **Hands-on time:** 15 minutes. **Total time:** 15 minutes.*

**Coconut milk adds a rich, creamy texture to this cold-weather soup (even though we've opted for low fat!). But be sure to add the coconut milk at the end of cooking, as it will curdle and separate if boiled.**

INGREDIENTS:

- 1 Tbsp coconut oil
- 1 medium white onion, diced
- ½ tsp ground cinnamon
- ½ tsp chile powder
- ½ tsp ground cumin
- Pinch ground nutmeg
- 3 cups low-sodium chicken broth
- 3 cups pumpkin purée or organic pure pumpkin (or try squash or sweet potato)
- 1 Tbsp fresh lime juice
- 1 cup light coconut milk
- Sea salt and fresh ground black pepper, to taste
- ¾ cup nonfat plain Greek yogurt
- 6 Tbsp raw pumpkin seeds

INSTRUCTIONS:

ONE: Heat oil in a large saucepan on medium-high. Add onion and cook, stirring frequently, until softened and translucent, about 5 minutes. Add cinnamon, chile powder, cumin and nutmeg and cook for about 1 minute, stirring frequently, until fragrant. Add broth and pumpkin and whisk until incorporated and smooth, adding up to 1 cup water if broth is too thick (soup should coat the back of a spoon). Bring to a boil, reduce heat to medium-low and simmer for 5 minutes, stirring frequently. Remove from heat and add lime juice. Stir in coconut milk and season with salt and pepper.

TWO: Ladle 1½ cups soup into each of 6 bowls. Top each with 2 Tbsp yogurt and 1 Tbsp pumpkin seeds and serve immediately.

*Nutrients per 1⅓-cup serving: Calories: 189, Total Fat: 11 g, Sat. Fat: 5 g, Carbs: 17 g, Fiber: 5 g, Sugars: 5 g, Protein: 10 g, Sodium: 82 mg, Cholesterol: 0 mg*

**NUTRITIONAL BONUS: Five grams of saturated fat per serving may seem high, but coconut milk contains a favorable type of saturated fat called lauric acid, which is easily metabolized by the body.**

# Dill & Scallion Whole-Grain Matzo Ball Soup

*Serves 4. **Hands-on time:** 45 minutes. **Total time:** 1 hour, 30 minutes (plus 2 hours to chill Matzo batter and overnight to chill stock).*

**Matzo Ball Soup is a traditional Jewish comfort food dish of home-made chicken broth and dumplings known as matzo balls. Usually made from whole eggs, chicken fat and matzo meal, these little dumplings pack a heavy, calorie-dense punch. Matzo meal is a bread-crumb-like ingredient made from matzo, an unleavened white flour flatbread. We've used whole-grain matzo meal, substituted arrow-root for the egg yolks and olive oil for the chicken fat. Look for whole grain matzo meal in the Kosher section of your grocery store or at a Jewish bakery or deli.**

## INGREDIENTS:

### HOMEMADE CHICKEN STOCK

- 4 lb raw chicken bones
- 3 stalks celery, chopped
- 3 medium carrots, peeled and chopped
- 1 medium yellow onion, peeled and chopped
- 1 medium leek, white and light green parts only, chopped and rinsed well
- 6 sprigs each fresh thyme and flat-leaf parsley
- 8 whole black peppercorns
- 2 bay leaves
- 2 cloves garlic
- Sea salt and fresh ground black pepper, to taste

### MATZO BALLS

- 1 large egg, whisked
- 1 Tbsp arrowroot powder
- 2 Tbsp olive oil or refrigerated olive oil spread, softened
- 2 Tbsp chopped fresh dill
- 3 Tbsp minced scallions
- ¾ tsp sea salt
- ½ tsp fresh ground black pepper
- 1 cup plus 3 Tbsp whole-grain Matzo meal, divided
- 1 medium leek, white and light green parts only, chopped and rinsed well
- 4 tsp chopped fresh flat-leaf parsley

## INSTRUCTIONS:

ONE: Prepare Homemade Chicken Stock: In a 10-qt stockpot, add chicken bones, celery, carrots, onion, leek, thyme, parsley, peppercorns, bay leaves and garlic. Add enough cold water so that ingredients are submerged by 2 inches. Bring to a gentle simmer on high heat but not to a full rolling boil. Reduce heat to medium-low and simmer for 3 hours. Skim impurities and grey foam from top of stock with a ladle and discard, about every 15 to 20 minutes, until very little foam and impurities form on top. Do not stir stock.

TWO: Set up an ice bath in your sink or a large container. Strain stock through a fine mesh strainer into a heatproof sealable container, gently pressing on solids to extract liquid; discard solids. Immerse container into ice bath, stirring stock occasionally to cool quickly and evenly. Cover stock and refrigerate overnight.

THREE: Remove stock from fridge. Remove and discard solidified fat layer on top of stock. (Stock may be stored, covered and refrigerated, for 3 days or frozen for 3 to 4 months.)

FOUR: Prepare Matzo Balls: In a medium bowl, whisk together egg, arrowroot, ½ cup Homemade Chicken Stock, oil, dill, scallions, salt, pepper and 1 Tbsp water. Using a fork, stir in 1 cup matzo meal until incorporated. Cover and refrigerate batter until smooth, 2 to 3 hours.

FIVE: Bring a large pot of salted water to a boil over high heat. Reduce heat to medium-low so that water just barely simmers.

SIX: Wet hands with cold water. Scoop 2 Tbsp matzo batter into your hands and gently form into a ball. Carefully immerse ball into water with a slotted spoon and simmer for 5 minutes. If ball falls apart in water, stir more matzo meal into batter, 1 Tbsp at a time, and retest. Once test ball holds together, continue to form remaining matzo batter into balls, placing them onto a parchment-lined baking sheet.

SEVEN: Using a slotted spoon, immerse all matzo balls into water. Cover and simmer for about 40 to 50 minutes. Do not allow water to boil. (Do not store matzo balls in stock after cooking, as they will disintegrate.)

EIGHT: While matzo balls are simmering, in a large saucepan, bring remaining Homemade Chicken Stock and leek to a boil on high heat. Reduce heat to medium and simmer for 10 minutes.

NINE: Divide matzo balls among 4 soup bowls. Season stock with salt and pepper. Divide leeks and stock evenly among bowls, and sprinkle each with 1 tsp parsley.

Nutrients per serving (3 matzo balls and 2 cups stock): *Calories: 241, Total Fat: 2 g, Sat. Fat: 0.5 g, Monounsaturated Fat: 0.5 g, Polyunsaturated Fat: 0.5 g, Carbs: 52 g, Fiber: 5 g, Sugars: 7 g, Protein: 7 g, Sodium: 469 mg, Cholesterol: 52 mg*

## Nutritional Bonus:

**Regular matzo meal is made with refined white flour and contains virtually no fiber. By simply swapping whole-grain matzo meal, we increased the fiber in each serving by 4 g.**

**Nutritional Bonus:**
Clams are one of the highest sources of iron and vitamin B12. Iron helps transport oxygen around the body and B12 supports heart and circulatory health. Clams contain about 24 g of iron (over 100% RDA) in a 100 g serving, compared to less than 2 g for the same size serving of lean beef. Clams also win out in the B12 category with a whopping 98 g (560% RDA) compared to beef at only 6 g.

Creole Manhattan Clam Chowder

# Creole Manhattan Clam Chowder

*Serves 6. Hands-on time: 20 minutes. Total time: 1 hour.*

**The secret to this spicy broth is the addition of Creole aromatic spices – smoked paprika, cayenne pepper, oregano and thyme.**

## INGREDIENTS:

- 6 lb clams in shells, scrubbed very well and rinsed under cold running water (or 1 cup jarred clams, 2 cups clam juice and 2 cups water)
- 2 tsp olive oil
- 1 medium yellow onion, diced
- 1 medium carrot, peeled and diced
- 2 stalks celery, diced
- ½ green bell pepper, diced
- 2 cloves garlic, minced
- 1 bay leaf
- ½ tsp each dried oregano leaves and thyme leaves
- ½ tsp smoked hot paprika (or ½ tsp smoked sweet paprika and ¼ tsp ground cayenne pepper)
- 2 Yukon gold potatoes, peeled and diced (about 2½ cups)
- 1 cup low-sodium chicken broth
- 2 cups boxed diced tomatoes, no salt added (TRY: Pomi Chopped Tomatoes)
- Sea salt and fresh ground black pepper, to taste
- 2 Tbsp chopped fresh flat-leaf parsley

## INSTRUCTIONS:

ONE: In a large stockpot, bring 1½ cups water to a boil. Add clams, cover and allow to steam for 10 to 15 minutes, stirring once, until most of clams are open. Discard any that remain closed or have cracked shells. Transfer clams to a large bowl and strain over a fine mesh strainer, reserving liquid. (You should have about 4 cups liquid.) Wash stockpot to remove any impurities. (If using jarred clams, begin at Step Three.)

TWO: Reserve 18 clams in shells. Using your hands, remove remaining clams from shells; they should slide out easily. Discard shells, coarsely chop clams and set aside.

THREE: Heat oil in stockpot on medium-high. Add onion, carrot, celery, bell pepper and garlic and cook, stirring frequently, until fragrant and onions are translucent, about 6 minutes. Add bay leaf, oregano, thyme and paprika and cook, stirring frequently, about 2 minutes. Increase heat to high and add potatoes, broth and reserved clam cooking liquid. Bring to a boil, reduce heat to medium and simmer for 15 to 18 minutes, until potatoes are tender and broth has thickened slightly. Add tomatoes and continue to simmer for about 15 minutes. Remove from heat, remove and discard bay leaf, and stir in shucked clams and reserved 18 clams in shells to warm. Season with salt and black pepper and stir in parsley.

FOUR: To serve, divide clams in shells evenly among 6 shallow soup bowls. Ladle in 1½ cups chowder and enjoy.

*Nutrients per 1½-cup serving: Calories: 450, Total Fat: 6.5 g, Sat. Fat: 1 g, Omega-3s: 680 mg, Omega-6s: 330 mg, Carbs: 32 g, Fiber: 3 g, Sugars: 4 g, Protein: 62 g, Sodium: 348.5 mg, Cholesterol: 154 mg*

# Sheet-Pan Soup

*Serves 6.*

**Cookbook author, food adventurer and host of *Glutton for Punishment* Bob Blumer shared this super-simple recipe for roasted vegetable Sheet-Pan Soup exclusively with *Clean Eating*.**

## INGREDIENTS:

- 3 Tbsp olive oil
- 1 large eggplant, peeled and chopped into 1-inch cubes
- 3 celery stalks, chopped into 1-inch pieces
- 3 carrots, chopped into 1-inch pieces
- 3 shallots, quartered
- 6 cloves garlic
- 2 Yukon gold potatoes, peeled and chopped into 1-inch cubes
- 1 tsp sea salt
- 6 cups vegetable or chicken broth
- 6 sage leaves

## INSTRUCTIONS:

ONE: Preheat oven to 425°F.

TWO: In a large bowl, add oil, eggplant, celery, carrots, shallots, garlic, potatoes and salt; toss thoroughly to coat. Spread vegetables onto a large sheet pan and roast for 1 hour, flipping vegetables occasionally, until they begin to brown. Remove pan from oven and let cool.

THREE: In a blender, add vegetables and broth in manageable batches. Purée, then pass mixture through a strainer into a large pot or serving bowl and discard solids. Spoon soup into individual bowls, garnish with sage leaves and serve.

*Nutrients per 1 cup serving: Calories: 202, Total Fat: 9 g, Sat. Fat: 1 g, Monounsaturated Fat: 7 g, Polyunsaturated Fat: 1 g, Carbs: 26 g, Fiber: 5 g, Sugars: 5 g, Protein: 3 g, Sodium: 515 mg, Cholesterol: 0 mg*

# Your Guide to Winter Produce

Unless you're lucky enough to fly south for the winter, local produce may be difficult to come by December through February. Here's how to choose your produce like a pro, plus tips for keeping it fresh at home.

## PEARS
**(bosc, comice, concorde, green anjou, red anjou)**

At the market: Feel for firm skin with no bruises or punctures; mottled color is OK.

At home: To ripen fully, store at room temperature just until skin yields to gentle pressure; eat immediately.

## WINTER SQUASH
**(butternut, acorn, spaghetti)**

At the market: Look for smooth, firm skin and squash heavy for its size.

At home: Store in a cool, dry place on several layers of newspaper for up to 2 months.

## HEARTY GREENS
**(kale, collards, mustard, turnip)**

At the market: Opt for crisp, deep green leaves with no discoloration and freshly cut stems.

At home: Refrigerate unwashed greens in plastic bags in the crisper drawer for up to 3 days.

## CITRUS
**(oranges, grapefruits, pomelos)**

At the market: Look for shiny skin without soft spots and a pleasing citrus scent. Color and scarring are not indicators of quality.

At home: Store oranges in a cool place for up to 4 days; refrigerate for 1 week. Grapefruit and pomelos will keep for 1 to 2 weeks at room temperature or 2 to 3 weeks in the refrigerator.

# What's Growing Where You Live?

Filling your plate with foods grown close to home supports farmers in your region and reduces the environmental impact of transporting produce long distances. In very cold climates, hearty picks such as winter squash, potatoes and pears from the fall harvest are available throughout the winter months.

**WINTER SALAD GREENS (radicchio, frisée, endive)**

At the market: Dense, crisp heads that feel firm, not spongy, are best. Paler endive leaves indicate less bitter flavor.

At home: Refrigerate unwashed greens in plastic bags in the crisper drawer for up to 5 days; 1 week for radicchio.

**ROOT VEGETABLES (parsnips, turnips, rutabaga)**

At the market: Choose parsnips with unshriveled, even-colored beige skin; medium-size turnips and rutabagas with smooth, firm skin.

At home: Refrigerate, unpeeled, in plastic bags in the crisper drawer for up to 2 weeks.

**NORTHWEST**

Pears, apples, cabbage, hearty greens, winter squash, root vegetables, onions, mushrooms, potatoes, sunchokes, spinach

**UPPER MIDWEST**

Onions, potatoes, sunchokes, root vegetables, winter squash, daikon

**NORTHEAST & MID-ATLANTIC**

Mushrooms, sprouts, apples, beets, cabbage, root vegetables, pears, potatoes

**SOUTHWEST**

Citrus, avocado, broccoli, hearty greens, mushrooms, cabbage, radishes

**MIDWEST**

Apples, mushrooms, winter squash, broccoli, turnips, parsnips, carrots, onions, spinach

**SOUTHEAST**

Citrus, avocado, arugula, cabbage, carrots, hearty greens, mushrooms, spinach, turnips, winter squash, cauliflower, radishes, celery

**NOTE:** Alaska and Hawaii experience unique growing seasons – Alaska's is severely restricted during winter months, while Hawaii's largely lasts year-round.

\* Please note that the availability of produce may vary based on environmental conditions.

# Snacks &
Starters,
Dips &
Spreads

Fish Fritters with Red Pepper
& Malt Vinegar Dipping Sauce, p. 110

One of the main principles behind *Clean Eating* is to enjoy five or six small meals each day to rev up the metabolism and keep your body energized, all while keeping hunger at bay. This means eating every two to three hours. Here, we offer a wide variety of snacks and starters to get you from one meal to the next without a hunger pang. Having loved ones over? Whip up a low-fat, low-cal Baked Spinach & Artichoke Dip that won't end in guilt. Is it your turn to have the book club over for dinner? Impress your guests with a mouthwatering and easy-to-pull-together Apple Walnut Bruschetta.

# Stuffed Banana Peppers
## WITH FRESH BASIL LIME SAUCE

*Serves 6.*

**This hearty starter is a favorite at rocker Chrissie Hynde's VegiTerranean, a dynamic vegan restaurant located in Akron, Ohio.**

### INGREDIENTS:

**RISOTTO**
- 2 Tbsp olive oil
- 1 medium yellow onion, finely diced
- 3 cups brown arborio or short-grain rice
- ¼ cup dry white wine or low-sodium vegetable broth
- Olive oil cooking spray

**PEPPERS**
- 6 medium to large hot Italian banana peppers (NOTE: If you prefer less heat, use mild Hungarian wax peppers instead of the Italian peppers.)

- 1 cup Tofu Ricotta (recipe at right)
- 6 oz shredded soy mozzarella cheese
- 2 Tbsp olive oil

**BASIL LIME SAUCE**
- 2 cups low-sodium vegetable broth
- 1 clove garlic, minced
- 1 Tbsp minced shallot
- 2 tsp Sucanat
- 2 Tbsp fresh lime juice
- 1 Tbsp Earth Balance Buttery Spread with Olive Oil
- 1 cup fresh basil, chopped

### INSTRUCTIONS:

**ONE:** Prepare risotto: Heat oil in a large pot on medium. Add onion and sauté until soft and translucent, 5 to 7 minutes. In a separate pot, bring 6 cups water to a simmer.

**TWO:** Add rice to onion and stir with a wooden spoon until grains are opaque and very hot, but not browned. Pour in wine and stir until liquid is absorbed. Add 1 ladle of water from second pot and stir until absorbed. Add another ladle of water and continue process until 6 cups water have been used, always waiting for rice to absorb liquid before adding another ladleful. Once all water has been added and risotto is velvety and tender but still semi-firm to the bite, remove from heat. Let stand, stirring frequently, for 5 to 8 minutes, until thickened.

**THREE:** Transfer to a baking sheet and spread risotto out to cool for 1 hour. Risotto can be made 3 days in advance and kept, covered, in refrigerator. Bring to room temperature before proceeding.

**FOUR:** Prepare peppers: Preheat oven to 400°F. Mist a baking sheet with cooking spray.

**FIVE:** Cut off the top of each pepper, leaving top intact and setting it aside. Using a paring knife, create a slit down the center of each pepper, being careful not to slice all the way through. Scoop out seeds with a small spoon.

CONTINUED ON NEXT PAGE

**SIX:** In a large bowl, combine risotto, Tofu Ricotta and mozzarella. Gently stuff peppers with mixture, dividing evenly; do not overstuff or peppers will cook unevenly.

**SEVEN:** Heat oil in a large skillet on medium-high. Sauté stuffed peppers until browned on the bottom, about 3 to 5 minutes. Transfer peppers to prepared baking sheet and bake for 10 minutes or until heated through.

**EIGHT:** Prepare basil lime sauce: Pour out excess oil from skillet used to sauté peppers. Place skillet on medium-high heat and add broth, garlic, shallot, Sucanat and lime juice. Bring to a simmer and cook until mixture reduces by half, about 8 minutes. Remove from heat and slowly stir in olive oil spread. When sauce has cooled and thickened slightly, stir in basil.

**NINE:** Arrange peppers on a serving platter. Spoon basil lime sauce over top. Garnish with additional basil, if desired. Serve immediately.

Nutrients per serving (1 pepper, 1 cup risotto mixture, 2 Tbsp sauce): *Calories: 534, Total Fat: 15 g, Sat. Fat: 2 g, Monounsaturated Fat: 7 g, Polyunsaturated Fat: 3 g, Carbs: 90 g, Fiber: 10 g, Sugars: 5 g, Protein: 18 g, Sodium: 470 mg, Cholesterol: 0 mg*

# Tofu Ricotta

*Makes 1½ cups.*

### INGREDIENTS:

- 8 oz firm tofu
- ½ tsp minced garlic
- ½ tsp minced shallot
- ½ tsp plum vinegar
- 1 Tbsp fresh lemon juice
- 1 Tbsp extra-virgin olive oil
- 1 tsp nutritional yeast flakes
- ½ tsp chopped fresh basil
- ½ tsp chopped fresh parsley
- Kosher salt and fresh cracked black pepper, to taste

### INSTRUCTIONS:

**ONE:** Press tofu through a potato ricer into a large bowl. Or, alternatively, mash tofu with your hands until crumbly. Add remaining ingredients and mix well, until mixture is the consistency of ricotta cheese.

Nutrients per ¼-cup serving: *Calories: 42, Total Fat: 2 g, Sat. Fat: 0.25 g, Monounsaturated Fat: 1 g, Polyunsaturated Fat: 1 g, Carbs: 1 g, Fiber: 0.5 g, Sugars: 0.25 g, Protein: 4 g, Sodium: 22 mg, Cholesterol: 0 mg*

**Stuffed Banana Peppers**

# Apple Walnut Bruschetta

*Serves 6. **Hands-on time:** 15 minutes. **Total time:** 45 minutes.*

**Here's a perfect rustic recipe packed with taste. To cut about 20 minutes from total prep time, you can roast the garlic up to two days in advance, remove cloves from skins and store in a sealable container in the refrigerator until ready to use.**

## INGREDIENTS:

- 2 heads garlic
- 2 Granny Smith apples, unpeeled, cored and sliced ½ inch thick
- ½ cup crumbled goat cheese (3 oz)
- ½ whole-grain baguette (5 oz)
- ¼ cup coarsely chopped unsalted walnuts, toasted

**NOTE: To toast walnuts, place them on a parchment-lined baking tray and cook in a 350°F oven for 8 to 10 minutes or until light golden brown, stirring once. Toast a few cups at a time, then store them in a sealed container in the fridge or freezer for a quick addition to meals and snacks.**

## INSTRUCTIONS:

**ONE:** Ensure 2 racks are in place in oven, in middle and bottom third positions. Preheat oven to 350°F. Slice about ¼ inch off the top of each head of garlic, making sure to expose each clove. Wrap garlic in aluminum foil and place on a baking tray. Roast on top rack in oven for 30 to 35 minutes or until garlic is soft and fragrant.

**TWO:** Meanwhile, arrange apples in a single layer on a parchment-lined baking tray. Place in oven alongside garlic for about 15 minutes or until soft and light golden brown. Remove from oven and let cool at room temperature.

**THREE:** Remove garlic from oven, open aluminum foil and let garlic cool to room temperature. Using the tip of a paring knife, remove roasted cloves from the skins and transfer to a medium bowl, discarding skin. Mash garlic lightly with a fork and add cheese. Mix until combined but garlic chunks are still visible; set aside.

**FOUR:** Slice baguette into 18 thin pieces. Arrange baguette slices on another baking tray and toast on bottom rack in oven for 6 to 8 minutes or until golden brown and crisp, flipping bread once halfway through cooking.

**FIVE:** To assemble, spread each toasted baguette slice with about 2 tsp garlic-cheese mixture. Place apple slices over top of garlic-cheese mixture, dividing evenly, then sprinkle with walnuts. Serve immediately.

**Nutrients per 3 bruschetta:** *Calories: 164, Total Fat: 7 g, Sat. Fat: 3 g, Carbs: 21 g, Fiber: 5 g, Sugars: 6 g, Protein: 4 g, Sodium: 162 mg, Cholesterol: 6 mg*

# Chicken Blue Cheese Stuffed Potatoes

*Serves 6. **Hands-on time:** 25 minutes. **Total time:** 1 hour, 25 minutes.*

The combination of blue cheese, spinach and chicken makes these stuffed potatoes a unique one-dish meal.

**TIP:** Don't be intimidated by this recipe's cooking time. You can make the potatoes the night before when you have a bit more time on your hands and store them in the refrigerator. The next day, warm them up by placing them in a 325°F oven for 25 minutes.

## INGREDIENTS:

- 6 russet potatoes (about 1½ lb), peel left on and scrubbed well
- Olive oil cooking spray
- ½ lb boneless, skinless chicken breasts (about 2 breasts), chopped into ¼-inch pieces
- ½ tsp sea salt, divided
- ¼ tsp fresh ground black pepper
- 2 tsp olive oil
- 3 oz baby spinach (about 1¾ cups)
- ½ small yellow or red onion, chopped (about ¼ cup)
- ¼ cup reduced-fat blue cheese, crumbled
- 2 Tbsp low-fat cream cheese
- 1 tsp fresh lemon juice

## INSTRUCTIONS:

**ONE:** Preheat oven to 400°F. With a fork, poke holes in potatoes. Wrap potatoes separately in foil and bake in a large baking dish misted with cooking spray for 45 minutes to 1 hour or until tender; let cool at least 15 minutes.

**TWO:** Season chicken with ¼ tsp salt and pepper. Heat oil in a large skillet over medium-high. Add chicken and cook for 5 to 7 minutes or until cooked through; remove from skillet and set aside. Add spinach and onion to same skillet and sauté over medium heat until spinach is wilted. Remove from heat; set aside.

**THREE:** Cut potatoes in half lengthwise. Carefully scoop out centers, leaving ¼-inch-thick shells. In a large mixing bowl, mash potato meat; set aside.

**FOUR:** Stir chicken and spinach mixture into potato meat. Add blue cheese, cream cheese, lemon juice and remaining ¼ tsp salt, stirring well. Spoon mixture into potato shells, dividing evenly, and place potatoes, cut side up, on a baking sheet misted with cooking spray.

**FIVE:** Bake at 400°F for 10 to 15 minutes or until lightly browned and thoroughly heated.

*Nutrients per potato (2 filled halves): Calories: 252, Total Fat: 4 g, Sat. Fat: 2 g, Monounsaturated Fat: 1.5 g, Polyunsaturated Fat: 0.25 g, Carbs: 40 g, Fiber: 3 g, Sugars: 2 g, Protein: 14 g, Sodium: 219 mg, Cholesterol: 25 mg*

# Banana Roll-Ups

*Serves 8. **Hands-on time:** 10 minutes. **Total time:** 20 minutes.*

**It's not just the bananas' mood-boosting tryptophan that will make you smile – this fun recipe requires just 10 minutes of hands-on time and contains only 180 calories per serving.**

## INGREDIENTS:

- 1 8-oz pkg low-fat cream cheese, softened
- 2 Tbsp pure maple syrup or raw honey
- ½ tsp ground cinnamon
- ½ tsp ground nutmeg
- Olive oil cooking spray
- 2 large ripe bananas, peeled and sliced
- 4 whole-wheat tortillas (8 inches each)

### TOPPING (OPTIONAL):

- 1 banana, sliced
- ¼ cup fresh mint
- ¼ cup pure maple syrup

## INSTRUCTIONS:

**ONE:** In a medium mixing bowl, combine cream cheese, maple syrup, cinnamon and nutmeg, stirring well.

**TWO:** Heat a large nonstick skillet coated with cooking spray over medium-high. Spread 1 Tbsp cream cheese mixture on each tortilla and top each with quarter of banana slices; roll up tortillas. Place 2 roll-ups in skillet and cook 2 minutes per side or until tortillas are lightly browned and crisp. Remove from pan and keep warm. Repeat procedure with remaining roll-ups. Cut each roll-up in half.

**THREE:** If desired, prepare topping: Heat additional banana slices in large nonstick skillet for 1 to 2 minutes per side or until lightly browned. Top roll-ups with additional banana slices, mint and maple syrup.

*Nutrients per ½ roll-up (not including topping): Calories: 180, Total Fat: 7 g, Sat. Fat: 3 g, Monounsaturated Fat: 1.5 g, Polyunsaturated Fat: 0.25 g, Carbs: 24 g, Fiber 2 g, Sugars: 8 g, Protein: 6 g, Sodium: 171 mg, Cholesterol: 16 mg*

**NUTRITIONAL BONUS: Bananas are a rich source of tryptophan, which may help improve your mood. The essential amino acid (essential meaning that the body cannot produce any on its own) is vital in the production of serotonin, a chemical involved in mood regulation.**

# Corn Bread Muffins

*Makes* 9 muffins. *Hands-on time:* 10 minutes. *Total time:* 25 minutes.

**A basketful of these warm muffins will add a cozy, comforting feel to your family dinner table.**

INGREDIENTS:

- ¾ cup skim milk
- ½ cup sun-dried tomatoes, chopped
- ½ cup fine corn flour
- ½ cup white whole-wheat flour
- 1 tsp low-sodium baking powder
- 1 cup fresh or frozen corn (if frozen, thaw prior to use; kernels from about 2 cobs)
- 1 jalapeño pepper, seeded and minced
- 2 egg whites
- 1 Tbsp raw honey
- Olive oil cooking spray
- 1½ oz low-fat cheddar cheese, grated (about ¼ cup)

INSTRUCTIONS:

ONE: Preheat oven to 350°F. In a small saucepan, mix milk and tomatoes. Place over high heat. As soon as milk starts to bubble around edges of saucepan, turn off heat. Set aside.

TWO: In a large bowl, add both flours and baking powder; mix well to combine. Make a well in center of flour mixture. Add corn, jalapeño, egg whites, honey and milk-tomato mixture. Mix with a wooden spoon until wet ingredients are just combined with dry ingredients.

THREE: Coat a muffin tin with cooking spray. Fill nine cups three-quarters of the way with batter and sprinkle cheese over top of each, dividing evenly. Bake for 10 to 12 minutes, until muffins puff and a toothpick comes out clean when inserted in centers. Transfer muffins to a wire rack. Serve immediately or cool completely before storing in an airtight container for up to 3 days.

Nutrients per muffin: *Calories: 102, Total Fat: 1 g, Sat. Fat: 0.25 g, Carbs: 19 g, Fiber: 2 g, Sugars: 4 g, Protein: 4.5 g, Sodium: 106 mg, Cholesterol: 1 mg*

# Garlicky Mussels
## WITH SPICY LIME CILANTRO BROTH

*Serves* 4. *Hands-on time:* 15 minutes. *Total time:* 25 minutes.

**In this recipe, cilantro and lime are used to healthfully brighten up the seafood broth, while adding fragrance and flavor. Serve a batch of comforting Corn Bread Muffins (see left) alongside this dish and you'll be able to soak up every last drop of flavorful broth.**

INGREDIENTS:

- 1½ lb tightly closed raw mussels (about 36 small mussels)
- 2 tsp olive oil
- 1 red bell pepper, seeded and finely chopped
- 4 cloves garlic, minced
- 1 jalapeño pepper, seeded and minced
- Zest and juice 4 limes, divided
- 2 cups low-sodium chicken broth
- 2 pints cherry tomatoes, cut in half
- ½ packed cup cilantro leaves, chopped
- 6 scallions, bulb removed, white and green parts thinly sliced on the diagonal

INSTRUCTIONS:

ONE: Place mussels in a large bowl of cold water. Soak for 15 to 20 minutes. With your fingers or a slotted spoon, lift out mussels and place in a colander. Rinse under cold running water and discard any mussels that have opened. Check each mussel for a thread-like string hanging out of the shell (called the "beard"). To remove, use a tea towel and take hold of the beard. Pull firmly toward the hinge end of the shell and tug free.

TWO: Heat a large stockpot over medium-high. Add oil, bell pepper, garlic, jalapeño and lime zest. Reduce heat to medium and cook for 4 to 5 minutes, stirring occasionally, until pepper is soft. Add lime juice, broth and 1 cup water and bring to a boil. Add tomatoes and mussels. Cover and cook for 6 to 8 minutes, until shells open and mussels are cooked through. Sprinkle with cilantro and scallions and serve immediately.

**TIP: To keep herbs fresh for longer, wrap them in a dry paper towel and store in a sealable bag in the refrigerator.**

Nutrients per serving (1 cup broth and about 8 to 9 mussels): *Calories: 247, Total Fat: 7 g, Sat. Fat: 1 g, Carbs: 22 g, Fiber: 3 g, Sugars: 7 g, Protein: 25 g, Sodium: 537 mg, Cholesterol: 48 mg*

Garlicky
Mussels

# Baked Oysters

*Serves 6. **Hands-on time:** 30 minutes. **Total time:** 40 minutes.*

**Don't be scared away by the large amount of kosher salt in this recipe; it is not meant for consumption. Instead, the salt is used to keep the oysters stable while they bake, plus it also makes for a pretty presentation.**

## INGREDIENTS:

- 1 Tbsp natural buttery spread, divided
- 3 Tbsp whole-wheat panko bread crumbs
- 1 large shallot, finely chopped
- 1 cup watercress, finely chopped
- 1 cup baby spinach, finely chopped
- ⅛ tsp sea salt
- Fresh ground black pepper
- 1 to 2 cups coarse kosher salt
- 18 fresh oysters on the half shell (NOTE: Opt for east coast farmed oysters, if possible.)
- 2 Tbsp freshly grated Parmigiano-Reggiano cheese
- Lemon wedges, for serving, optional
- Hot sauce, for serving, optional

## INSTRUCTIONS:

**ONE:** Preheat oven to 450°F. Heat ½ Tbsp buttery spread in a large skillet on medium. When spread is melted, add panko. Cook, stirring frequently, until panko is lightly toasted, about 3 minutes. Transfer half of panko to a small bowl and set aside. Push remaining panko to side of skillet and add remaining ½ Tbsp buttery spread. When spread is melted, add shallot. Cook, stirring to blend with panko, until tender, about 2 minutes. Add watercress, spinach, sea salt and pepper. Cook until greens are wilted. Transfer mixture to another small bowl and let cool slightly.

**TWO:** In a large ovenproof skillet or shallow baking dish, arrange kosher salt in an even layer, about ½-inch thick. Drain any liquid from oysters and use a paring or cheese knife to loosen oyster so that it is no longer anchored to the shell. Nestle oysters (still on their half shells) in kosher salt to keep them from tipping. Top each oyster with about 1 tsp watercress mixture.

**THREE:** Add Parmigiano-Reggiano to bowl with reserved panko and combine. Sprinkle mixture lightly over each oyster, discarding any leftovers. Transfer oysters to oven and bake for 10 minutes or until edges of oysters curl slightly. Serve with lemon wedges and hot sauce, if desired.

**TIP: Save time by buying oysters from a fishmonger who will shuck them for you.**

*Nutrients per 3 oysters: Calories: 74, Total Fat: 3 g, Sat. Fat: 1 g, Carbs: 7 g, Fiber: 1 g, Sugars: 0.25 g, Protein: 4 g, Sodium: 191 mg, Cholesterol: 12 mg*

## How to Prepare Oysters for Baking

**ONE:** In a large ovenproof skillet or shallow baking dish, arrange kosher salt in an even layer, about ½-inch thick.

**TWO:** Drain any liquid from oysters and use a paring or cheese knife to loosen oyster meat so that it is no longer anchored to the shell.

**THREE:** Nestle oysters (still in their half shells) in kosher salt to keep them from tipping.

**FOUR:** Top each oyster with about 1 tsp of the watercress mixture. Mix the Parmigiano-Reggiano with remaining panko and sprinkle lightly over each oyster (discard any leftovers). Transfer oysters to oven and bake 10 minutes, or until edges of oysters curl slightly.

# Holy Moly Guacamole!

*Serves* 6.

**This guilt-free version is bright, chunky and full of flavor.**

## INGREDIENTS:

- 4 avocados, pitted and peeled
- 2 serrano peppers, seeded and minced
- ½ red onion, minced
- 1 garlic clove, minced
- ½ loosely packed cup minced cilantro
- Juice ½ lemon
- Juice ½ lime
- ½ tsp ground coriander
- 2 Tbsp extra-virgin olive oil
- Sea salt and fresh ground black pepper, to taste
- Salsa or diced tomatoes, optional

## INSTRUCTIONS:

In a large bowl, mix together first 10 ingredients and mash with a potato masher. Top with salsa or tomatoes, if desired. Enjoy with your favorite whole-grain tortilla chips.

*Nutrients per serving: Calories: 202, Total Fat: 18 g, Sat. Fat: 2.5 g, Monounsaturated Fat: 12 g, Polyunsaturated Fat: 2 g, Carbs: 10 g, Fiber: 7 g, Sugars: 1 g, Protein: 2 g, Sodium: 29 mg, Cholesterol: 0 mg*

# Tzatziki

*Makes* 3 cups. *Hands-on time:* 15 minutes. *Total time:* 15 minutes.

**This all-purpose dip can be served with raw veggies and sliced whole-wheat pitas or as a refreshing accompaniment to fish or chicken.**

## INGREDIENTS:

- 2 medium cucumbers, peeled and seeded
- 2 cups nonfat plain Greek yogurt
- 1 clove garlic, smashed
- 1 Tbsp fresh dill, finely minced
- 1 Tbsp fresh mint, finely minced
- ⅛ tsp sea salt
- ¼ tsp fresh ground black pepper
- ¼ tsp red wine vinegar

## INSTRUCTIONS:

**ONE:** Finely grate cucumbers and place in center of a clean cloth dishtowel. Gather up ends and twist to wring out liquid over sink until cucumber is dry (cucumbers will release about ⅔ cup liquid).

**TWO:** In a large bowl, gently fold cucumbers into yogurt. Mix in garlic, dill, mint, salt, pepper and vinegar. Chill for at least 1 hour before serving. Dip will keep for up to 2 days in refrigerator.

**TIP: For an even thicker tzatziki, try straining the yogurt through a cheesecloth in the refrigerator overnight.**

*Nutrients per ¼-cup serving: Calories: 20, Total Fat: 0 g, Sat. Fat: 0 g, Carbs: 3 g, Fiber: 0 g, Sugars: 2 g, Protein: 2 g, Sodium: 25 mg, Cholesterol: 0 mg*

# Fish Fritters
## WITH RED PEPPER & MALT VINEGAR DIPPING SAUCE

*Serves* 4. *Hands-on time:* 15 minutes. *Total time:* 30 minutes.

**Hot, salty, battered fried fish covered in malt vinegar is an English comfort-food dream, but when it comes to arterial blockage, this dish is a nightmare. On the lighter side, our cloud-like fish fritter still has the anticipated sour and salty flavor combo – minus most of the saturated fat!**

## INGREDIENTS:

### FRITTERS

- 1 medium head broccoli, cut into florets (about 6 cups)
- 3 jalapeño peppers, seeded and chopped
- ¼ tsp sea salt, divided
- 1 12-oz piece catfish or tilapia, cut into thirds
- ½ cup whole-wheat flour
- 1 oz part-skim mozzarella, grated
- 6 egg whites
- 2 Tbsp olive oil, divided

### DIPPING SAUCE

- ½ cup jarred sliced roasted red bell peppers
- ¼ cup malt vinegar
- 1 Tbsp nonfat Greek yogurt

## INSTRUCTIONS:

**ONE:** Prepare dipping sauce: Place all ingredients in a mini chopper or blender and blend until smooth; set aside.

**TWO:** Prepare fritters: Place broccoli, jalapeños and ⅛ tsp salt in a food processor; process until chunky. Add fish, flour and cheese and pulse 2 or 3 more times, until fish is broken up.

**THREE:** In a large bowl, add egg whites and remaining ⅛ tsp salt. Using an electric mixer on high speed, beat egg whites until they triple in volume and cling to the inside of the bowl when tilted. Add ¼ cup fish mixture to egg whites and gently fold them in once or twice with a rubber spatula. Add remaining fish mixture, folding gently for 5 or 6 turns so as to not deflate egg whites.

**FOUR:** Heat 2 large skillets over high heat. Add 1 Tbsp oil to each skillet and reduce heat to medium. Drop fish mixture into skillets in scant ¼-cup increments, spacing fritters 1 inch apart and cooking in batches, if necessary. Cook for 3 to 4 minutes per side, turning once, until both sides are crisp and brown. Transfer cooked fritters to a plate and cover with a paper towel. Serve immediately with dipping sauce.

*Nutrients per serving (3 fritters and 1 Tbsp sauce): Calories: 300, Total Fat: 10 g, Sat. Fat: 2 g, Monounsaturated Fat: 5 g, Polyunsaturated Fat: 1 g, Omega-3s: 320 mg, Omega-6s: 930 mg, Carbs: 22 g, Fiber: 7 g, Sugars: 2.5 g, Protein: 31 g, Sodium: 399 mg, Cholesterol: 22 mg*

For a photo of this recipe, see page 100.

# Mini Grilled Cheese Sandwiches

*Serves 8. **Hands-on time:** 20 minutes. **Total time:** 30 minutes.*

**Dating back to the 1920s, grilled cheese is one of North America's favorite comfort foods, loved by both young and old. But instead of simply slapping some cheese between two slices of bread – as usual! – why not add black beans and shredded chicken to the mix for a little Mexican infusion?**

## INGREDIENTS:

- 1 cup canned or cooked black beans, drained and rinsed (TIP: Opt for BPA-free cans.)
- 2 Tbsp chopped fresh cilantro leaves
- Sea salt and cayenne pepper, to taste
- 1 whole-grain baguette (10 oz)
- Olive oil cooking spray
- 8 oz low-fat cheddar cheese, shredded
- 8 oz grilled boneless, skinless chicken breast, shredded or thinly sliced

## INSTRUCTIONS:

**ONE:** Place beans, ¼ cup water and cilantro into the bowl of a 4-cup food processor; purée until smooth. Season with salt and cayenne. Scrape mixture into a sealable container, cover and set aside. (Mixture can be made ahead and stored in refrigerator for 1 to 2 days.)

**TWO:** Slice baguette into 32 pieces (about ¼ inch thick) and arrange in a single layer on a tray or cutting board. Spray each slice with cooking spray and flip over, misted side down.

**THREE:** Spread 1 tsp bean purée onto 16 of the baguette slices. Top each of remaining 16 slices with ½ oz cheese (about 1 Tbsp) and ½ oz chicken. Sandwich baguette slices together, topping each cheese-chicken slice with a bean purée slice, making a total of 16 sandwiches.

**FOUR:** Preheat a nonstick skillet over medium heat and mist with cooking spray. Place sandwiches into pan, cooking in batches. Cook for 2 to 3 minutes per side or until bread is light golden brown, cheese is melted and chicken is warm. Serve immediately.

*Nutrients per 2 sandwiches: Calories: 217, Total Fat: 6 g, Sat. Fat. 2 g, Curbs: 20 g, Fiber: 4 g, Sugars: 1 g, Protein: 18 g, Sodium: 365 mg, Cholesterol: 30 mg*

Baked Spinach & Artichoke Dip

THE BEST OF CLEAN EATING 2

# Baked Spinach & Artichoke Dip

*Serves* 10. **Hands-on time:** *35 minutes.* **Total time:** *1 hour, 5 minutes.*

**In this revamped version of the traditional creamy calorie bomb, the two titular veggies finally get the spinach dip they deserve.**

## INGREDIENTS:

- 1½ cups frozen cauliflower florets
- 4 oz ⅓-less-fat cream cheese
- 9 to 11 Tbsp low-fat milk, divided
- Olive oil cooking spray
- 1 medium onion, chopped
- 3 cloves garlic, minced
- 1 10-oz box frozen chopped spinach, thawed and squeezed to remove excess water
- 1 8-oz box frozen artichoke hearts, thawed and chopped
- ¼ packed cup fresh dill sprigs, thick stems removed
- ½ tsp sea salt, plus additional to taste
- ¼ tsp ground cayenne pepper, or to taste
- 5 scallions, chopped
- 2 oz reduced-fat Monterey Jack or mozzarella cheese, shredded (½ cup)

## INSTRUCTIONS:

**ONE:** Preheat oven to 350°F. Cook cauliflower according to package directions (you should be left with 1 cup cooked). Place cauliflower in the bowl of a food processor and add cream cheese and 3 Tbsp milk. Purée until smooth; transfer mixture to a large bowl.

**TWO:** Coat a nonstick skillet with cooking spray and heat on medium. Add onion and cook until lightly browned and soft, 8 to 10 minutes. Add garlic and cook for 1 minute more. Transfer mixture to food processor (no need to clean it after puréeing cauliflower mixture). Add spinach, artichokes, dill, ½ tsp salt and cayenne. Add 6 Tbsp milk, turn processor on and purée until mixture is easily spreadable. If necessary, add 2 Tbsp milk to thin. Transfer to bowl with cauliflower mixture. Add scallions and stir until thoroughly combined. Check seasoning and add additional salt or cayenne as needed.

**THREE:** Transfer mixture to an 8- or 9-inch square baking dish and cover with foil. Bake for 20 minutes. Discard foil and sprinkle with cheese. Bake for 10 minutes more, until cheese is melted and dip is heated through. Serve hot.

*Nutrients per serving (⅓ cup dip): Calories: 84, Total Fat: 4 g, Sat. Fat: 2 g, Carbs: 7.5 g, Fiber: 2.5 g, Sugars: 2 g, Protein: 5 g, Sodium: 250 mg, Cholesterol: 11 mg*

# Parmesan Popovers

*Makes* 18 popovers. **Hands-on time:** *10 minutes.* **Total time:** *40 to 50 minutes.*

**Whole milk, egg yolks and butter are what make traditional popovers high-saturated fat foods. Our version offers a golden, eggy, chewy yet healthy alternative that pairs well with soups and stews.**

## INGREDIENTS:

- 1 egg
- 3 egg whites
- 1 cup soft tofu, crumbled
- 1½ cups skim milk
  (or low-fat unsweetened soy, almond or rice milk)
- 2 Tbsp olive oil
- 1 cup kamut flour
- ½ cup quinoa flour
- 1 Tbsp baking powder
- ½ cup low-fat Parmesan cheese, grated
- Olive oil cooking spray

## INSTRUCTIONS:

**ONE:** Preheat oven to 425°F. Blend egg, egg whites, tofu, milk and oil in a blender until smooth.

**TWO:** In a medium bowl, whisk dry ingredients and Parmesan. Add wet ingredients to dry ingredients and whisk until smooth. Let sit 15 to 20 minutes. Preheat standard muffin tin or popover pan in oven for 5 minutes.

**THREE:** Mist hot muffin or popover pans with cooking spray. Fill cups three-quarters full with batter. Bake 10 minutes, reduce temperature to 350°F and bake an additional 5 to 7 minutes or until golden.

**OPTION: To make mini popovers, use a mini-muffin pan and reduce cooking time to 7 minutes at 425°F, then 4 to 5 minutes at 350°F.**

**TIP: Pass on the Parmesan and your popover batter can be used to make light, fluffy pancakes that are high in protein and calcium.**

*Nutrients per popover: Calories: 60, Total Fat: 3 g, Sat. Fat: 0.5 g, Carbs: 6 g, Fiber: 0 g, Sugars: 1 g, Protein: 3 g, Sodium: 60 mg, Cholesterol: 15 mg*

**NUTRITIONAL BONUS: Using tofu, skim milk and Parmesan cheese in these popovers increases their calcium content, offering 10% of your daily need per popover. The body stores 99% of its calcium in bones and teeth, while the other 1% is required for vital functions such as the expansion and contraction of muscles and blood vessels.**

# Baked Lobster & Brie Dip
## WITH LEMON ROSEMARY CRACKERS

*Serves 12. **Hands-on time:** 25 minutes. **Total time:** 1 hour, 5 minutes.*

**This is a decadent and rich dish that no one will guess is *CE*-approved! The Lemon Rosemary Crackers are perfect for many appetizers over the holidays and also make for a great hostess gift wrapped up in a beautiful little box. When shopping for ingredients, purchase fresh-cooked lobster meat from your local fishmonger. Many will even allow you to pick a live one and will cook it for you while you shop.**

## INGREDIENTS:

### DIP

- 2 tsp olive oil
- 2 cloves garlic, minced
- 6 cups baby spinach, lightly packed
- 1 cup shredded part-skim mozzarella cheese
- ½ cup nonfat plain Greek yogurt
- ½ cup low-fat plain cream cheese, softened
- 1 Tbsp fresh lemon juice
- Pinch ground cayenne pepper
- 1½ cups chopped cooked lobster meat
- 1½ cups low-fat Brie cheese, diced (about 7 oz)
- 2 Tbsp each chopped fresh chives and flat-leaf parsley
- Sea salt and fresh ground black pepper, to taste

### CRACKERS

- 1½ cups white whole-wheat flour, divided
- ¾ cup quinoa flour
- 1 Tbsp coarsely chopped fresh rosemary
- 2 tsp lemon zest
- 1 tsp baking powder
- 1 tsp sea salt
- ¼ cup olive oil
- 1 egg white, whisked until just foamy

## INSTRUCTIONS:

**ONE:** Preheat oven to 400°F. Ensure 2 racks are in top and bottom thirds of oven.

**TWO:** Prepare crackers: Reserve ¼ cup white whole-wheat flour for use when rolling out crackers. In a large bowl, whisk together 1¼ cups white whole-wheat flour, quinoa flour, rosemary, lemon zest, baking powder and salt. Make a well in the center of the flour and add oil. Using a whisk, stir in oil until mixture resembles coarse crumbs. Again, make a well and add ⅔ cup water. Gently fold in using a spatula until just barely combined. Transfer to a lightly floured surface and gently knead for about 30 seconds. Divide dough into 4 equal pieces and cover with a clean damp tea towel so that dough does not dry.

**THREE:** Place 1 piece of dough onto a lightly floured surface, leaving others covered. Roll into a ¹⁄₁₆-inch-thick oval, turning dough over and lightly re-flouring surface as needed. Place onto 1 of 2 parchment-lined baking sheets. Repeat with remaining dough, placing 2 ovals on each tray. Brush tops of each oval evenly with egg white. Place trays into oven on both top and bottom racks and bake for about 10 to 12 minutes, rotating trays and switching rack placement once halfway through baking, until golden. Remove crackers from oven and let cool (but leave oven on). Break into 2- to 3-inch pieces, cover and reserve.

**FOUR:** Prepare dip: Reduce oven temperature to 375°F. In a large skillet, heat oil on medium-high. Cooking in batches if necessary, add garlic and spinach and cook for 1 to 2 minutes, until spinach is just wilted. Transfer to a colander, allow to cool for 2 to 3 minutes and gently press to drain excess water. Cool to room temperature and transfer to a large mixing bowl. Set aside.

**FIVE:** Add mozzarella, yogurt, cream cheese, lemon juice and cayenne to the bowl of a food processor and pulse until thoroughly combined. Using a spatula, scrape cheese mixture into bowl with spinach. Stir in lobster, Brie, chives and parsley. Season with salt and pepper.

**SIX:** Transfer dip to a shallow ovenproof casserole dish and place dish on a baking tray. Heat in oven for 15 to 18 minutes, until hot and bubbling. Remove from oven and let rest for 3 to 4 minutes. Serve with Lemon Rosemary Crackers for dipping.

**Nutrients per serving (⅓ cup dip and ¹⁄₁₂ of crackers):** *Calories: 256, Total Fat: 12 g, Sat. Fat: 3 g, Monounsaturated Fat: 5 g, Polyunsaturated Fat: 1 g, Carbs: 21 g, Fiber: 4 g, Sugars: 1 g, Protein: 16 g, Sodium: 481 mg, Cholesterol: 33 mg*

## Nutritional Bonus:
**This decadent dip may seem indulgent, but it is nutritionally so much better than any traditional hot cheese dip that can contain more than 55 g of fat and over 1,000 calories per serving! Each serving also packs 17 g of protein largely due to the lobster and quinoa flour.**

# Citrus Scones

*Makes 24 scones. Hands-on time: 15 minutes. Total time: 30 to 35 minutes.*

Originating in the UK, scones are widely popular throughout Europe as a teatime snack. Easier to make than traditional scones, our soft, light, slightly sweet treats are packed with citrus flavor. Omitting the butter and cream of classic scones and replacing them with healthier ingredients may make these baked goods less flaky, but the benefit of a high-protein, high-fiber, zero-saturated-fat snack is worth the trade. And your taste buds won't miss the fatty stuff.

## INGREDIENTS:

- ⅔ cup skim milk
- Juice each ½ lemon, ½ lime and ½ orange (⅓ cup total juice)
- 1½ cups spelt flour
- 1 cup brown rice flour, finely ground
- 1 tsp baking powder
- ½ tsp baking soda
- ⅓ cup Sucanat
- Zest each ½ lemon, ½ lime and ½ orange (1 Tbsp total zest)
- 2 egg whites
- ¼ cup olive oil
- 1 tsp pure vanilla extract
- Olive oil cooking spray

## INSTRUCTIONS:

**ONE:** Preheat oven to 350°F. In a small bowl, combine milk and citrus juice. Let sit 5 minutes.

**TWO:** In a medium bowl, whisk flours, baking powder, baking soda, Sucanat and zest.

**THREE:** Add egg whites, oil and vanilla to milk mixture and blend well. Add wet ingredients to dry ingredients and combine. Do not over mix.

**FOUR:** Mist 2 baking sheets with cooking spray. Spoon one-third of dough onto a baking sheet and spread in a circle, 1 inch thick. Repeat with remaining dough. (There will be 2 circles on 1 sheet and 1 on the other.) Bake 15 to 20 minutes or until scones are golden. Cut each circle into 8 wedges and serve.

**OPTION: Dough can also be dropped by rounded tablespoon to make biscuit-style scones.**

**OPTION: For a fiber boost, substitute oat flour for brown rice flour.**

*Nutrients per scone: Calories: 90, Total Fat: 2.5 g, Sat. Fat: 0 g, Carbs: 14 g, Fiber: 1 g, Sugars: 3 g, Protein: 2 g, Sodium: 35 mg, Cholesterol: 0 mg*

# Chive Goat Cheese Soufflés

*Serves 4. Hands-on time: 35 minutes. Total time: 55 minutes.*

We've reduced the number of egg yolks and replaced the butter with just a tablespoon of extra-virgin olive oil, so these impressive little soufflés will fit comfortably into your healthy lifestyle.

## INGREDIENTS:

- 2 tsp natural buttery spread (TRY: Earth Balance Buttery Spread with Olive Oil)
- 3 Tbsp finely crushed whole-wheat bread crumbs
- 1 large egg, separated
- 2 large egg whites (do not use pre-packaged whites)
- ¼ tsp dry mustard powder
- ¼ tsp sea salt
- Fresh ground black pepper, to taste
- ¼ tsp cream of tartar
- 1 Tbsp extra-virgin olive oil
- 3 scallions, thinly sliced (about ⅓ cup)
- 2 Tbsp white whole-wheat flour
- ⅔ cup low-fat milk
- 3 Tbsp chopped chives
- 2 oz goat cheese, crumbled

## INSTRUCTIONS:

**ONE:** Position 1 rack in center of oven. Preheat oven to 375°F. Thoroughly coat the insides of 4 6-oz ramekins with buttery spread. Divide bread crumbs evenly among ramekins. One at a time, gently shake ramekins to coat with bread crumbs, discarding any that don't adhere.

**TWO:** Place egg yolk in a large mixing bowl. Add 3 whites to another large mixing bowl, preferably stainless steel. To the yolk, add mustard powder, salt and a few grinds of pepper; set aside. To the whites, add cream of tartar and set aside.

**THREE:** Heat oil in a small saucepan on medium-low. Add scallions and cook until soft, about 2 minutes. Add flour and cook, stirring constantly, for 1 minute. Slowly pour in milk while continuing to whisk. Increase heat to medium and whisk constantly until mixture thickens, 1 to 2 minutes (do not allow milk to boil). Remove from heat.

**FOUR:** Add a spoonful of milk mixture to egg yolk and whisk to combine (this prevents yolk from overheating). Add remaining milk mixture and whisk again. Using an electric mixer, beat egg whites on high speed until stiff peaks form, 2 to 3 minutes.

**FIVE:** Fold chives and cheese into yolk mixture, then add about one-third of egg whites. Using a rubber spatula, gently fold whites into yolks, just until combined (do not over mix; a few white streaks should remain visible). Fold in remaining egg whites in 2 more batches. Divide mixture evenly among prepared ramekins. Bake directly on oven rack for 18 to 19 minutes or until tops are puffed and golden brown. Transfer ramekins to table right away, as tops will start to deflate almost immediately. Soufflés will be very hot, so wait 5 to 10 minutes, then enjoy!

*Nutrients per soufflé: Calories: 172, Total Fat: 10 g, Sat. Fat: 4 g, Monounsaturated Fat: 4 g, Polyunsaturated Fat: 1 g, Carbs: 11 g, Fiber: 1 g, Sugars: 3 g, Protein: 9 g, Sodium: 357 mg, Cholesterol: 14 mg*

**Chive Goat Cheese Soufflés**

# Stop Mindless Eating

Here are Tosca's top tips for planning for hunger and knowing what to eat on the go.

Tosca Reno, *Clean Eating* columnist and bestselling author of *The Eat-Clean Diet®* series, shares her strategies for successful snacking.

**I'm good at starting my day with a clean breakfast that my husband makes for me, followed by a clean snack and a lunch that I pack using the previous night's leftovers. But after lunch, everything falls apart. Is it my lack of willpower or am I missing something important in my diet?**

As with all habits, to make them routine you must practice good planning and then implement them. Change comes after you have repeated the new behavior so often it then becomes a lifestyle. It is easy to get through the morning in your case because you have picked up steam by having a clean breakfast your husband has prepared for you (lucky girl!), and then using up clean leftovers for lunch. The reason "everything falls apart" is because in all likelihood you have not packed enough food to get you through the afternoon. Figuring out the number of meals you will eat after lunch and planning for them can easily correct this. Take a few more dinner leftovers with you if there is enough or do what I do and make planned leftovers. I take extra boiled eggs from breakfast or I purposely make extra oatmeal pancakes and bring a few with me for the afternoon. Pair them with some crackers and hummus or some raw veggies and you'll be more than fine.

**What are some easy snack foods I can take with me to work? I don't have a refrigerator, so I am limited in the food I can take.**

When I travel, I run into this very problem. Luckily, with a little planning, it is easy to be prepared for hunger pangs no matter where you are. Here is what I pack for airplane travel that may work well for those of you who don't have a way to keep foods cool:

- Several baggies (or enough for the day) of premeasured ½-cup **oatmeal** servings (you can get hot water anywhere), each mixed with 2 tablespoons ground **flaxseed**, 2 tablespoons **wheat germ**, ¼ cup **raisins or dried cranberries** and a scoop of **protein powder** and a spoon.

- A baggie containing a mix of **herbal teas** (again, you can get hot water anywhere).

- A bar of **dark chocolate**, which I eat in small pieces – not all at once (70% cocoa or darker is healthiest).

- A package of **clean crackers** – I like Ryvita. There are numerous kinds of this wonderful crisp snack bread that work well in an *Eat-Clean Diet®* lifestyle (my personal favorite is the muesli or sunflower seed kind).

- A mixture of **nuts, seeds and dried fruits**, also premeasured in several small baggies.

- A small jar of **natural peanut butter**.

- **Apples and oranges** because they keep well.

- A small bag of **pitted dates**.

- And, of course, I carry **water** at all times.

With this kind of food at the ready, you will never have to go hungry – or be at the mercy of dreaded airplane food. I pack these foods into my carry-on and I also have them at my office. You will always be prepared for hunger this way.

# Main Courses

Catfish Fillets with
Warm Corn Relish, p. 167

# Beef, Pork & Lamb

Coming up with delicious and healthy dinner ideas on a daily basis isn't always easy. Lucky for you, the following pages contain a delectable array of our very best main-dish ideas for beef, pork and lamb. We've got cleaned-up classics (Spaghetti & Meatball Casserole), crowd pleasers (Ratatouille Sloppy Joes), exotic options (Moroccan Braised Beef) and comfort food with a twist (Thai Meatloaf). We hope you feel a little less stressed already!

## Thai Meatloaf
### WITH CRISPY-BAKED NOODLES

*Serves* 4. **Hands-on time:** *30 minutes.* **Total time:** *50 minutes.*

**By adding sautéed mushrooms and whole-wheat bread crumbs to this meatloaf, you'll lend a bit of extra flavor, texture and moisture.**

### INGREDIENTS:

- Olive oil cooking spray
- 1 whole-wheat pita (7 inches in diameter)
- 4 oz whole-wheat spaghetti
- 2 tsp extra-virgin olive oil, divided
- 8 oz button mushrooms, sliced
- 2 cloves garlic, minced
- 1 small yellow onion, diced
- ¾ lb lean ground pork
- 1 egg
- 1 tsp ground ginger
- 1 tsp low-sodium soy sauce
- 10 stems fresh cilantro, minced, plus more for garnish
- 1 carrot, peeled and sliced into thin circles
- 1 green onion, trimmed and sliced into thin circles

### INSTRUCTIONS:

ONE: Lightly mist a 9 x 5-inch glass loaf pan with cooking spray and set aside. Cover a baking sheet with a piece of parchment paper and set aside. Adjust oven racks to leave about 4 inches of space between top and bottom racks. Preheat oven to 350°F.

TWO: Rip pita into bite-sized pieces and place them in the bowl of a food processor. Process for about 1 minute or until pita pieces have become medium-fine bread crumbs. Set aside.

THREE: Prepare spaghetti according to package directions. Drain well and toss with 1 tsp oil. Lay pasta out onto prepared baking sheet, spreading individual noodles out as much as possible so there are no noodle nests or lumps. Set aside.

FOUR: Heat remaining 1 tsp oil in a large nonstick pan on medium for 1 minute. Add mushrooms and cook for 5 minutes, stirring occasionally. Drain and set aside.

FIVE: In a large mixing bowl, combine garlic, yellow onion, pork, egg, ginger, soy sauce, 2 Tbsp water and cilantro; mix well. Add 1 cup reserved bread crumbs and mix again. Gently fold in mushrooms. Mold mixture into the shape of the loaf pan, then place in pan.

SIX: Place loaf pan on top rack and baking sheet with noodles on lower rack of oven. Bake for 20 to 25 minutes or until a toothpick inserted into center of meatloaf comes out clean and meat feels firm when pressed; do not over-bake. If noodles are not crispy when pressed, bake for another 5 minutes.

SEVEN: Pull apart noodles, creating 4 portions. Divide meatloaf into 4 equal servings. Serve meatloaf alongside noodles, scattering carrot and green onion over top of noodles before serving. Garnish with cilantro.

**Nutrients per serving (6 oz meatloaf and 1 oz pasta):** *Calories: 347, Total Fat: 7 g, Sat. Fat: 2 g, Monounsaturated Fat: 2.5 g, Polyunsaturated Fat: 1 g, Carbs: 36 g, Fiber: 6 g, Sugars: 4 g, Protein: 35 g, Sodium: 253 mg, Cholesterol: 120 mg*

# Beef Stir-Fry
## WITH CARAMELIZED ONIONS & BELL PEPPERS

*Serves 4. **Hands-on time:** 15 to 20 minutes. **Total time:** 15 to 20 minutes.*

**Sure to appear on your weekly menu over and over again, this simple-to-prepare stir-fry boasts incredible depth of flavor. The sweet and tender caramelized onions and bell peppers pair perfectly with the smokiness of roasted red peppers and lemony basil.**

## INGREDIENTS:

- 1 cup quinoa
- 1 Tbsp olive oil
- 1 cup chopped yellow onion
- 3 cloves garlic, minced
- 1 each yellow, orange and green bell pepper, chopped
- 1 cup chopped roasted red peppers
- 1 lb lean beef tenderloin, trimmed of visible fat and cut into thin strips
- 1 cup low-sodium beef broth
- ¼ cup chopped fresh basil
- Sea salt and fresh ground black pepper, to taste

## INSTRUCTIONS:

ONE: Cook quinoa according to package directions; set aside.

TWO: Meanwhile, heat oil in a wok or large skillet on medium-high. Add onion and garlic and cook for 2 to 3 minutes, until onions are soft. Add bell peppers and roasted peppers and cook for 2 minutes, until onions are golden brown. Add beef and cook for another 2 minutes, stirring frequently. Add broth and bring to a simmer over same heat. Simmer for 2 minutes, until steak is cooked through. Remove from heat, stir in basil and season with salt and pepper. Serve beef mixture over quinoa.

**Nutrients per serving (1½ cups beef mixture and ½ cup quinoa):** *Calories: 377, Total Fat: 11 g, Sat. Fat: 2 g, Carbs: 40 g, Fiber: 6 g, Sugars: 7 g, Protein: 31 g, Sodium: 316 mg, Cholesterol: 60 mg*

**Nutritional Bonus:**
Made from soybeans fermented with B12-synthesizing bacteria, miso is regarded as a protein source even in small amounts. Just 1 Tbsp of miso paste contains an impressive 2 g of protein!

**Beef Tenderloin**

# Beef Tenderloin
## WITH MISO-MUSHROOM GRAVY & SMASHED REDSKIN POTATOES

**Serves 6. Makes** *2½ cups Miso-Mushroom Gravy and 4½ cups Smashed Potatoes.*
**Hands-on time:** *45 minutes.* **Total time:** *1 hour (plus 1 hour for marinating).*

**Searing and roasting beef tenderloin in one piece instead of cutting it into steaks helps keep the meat juicy and flavorful. It can also make for an impressive presentation if carved at the table.**

### INGREDIENTS:

- 1½ lb center-cut beef tender-loin, trimmed of visible fat
- 4 tsp olive oil, divided
- 1 medium white or red onion, thinly sliced
- 1 each red and yellow bell pepper, thinly sliced
- Sea salt and fresh ground black pepper, to taste
- 1 lb fresh baby spinach

### BEEF MARINADE

- 2 tsp olive oil
- 1 Tbsp low-sodium tamari
- 1 Tbsp balsamic vinegar
- 2 cloves garlic, minced
- 1 tsp ground cumin
- ½ tsp smoked sweet paprika

### MISO-MUSHROOM GRAVY

- 2 tsp olive oil
- 2 cloves garlic, minced
- 1 cup thinly sliced cremini mushrooms
- 3 Tbsp whole-wheat flour
- 2 cups low-sodium beef or chicken broth, divided
- 3 Tbsp white miso paste
- Sea salt and fresh ground black pepper, to taste

### SMASHED POTATOES

- 1½ lb mini redskin potatoes
- ½ tsp sea salt, plus additional to taste
- ½ cup nonfat plain Greek yogurt
- 3 Tbsp fresh lemon juice
- 2 Tbsp chopped fresh chives
- Fresh ground black pepper, to taste

### INSTRUCTIONS:

**ONE:** Pat beef dry with paper towel. Prepare marinade: In a small bowl, stir together oil, vinegar, garlic, cumin and paprika. Place beef into a resealable plastic bag. Pour marinade into bag, remove excess air from bag to ensure beef is completely coated, seal and refrigerate for a minimum of 1 hour or up to 24 hours.

**TWO:** Prepare Miso-Mushroom Gravy: In a medium pot, heat oil on medium. Add garlic and mushrooms and cook, stirring frequently, until softened, about 5 minutes. In a small bowl, add flour and ½ cup broth. Whisk to combine and ensure there are no lumps. Add mixture to pot and stir constantly, about 3 minutes. Add remaining 1½ cups broth to pot and whisk to combine. Increase heat to medium-high and bring to a boil. Reduce heat to medium-low, whisk in miso paste and allow sauce to cook until thickened, about 10 minutes. Taste and adjust seasoning with salt and pepper. Remove from heat, cover and keep warm.

**THREE:** Prepare smashed potatoes: In a medium pot, add potatoes and cover with cold water. Bring to a boil on high heat, add salt and cook until potatoes are tender when pierced with a fork, about 10 minutes. Remove from heat and drain water, then return potatoes to pot and coarsely smash with a potato masher or fork. Fold in yogurt, lemon juice and chives. Season with salt and pepper. Remove from heat, cover and keep warm until ready to serve.

**FOUR:** Preheat oven to 400°F. Heat a large ovenproof skillet (or cast-iron pan) on medium-high. Add 2 tsp oil and beef to pan and sear for about 2 minutes per side, until outside of beef is golden brown. Transfer beef to a parchment- or foil-lined baking sheet and roast in oven for 15 minutes for medium-rare doneness or 18 to 20 minutes for medium (or until internal temperature reaches 125°F or 130°F, respectively). Remove from oven, cover loosely with foil and allow beef to rest for 10 minutes.

**FIVE:** Meanwhile, heat remaining 2 tsp oil in a new skillet on medium-high. Add onions and bell peppers and cook, stirring frequently until tender, about 6 minutes. Season with salt and pepper.

**SIX:** In a saucepan, add about 2 inches of water, fit with a steamer insert and bring water to a boil. Add spinach to steamer, cover and steam for about 1 minute or until spinach is wilted. Transfer to a mixing bowl and season with salt and pepper.

**SEVEN:** To serve, carve beef into 6 equal medallions. Scoop about ⅔ cup smashed potatoes onto each plate and serve with beef, sautéed peppers and onions and spinach. Drizzle with Miso-Mushroom Gravy and serve immediately.

**Nutrients per serving (4 oz beef, ¾ cup potatoes, ⅓ cup gravy, ¼ cup bell pepper-onion mixture, 2½ oz spinach):** *Calories: 370, Total Fat: 11.5 g, Sat. Fat: 2.5 g, Monounsaturated Fat: 6 g, Polyunsaturated Fat: 1 g, Carbs: 40 g, Fiber: 7.5 g, Sugars: 7 g, Protein: 32 g, Sodium: 717 mg, Cholesterol: 60 mg*

# Creole Dirty Rice
## WITH ANDOUILLE SAUSAGE & RED BEANS

*Serves 6. Hands-on time: 1 hour.*
*Total time: 2½ hours (plus overnight soaking of beans) or see our time-saving tip below!*

**Our version of dirty rice doesn't have the typical heat of most Creole dishes, but if your family likes it hot, you can always double the amount of Cajun seasoning and add a bit of cayenne pepper.**

### INGREDIENTS:

- 1 cup brown rice
- 7 oz deli-fresh smoked lean andouille sausage
- Olive oil cooking spray
- 1 medium yellow onion, diced
- 1 green bell pepper, cored, seeded and diced
- 3 cloves garlic, minced
- 8 oz dried red beans, soaked overnight in water in a covered pot
- 1 bay leaf
- 2 tomatoes, preferably Roma, cored, seeded and finely chopped
- 1½ tsp Cajun seasoning
- Sea salt and fresh ground black pepper, to taste
- 4 Tbsp fresh cilantro, minced

### INSTRUCTIONS:

**ONE:** Cook brown rice according to package directions. Remove from heat and set aside.

**TWO:** In a medium pot, cover sausage with about 3 inches of water. Bring to a boil, then allow to boil for 10 minutes. Remove from heat, drain and let cool for 5 minutes before slicing sausage.

**THREE:** Heat a large pot on medium-high. Mist with cooking spray and add onion, green pepper and garlic. Sauté for about 5 minutes or until vegetables are cooked through. Drain soaked beans and rinse with cold water. Add beans, bay leaf and 3 cups water to pot with vegetables. Bring to a boil, then let boil for 20 minutes before reducing heat to medium-low. Cook until beans are soft, stirring occasionally and adding more water as it evaporates, about 2 hours. When beans are cooked through and water has reduced to less than 1 cup, add tomatoes and cook for at least 15 more minutes.

**FOUR:** Remove bay leaf. Stir in Cajun seasoning, cooked rice and sausage and cook for about 10 minutes. Season with salt and pepper and garnish with cilantro before serving.

**TIP:** We've opted for dried beans instead of canned to avoid chemicals such as bisphenol A (BPA), which may be hiding in the can's lining. However, if you're running short on time, feel free to go with canned beans but look for brands that choose BPA-free cans and remember to drain and rinse the beans first. If you use canned beans in our Creole Dirty Rice, you will only need to warm them up for about 5 to 10 minutes instead of cooking them for 2 hours. And, you can reduce the water from 3 cups to ½ cup.

*Nutrients per 1-cup serving: Calories: 292, Total Fat: 2 g, Sat. Fat: 0.5 g, Carbs: 53 g, Fiber: 4 g, Sugars: 4 g, Protein: 15 g, Sodium: 427 mg, Cholesterol: 7 mg*

---

# Dusted Pork Cutlets
## WITH BALSAMIC-DRENCHED RAISINS & MAPLE SQUASH

*Serves 4. Hands-on time: 35 minutes. Total time: 55 minutes.*

**If you think dried fruit is only good in trail mix, think again! Balsamic-simmered raisins are the perfect companion for these crispy cutlets.**

### INGREDIENTS:

- 1 acorn squash (about 1½ lb)
- 1 Tbsp pure maple syrup
- 1 egg
- ½ cup fine-ground cornmeal
- 1 lb pork tenderloin, trimmed of visible fat, cut into 1-inch-thick medallions
- 1 Tbsp extra-virgin olive oil
- 2 Tbsp balsamic vinegar
- ¼ lb unsweetened raisins (about ¾ cup)

### INSTRUCTIONS:

**ONE:** Preheat oven to 375°F. Cover a baking sheet with aluminum foil and set aside.

**TWO:** Cut squash in half with a heavy 8-inch chef's knife. Scrape out and discard seeds and stringy fibers. Place squash halves cut side up on prepared sheet. Pour 1½ tsp maple syrup onto each half. Bake for 40 minutes, until edges are brown and center begins to wrinkle.

**THREE:** Crack egg into a flat-bottomed soup bowl. Lightly whisk egg with a fork. Place cornmeal in a separate flat-bottomed bowl.

**FOUR:** Dip each pork medallion into egg and then into cornmeal, evenly coating all sides. Place medallions on a plate.

**FIVE:** Heat oil in a large nonstick pan for 1 minute on medium. Add medallions and cook for 4 minutes or until pink juices are released. Flip each piece over and cook for another 4 minutes or until juices run clear and both sides of medallions are golden brown. Remove pan from heat.

**SIX:** Remove pork from pan and set aside. Add vinegar, raisins and 2 Tbsp water to pan and place back on heat. Simmer mixture for 10 minutes on low heat, stirring occasionally to deglaze pan. Raisins will soak up cooking liquid and double in size.

**SEVEN:** When squash halves are done, carefully remove them from oven. Let squash cool for at least 10 minutes before handling. Pour any pooled maple syrup from centers of the halves into a bowl and reserve. Cut each half in half again. To serve, drizzle reserved syrup over squash and serve alongside 4 oz pork and approximately ⅓ cup balsamic-drenched raisins.

**ROAST THOSE SEEDS!** Roasting seeds from your squash is easier than you think. Simply rinse well, place in a medium pot and cover with 2 inches of cold water. Place pot on medium-low heat and simmer, covered, for 1 hour. Drain, then toss simmered seeds with a drizzle of extra-virgin olive oil and a pinch of sea salt, then spread them out on a baking tray lined with parchment paper. Bake at 250°F for 1 hour. Let cool and store in an airtight container for up to 1 week.

*Nutrients per serving (4 oz pork, ¼ squash and ⅓ cup raisins): Calories: 390, Total Fat: 8 g, Sat. Fat: 2 g, Monounsaturated Fat: 4 g, Polyunsaturated Fat: 1 g, Carbs: 51 g, Fiber: 5 g, Sugars: 22 g, Protein: 29 g, Sodium: 93 mg, Cholesterol: 126 mg*

Dusted Pork Cutlets

Moroccan
Braised
Beef

# Moroccan Braised Beef
WITH ROOT VEGETABLES

*Serves 4.* **Hands-on time:** *45 minutes.* **Total time:** *2 hours, 25 minutes.*

**Beef chuck is affordable and ideal for braising – it becomes incredibly tender when cooked slowly. Look for lean cuts with fine marbling.**

## INGREDIENTS:

- 2 navel oranges, divided
- 1¼ lb lean beef chuck, trimmed of visible fat
- ½ tsp sea salt, plus additional to taste, divided
- Fresh ground black pepper, to taste
- 4 to 5½ tsp olive oil, divided
- ½ medium onion, chopped (about ½ cup)
- 1½ tsp ground cumin
- 1½ tsp ground coriander
- 1½ tsp ground cinnamon
- ⅛ to ¼ tsp ground cayenne pepper, depending on desired heat level
- 3 cloves garlic, chopped
- 1½ Tbsp tomato paste
- 2¾ cups low-sodium chicken broth, divided
- 1 small turnip, peeled and cut into ¾-inch pieces (about 1 cup)
- 3 medium parsnips, peeled and cut into ½-inch pieces (about 1 cup)
- 2 medium carrots, peeled and cut into ½-inch pieces (about 1 cup)
- 12 dried plums
- ¾ cup whole-wheat couscous
- 3 scallions, thinly sliced

## INSTRUCTIONS:

**ONE:** Preheat oven to 350°F. With a vegetable peeler, remove peel from one of the oranges in thick strips. Scrape off and discard any white pith from underside of peel, cover peel with plastic wrap. Cut orange and squeeze juice into a bowl; discard orange and set juice aside.

**TWO:** Cut beef into 1-inch pieces. Pat dry and season with ¼ tsp salt and pepper. In a large ovenproof pot with a lid, heat 1½ tsp oil on medium-high. Add as many beef pieces as you can without crowding the pot (at least ½ inch apart). Brown beef on all sides (about 2 minutes per side). Transfer to a plate and repeat with more oil and remaining beef.

**THREE:** Drain fat from pot. Add 1 tsp oil and heat over medium. Add onion and cook about 5 minutes. Add cumin, coriander, cinnamon and cayenne; stir and cook for about 2 minutes. Add garlic and tomato paste; stir and cook for 2 more minutes. Add 1¾ cups broth and reserved orange peel and juice; bring to a simmer. Add beef and any juices. As soon as liquid returns to a simmer, cover and transfer to oven; cook for 45 minutes.

**FOUR:** Remove pot from oven and add remaining 1 cup broth, turnip, parsnips and carrots. Cover and return to oven for 30 minutes. Remove pot again and add plums. Return to oven and cook 15 to 25 more minutes. Check seasoning and add salt and pepper, if needed.

**FIVE:** About 15 minutes before beef is done, bring 1 cup water and ¼ tsp salt to a boil. Stir in couscous, cover, remove from heat and set aside for 5 to 10 minutes. Fluff with a fork and divide among 4 bowls. Add beef and vegetables and top with scallions and zest of remaining orange.

**Nutrients per serving (about 1½ cups beef mixture and ¾ cup couscous):**
*Calories: 492, Total Fat: 13 g, Sat. Fat: 3 g, Monounsaturated Fat: 7 g, Polyunsaturated Fat: 1 g, Carbs: 64 g, Fiber: 10 g, Sugars: 19 g, Protein: 34 g, Sodium: 422 mg, Cholesterol: 50 mg*

# Slow & Smothered Beef Steaks
WITH RUSTIC POTATO-CAULIFLOWER MASH

*Serves 4.* **Hands-on time:** *17 minutes.* **Total time:** *1 hour, 22 minutes.*

**This recipe's hour-plus cooking time is merely one of the steps meant to ensure your meat is tender and savory. Toasting the flour adds depth of flavor, while tenderizing the beef further reduces toughness.**

## INGREDIENTS:

- 2 Tbsp finely chopped fresh parsley, for garnish

**STEAKS**

- 2 Tbsp white whole-wheat flour
- Olive oil cooking spray
- 1 lb lean top round beef, trimmed of fat, tenderized and cut into 4 pieces
- 1 cup thinly sliced onion
- 2 cups low-sodium beef broth
- 1 Tbsp Worcestershire sauce
- 2 dried bay leaves
- ½ tsp fresh ground black pepper
- ¼ tsp sea salt

**POTATOES**

- 12 oz Yukon gold potatoes, diced (peeled, if desired)
- 8 oz fresh or frozen cauliflower florets (thawed, if frozen)
- 3 Tbsp skim milk
- ½ tsp garlic powder
- ¼ tsp each sea salt and fresh ground black pepper
- 1 Tbsp extra-virgin olive oil

**TENDERIZING TIP: Save yourself time and trouble by asking your butcher to tenderize the beef for you. Or, you can also get hands-on and use a meat mallet, rolling pin or bottom of a heavy skillet to pound the beef to ¼-inch thickness.**

## INSTRUCTIONS:

**ONE:** Preheat oven to 325°F. Prepare steaks: Heat a large nonstick skillet on medium-high. Add flour and cook for 2 minutes or until golden brown, stirring constantly. Immediately transfer from skillet to a small bowl.

**TWO:** Coat skillet with cooking spray and return to medium-high. Add steaks and cook for 2 minutes on one side, until browned, and set aside on a plate. Coat skillet again with cooking spray, add onion and cook for 4 minutes or until edges begin to brown. Sprinkle flour evenly over top of onions, stir until well coated. Gradually add broth, stirring constantly. Stir in Worcestershire, bay leaves, pepper and salt. Return beef and any accumulated juices on plate to skillet, cooked side up. Spoon broth mixture over beef and bring to a boil. Then reduce heat to medium-low, cover and cook for 1 hour, 15 minutes or until beef is very tender.

**THREE:** Meanwhile, prepare potatoes: Fill a pot with 1 inch of water and fit with a steamer basket. Place potatoes and cauliflower in steamer basket and bring water to a boil on high heat. Cover and cook until potatoes are tender, about 7 to 8 minutes. Transfer potato-cauliflower mixture to a large bowl and mash roughly with a potato masher or whisk. Stir in remaining ingredients.

**FOUR:** To serve, divide potato-cauliflower mixture evenly among 4 plates. Add 1 steak to each and spoon gravy over top. Garnish with parsley.

**Nutrients per serving (3 oz steak, ½ cup potato-cauliflower mixture, ¼ cup onion gravy):** *Calories: 285, Total Fat: 8 g, Sat. Fat: 2.5 g, Monounsaturated Fat: 5 g, Polyunsaturated Fat: 1 g, Carbs: 20 g, Fiber: 4 g, Sugars: 5 g, Protein: 31 g, Sodium: 402 mg, Cholesterol: 50 mg*

# Pot Roast
## WITH CARROT, FENNEL & SWEET POTATO ROSTI

*Serves* 16. **Makes** *8 cups vegetables, 3 lb beef and 4 cups beef jus.*
**Hands-on time:** *40 minutes.* **Total time:** *4 hours, 45 minutes.*

**There's nothing like the aroma of roast beef filling your home on a chilly day. This recipe makes enough to serve a crowd or it can be used for a smaller dinner with plenty of leftovers.**

### INGREDIENTS:

- 32 whole cherry tomatoes on the vine
- 3 Tbsp olive oil, divided
- 4 lb beef pot roast (shoulder pot roast or bottom round roast), trimmed of visible fat
- 1 Tbsp each chopped fresh rosemary, thyme and sage
- 2 cloves garlic, minced
- 1¼ tsp each kosher salt and fresh ground black pepper, divided
- 2 medium yellow onions, diced
- 3 cups low-sodium beef broth
- 1 cup boxed diced tomatoes (TRY: Pomi Chopped Tomatoes)
- 2 bay leaves
- 2 medium carrots, peeled and cut into 2-inch chunks
- 2 small fennel bulbs, stems trimmed and cut into 4-inch chunks
- 2 medium sweet potatoes, peeled
- 1 medium Yukon gold potato, peeled
- 2 Tbsp chopped fresh chives
- Olive oil cooking spray

### Nutritional Bonus:
**Like turkey, beef is high in tryptophan, one of the 10 essential amino acids that the body needs to synthesize protein. Just 4 oz of beef contains about 112% of the daily RDA for tryptophan, almost the same amount as turkey. Tryptophan also helps regulate appetite, elevates mood and aids a good night's sleep.**

### INSTRUCTIONS:

**ONE:** Position rack in bottom third of oven. Preheat oven to 400°F.

**TWO:** Arrange cherry tomatoes on a parchment-lined baking sheet and drizzle with 1 tsp oil. Roast tomatoes for about 20 minutes or until skin just begins to split. Cover and refrigerate until needed. Reduce oven heat to 350°F.

**THREE:** Pat beef dry with paper towels. In a large bowl, combine rosemary, thyme, sage, garlic, 2 tsp oil, 1 tsp salt and 1 tsp pepper. Place beef in bowl and turn to coat, rubbing seasoning into meat on all sides.

**FOUR:** In a 6- to 8-qt Dutch oven, heat remaining 2 Tbsp oil on medium-high. Add beef and sear on all sides until medium-brown and caramelized, 3 to 4 minutes per side. Remove beef from pot and set aside.

**FIVE:** Add onions to pot and cook for 4 to 6 minutes, stirring frequently and scraping brown bits from bottom of pot with a wooden spoon. Add broth and diced tomatoes and stir, scraping any remaining brown bits from bottom of pot. Return beef to pot, add bay leaves and cover pot with lid or lightly with foil; place in oven.

**SIX:** Roast for about 3 hours, carefully turning beef over in pot halfway through cooking. Add carrots and fennel to broth and cook for 30 minutes more, until beef is tender when pierced with a fork.

**SEVEN:** Meanwhile, begin preparing rosti: Coarsely grate potatoes with a cheese grater (or julienne with a mandoline) and place into center of a clean, dry towel. Working over the sink, fold towel over potatoes and twist well to squeeze out all excess water. Transfer potatoes to a bowl and stir in chives, remaining ¼ tsp salt and ¼ tsp pepper. Scoop ⅓ cup potato mixture onto a parchment-lined baking sheet and press down until about ¼ inch thick. Repeat with remaining potato mixture to make 16 rosti, evenly spacing each about ½ inch apart on sheet. Mist with cooking spray and bake in oven once beef is done, for about 15 to 20 minutes, until light golden brown.

**EIGHT:** Transfer beef to a cutting board, cover loosely with aluminum foil and let rest for 15 minutes. Remove tomatoes from fridge and let warm to room temperature. Using a slotted spoon, transfer carrot-fennel mixture to a serving dish and keep warm. Skim and discard any visible fat from surface of stock in pan.

**TEN:** Using scissors, snip cherry tomatoes apart, leaving ¼-inch stem on each tomato. Thinly slice beef and place 3 oz beef, ½ cup vegetables, ¼ cup jus, 1 potato rosti and 2 cherry tomatoes onto each plate.

**Nutrients per serving (3 oz beef, ½ cup vegetables, ¼ cup jus, 1 rosti, 2 tomatoes):** *Calories: 261, Total Fat: 13 g, Sat. Fat: 4 g, Monounsaturated Fat: 2 g, Polyunsaturated Fat: 1 g, Carbs: 12 g, Fiber: 3 g, Sugars: 3 g, Protein: 22 g, Sodium: 276 mg, Cholesterol: 66 mg*

Pot Roast

Carrot, Fennel & Sweet Potato Rosti

# Ratatouille Sloppy Joes

***Serves** 8. **Hands-on time:** 25 minutes. **Total time:** 1 hour, 25 minutes.*

We've combined two vastly different comfort-food classics by folding the flavor, color and nutrition of ratatouille, a traditional French vegetable stew, into an all-American favorite – Sloppy Joes – using our Everyday Marinara Sauce as a base. A French flair and the use of bison help add a touch of sophistication to this typically messy sandwich.

## INGREDIENTS:

- 1 tsp olive oil
- 1 lb extra-lean ground bison (or extra-lean ground beef)
- 3 cloves garlic, minced
- 1 medium onion, diced
- 2 tsp chile powder
- ¾ tsp mustard powder
- ⅛ tsp ground cayenne pepper
- 1 sweet red bell pepper, diced
- 1 medium zucchini, diced
- 1 small eggplant (¾ lb), diced
- 1½ cups Everyday Marinara Sauce (see recipe, p. 133)
- 1 Tbsp Sucanat or raw honey
- Sea salt and fresh ground black pepper, to taste
- 8 thin whole-grain sandwich buns, toasted

## INSTRUCTIONS:

**ONE:** Heat a large nonstick sauté pan on medium-high. Add oil, bison, garlic and onion and cook for 5 to 8 minutes, breaking up meat with a spoon while cooking, until no liquid remains and bison is browned. Add chile powder, mustard and cayenne, stir well and continue to cook for 1 more minute. Pour bison mixture into a bowl and set aside.

**TWO:** Return pan to heat and add bell pepper, zucchini and eggplant, stir and sauté for 3 to 4 minutes. Add bison mixture back to pan, stir well and reduce heat to medium. Cook for an additional 10 to 12 minutes, stirring often, or until all vegetables are tender and cooked throughout.

**THREE:** Add Everyday Marinara Sauce, 2 Tbsp water and Sucanat to pan, stirring until meat and vegetables are coated. Cook until sauce is hot and bubbling. Season with salt and pepper. To serve, sandwich ¾ cup bison mixture between each bun.

**Nutrients per 1 filled Sloppy Joe sandwich (including ¾ cup filling):** *Calories: 232, Total Fat: 5 g, Sat. Fat: 1 g, Monounsaturated Fat: 3 g, Polyunsaturated Fat: 1 g, Carbs: 30 g, Fiber: 5 g, Sugars: 10 g, Protein: 18 g, Sodium: 255 mg, Cholesterol: 30 mg*

# Everyday Marinara Sauce

*Makes about 6 cups.* **Hands-on time:** *25 minutes.* **Total time:** *1 hour, 25 minutes.*

**This versatile, robust sauce is a great staple to have on hand in your fridge or freezer. What could be easier than cooking up whole-grain noodles, slicing a grilled chicken breast and topping it all with some warmed sauce? And feel free to jazz up our recipe with your favorite herbs and spices.**

## INGREDIENTS:

- 12 medium Roma tomatoes or 5 cups jarred diced or strained plum tomatoes (no salt or sugar added)
- 1 Tbsp olive oil
- 4 cloves garlic, chopped
- 1 medium white onion, diced
- 2 medium carrots, peeled and diced
- 2 celery stalks, diced
- 1 Tbsp tomato paste
- 2 sprigs fresh oregano, stems removed (about 2 Tbsp leaves)
- 8 basil leaves
- ⅛ tsp red chile flakes, optional
- 1 Tbsp raw honey
- Sea salt and fresh ground black pepper, to taste

NOTE: If using jarred diced or strained tomatoes, begin instructions at Step Three.

## INSTRUCTIONS:

ONE: Bring a pot of water to boil over high heat. Using a small knife, remove each tomato core and cut a tiny X into the bottom end of each tomato. In a large bowl, prepare an ice bath. Immerse tomatoes into boiling water for 1 to 2 minutes or until skins begin to come off. Remove tomatoes with a slotted spoon and immerse into ice bath for about 1 minute or until cooled.

TWO: Once cooled, remove tomatoes from ice bath and remove skin by peeling it back from X in the bottom. Slice tomatoes in half, scoop out and discard seeds. Coarsely chop tomatoes and place into a bowl.

THREE: In a medium saucepot, heat oil over medium-high. Add garlic, onion, carrots and celery and sauté until onion becomes translucent and vegetables are softened. Add tomatoes, tomato paste, oregano, basil and chile flakes, if desired, and cook, stirring frequently, until sauce comes to a boil. Reduce heat to medium-low and simmer for 45 minutes to 1 hour, stirring occasionally.

FOUR: Remove saucepot from heat and carefully purée mixture with a hand blender or in a food processor until smooth. Add honey and season with salt and pepper; mix well.

FIVE: Ladle mixture into resealable containers, let cool to room temperature, cover and refrigerate until needed. Sauce can be kept, refrigerated, for up to 5 days or frozen for up to 2 months.

**Nutrients per 1-cup serving:** *Calories: 70, Total Fat: 2.5 g, Sat. Fat: 0.25 g, Carbs: 12 g, Fiber: 2.5 g, Sugars: 8 g, Protein: 2.5 g, Sodium: 49 mg, Cholesterol: 0 mg*

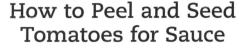

# How to Peel and Seed Tomatoes for Sauce

ONE: Bring a pot of water to a boil over high heat. While water is boiling, use a small knife to remove each tomato core and cut a small X into the bottom of each tomato.

TWO: Prepare an ice bath in a large bowl. Immerse tomatoes into boiling water for 1 to 2 minutes or until skin begins to come off. Remove tomatoes with a slotted spoon and immerse into ice bath for about 1 minute or until cooled.

THREE: Once cooled, remove tomatoes from water and remove skin by peeling it back from the X in the bottom.

FOUR: Slice tomatoes in half and use a spoon to scoop out and discard seeds, leaving middle rib intact.

# Flank Steak & Fries

*Serves 1. Hands-on time: 15 minutes. Total time: 30 to 33 minutes.*

Roasted sweet potato and parsnip fries put a festive (not to mention antioxidant-rich) spin on our steak frites, a Parisian bistro dish. For faster cooking and crispier results, cut the fries slim and vary the proportions of sweet potato to parsnip, depending on your personal preference.

## INGREDIENTS:

- ¼ lb buffalo or beef flank steak (or hanger or skirt steak)
- Sea salt and fresh ground black pepper, to taste
- 1 small sweet potato, scrubbed and cut into French-fry-sized strips (about ¼ x ¼ x 3 inches)
- 1 medium parsnip, scrubbed and cut into French-fry-sized strips (about ¼ x ¼ x 3 inches)
- 3 tsp olive oil, divided
- 2 cloves garlic, very finely minced
- ½ tsp chipotle pepper powder
- 7 dinosaur kale leaves, lower stems removed (Substitution: curly kale)

## INSTRUCTIONS:

ONE: Preheat oven to 400°F. Place an ovenproof skillet in oven to preheat, about 5 minutes. Season steak with salt and pepper, and set aside.

TWO: Combine potatoes and parsnips on a baking sheet. Drizzle with 1 tsp oil and sprinkle with garlic, then toss or mix with your hands to coat potatoes and parsnips. Sprinkle with chipotle powder and arrange in a single layer on baking sheet, leaving a third of the baking sheet empty for kale chips. Place baking sheet in oven and bake fries for 15 to 18 minutes, until lightly browned and crispy.

THREE: Meanwhile, remove skillet from oven and add 1 tsp oil. Sear steak on one side in hot skillet (not over stove top), then turn steak over and return pan to oven. Cook for 10 to 12 minutes, depending on thickness and desired doneness, until steak is medium-rare to medium.

FOUR: While steak and potatoes are cooking, stack kale leaves on a cutting board and cut crosswise into 2-inch-wide pieces. Drizzle with remaining 1 tsp oil and rub with your hands to lightly coat leaves. Place kale on baking sheet with fries during the last 6 to 8 minutes of cooking time and cook until crispy, being careful not to burn it.

FIVE: To serve, place steak on a serving plate. Arrange kale and half of potato-parsnip fries around steak, and serve immediately. Remaining half of fries can be kept for 3 days in refrigerator in a sealed container; re-warm under a hot broiler for 2 to 3 minutes before serving.

*Nutrients per serving (¼ lb buffalo flank steak, 1 cup kale chips, ½ of fries): Calories: 362, Total Fat: 18 g, Sat. Fat: 3.5 g, Monounsaturated Fat: 12 g, Polyunsaturated Fat: 2 g, Carbs: 28 g, Fiber: 5 g, Sugars: 4 g, Protein: 28 g, Sodium: 244 mg, Cholesterol: 50 mg*

# Grilled Lamb Loin Chops
## WITH CHERVIL TZATZIKI & EGGPLANT-HERB SALAD

*Serves 4. Hands-on time: 25 minutes. Total time: 55 minutes.*

**To save time, you can work on the salad while the cucumber drains and have your grill preheated and waiting for you (not vice versa).**

## INGREDIENTS:

- 4 large bone-in lamb loin chops (about 1½ lb), trimmed of all but a thin layer of visible fat
- ¼ tsp sea salt
- Fresh ground black pepper, to taste

### CHERVIL TZATZIKI

- 1 6-inch piece English cucumber, peeled
- Pinch sea salt
- ¾ cup nonfat plain Greek yogurt
- 2 Tbsp chopped chervil
- Fresh ground black pepper, to taste

### EGGPLANT-HERB SALAD

- Olive oil cooking spray
- 1 medium eggplant, cut into ½-inch chunks
- ⅛ tsp sea salt, plus additional to taste
- Fresh ground black pepper, to taste
- ½ Tbsp extra-virgin olive oil
- Juice ½ lemon
- 3 medium tomatoes, seeded and chopped
- 2 Tbsp chopped chervil
- 3 Tbsp chopped mixed herbs, such as mint, basil and thyme

## INSTRUCTIONS:

ONE: Prepare Chervil Tzatziki: Cut cucumber in half lengthwise. Scrape out seeds with a spoon and discard. Grate cucumber on large holes of a box grater. Place in a mesh sieve set over a bowl. Sprinkle with salt and drain for 10 to 15 minutes, pressing to extract any remaining liquid. Transfer cucumber to a clean bowl and add yogurt, chervil and pepper. Stir well and let rest at room temperature for 10 to 15 minutes. Serve immediately or chill for up to 2 hours; bring to room temperature before serving.

TWO: Prepare Eggplant-Herb Salad: Preheat broiler to high. Coat a rimmed baking sheet with cooking spray. Spread eggplant in a single layer on baking sheet and coat with cooking spray. Sprinkle with salt and pepper. Broil 6 to 8 inches from heat until lightly browned (6 to 8 minutes). Turn eggplant chunks and cook for 5 to 8 more minutes.

THREE: In a large bowl, whisk together oil and lemon juice. Add tomatoes and herbs, season with salt and pepper and toss to combine. Add eggplant and toss well. Serve immediately or keep covered at room temperature for up to 30 minutes.

FOUR: Prepare a charcoal or gas grill. Fifteen minutes before you are ready to cook, season lamb on both sides with salt and pepper, cover loosely and let rest at room temperature. Place lamb on medium-high, cover grill and cook to desired doneness. (**TIP:** Lamb is most tender at medium-rare, about 8 to 10 minutes per side.) Serve with Chervil Tzatziki and Eggplant-Herb Salad, trimming lamb of any remaining visible fat before enjoying.

*Nutrients per serving (1 lamb chop, ¼ cup tzatziki, ¾ cup salad): Calories: 230, Total Fat: 8 g, Sat. Fat: 3 g, Monounsaturated Fat: 3.5 g, Polyunsaturated Fat: 1 g, Carbs: 15 g, Fiber: 6.5 g, Sugars: 6 g, Protein: 24 g, Sodium: 276 mg, Cholesterol: 54 mg*

Chervil
Tzatziki

Grilled
Lamb Loin
Chops with
Eggplant
Herb Salad

**Nutritional Bonus:**
Often overlooked as a protein source, just 1 cup of baby lima beans contains about 24% of your recommended daily protein intake and 40% of your day's fiber! Like other legumes, the high fiber content (soluble fiber, in particular) helps lower cholesterol.

Smoked Paprika Pork Tenderloin

# Smoked Paprika Pork Tenderloin
## WITH SUCCOTASH

*Serves 4. **Hands-on time:** 15 minutes. **Total time:** 15 minutes.*

Succotash became popular during the Great Depression as an inexpensive corn-based dish that could be prepared with ingredients from the garden. It can take on many variations with the help of different herbs and vegetables, so experiment with what's in your fridge!

### INGREDIENTS:

- 1 Tbsp olive oil, divided
- ½ tsp smoked sweet paprika
- ¼ tsp ground cumin
- ½ tsp sea salt and fresh ground black pepper, divided
- 1 lb pork tenderloin, trimmed of visible fat and silver skin, sliced into 12 medallions
- ½ medium white onion, diced
- 1 red bell pepper, diced
- 1 cup frozen corn niblets, thawed and drained
- 1 cup frozen lima beans, thawed and drained
- 2 Tbsp chopped fresh cilantro

### INSTRUCTIONS:

**ONE:** In a medium bowl, mix 1 tsp oil, paprika, cumin and ¼ tsp each salt and pepper. Add pork to bowl and mix until pork is well coated. Set aside.

**TWO:** Heat 1 tsp oil in a large sauté pan on medium-high. Add onion and red pepper and sauté for 2 to 3 minutes, stirring frequently, until onion is softened and translucent. Add corn and beans to pan and cook for 3 more minutes, stirring frequently, until warmed. Transfer mixture to a bowl and toss with cilantro and remaining ¼ tsp each salt and pepper. Set aside and keep warm.

**THREE:** Carefully wipe pan with a paper towel. Return pan to stove top and heat remaining 1 tsp oil on medium-high. Add pork to pan, working in batches if necessary, and cook for 2 minutes per side for medium-doneness or 3 minutes per side for well done.

**FOUR:** To serve, scoop ⅔ cup corn-bean succotash onto each plate. Top succotash with 3 slices pork tenderloin and about 2 tsp pan juices.

*Nutrients per serving (4 oz pork and ⅔ cup succotash): Calories: 257, Total Fat: 6 g, Sat. Fat: 1 g, Monounsaturated Fat: 4 g, Polyunsaturated Fat: 1 g, Carbs: 20 g, Fiber: 4 g, Sugars: 3 g, Protein: 28 g, Sodium: 424 mg, Cholesterol: 74 mg*

# Pan-Seared Steaks

*Serves 4. **Hands-on time:** 5 minutes. **Total time:** 15 minutes.*

**Top these steaks with our tangy, delicious and clean Béarnaise Sauce (recipe below).**

### INGREDIENTS:

- Olive oil cooking spray
- 4 4-oz top round steaks, about ¾ inch thick, trimmed of visible fat
- ½ tsp each sea salt and fresh ground black pepper, or more to taste

### INSTRUCTIONS:

**ONE:** Coat a large nonstick skillet with cooking spray and heat on medium high. Sprinkle steaks with salt and pepper. Cook steaks to desired doneness, about 3½ minutes per side for medium or 3 minutes per side for medium rare.

**TWO:** Transfer steaks to a cutting board and let rest, loosely covered with foil, for 5 minutes. Slice on a diagonal, if desired, and arrange on plates.

*Nutrients per steak: Calories: 113, Total Fat: 4 g, Sat. Fat: 1.5 g, Monounsaturated Fat: 1.5 g, Polyunsaturated Fat: 0.5 g, Carbs: 0.25 g, Fiber: 0.25 g, Sugars: 0 g, Protein: 24 g, Sodium: 295 mg, Cholesterol: 50 mg*

# A Better Béarnaise Sauce

*Makes about 10 Tbsp. **Hands-on time:** 15 minutes. **Total time:** 20 minutes.*

### INGREDIENTS:

- ¼ cup white wine vinegar
- 2 Tbsp finely chopped shallots
- 1 Tbsp chopped fresh tarragon
- ½ cup low-sodium vegetable broth
- 1 large egg yolk
- 1½ tsp arrowroot
- Sea salt and fresh ground black pepper, to taste

### INSTRUCTIONS:

**ONE:** In a small saucepan, on medium-high, combine vinegar, shallots and tarragon. Cook until liquid is almost entirely evaporated, 3 to 4 minutes.

**TWO:** Meanwhile, fill a medium saucepan with 1 inch of water and bring to a boil on medium heat. Reduce to low to maintain a gentle simmer.

**THREE:** In a medium bowl whisk together broth, yolk and arrowroot. Stir in shallot mixture. Place over simmering water and cook, stirring and scraping bowl or pan occasionally (more constantly toward the end), just until mixture thickens, about 3 minutes. Remove from heat and add salt and pepper to taste. Cover and set aside until ready to use.

*Nutrients per 2½-Tbsp serving: Calories: 24, Total Fat: 1 g, Sat. Fat: 0.5 g, Monounsaturated Fat: 0.5 g, Polyunsaturated Fat: 0.25 g, Carbs: 3 g, Fiber: 0.25 g, Sugars: 0.5 g, Protein: 1 g, Sodium: 50 g, Cholesterol: 51 mg*

# Spaghetti & Meatball Casserole

**Serves** 6. **Hands-on time:** 25 minutes. **Total time:** 50 minutes.

**Much like lasagna, this casserole contains tomato-coated noodles with pockets of meat and herbs tucked in throughout. Kid-friendly spaghetti with bits of creamy pesto and bite-size meatballs make this a meal the whole family can appreciate.**

## INGREDIENTS:

- Olive oil cooking spray
- ½ lb whole-wheat spaghetti noodles (8 oz)
- 2 cloves garlic
- 1 cup fresh basil leaves (about 1 oz)
- 2 Tbsp olive oil
- 1 oz Parmigiano-Reggiano cheese, finely grated, divided
- ⅓ cup low-fat cottage cheese
- 6 oz extra-lean ground beef
- 1 Tbsp wheat germ
- 1 Tbsp skim milk
- ¼ cup finely diced red onion
- 2½ cups jarred strained and crushed tomatoes
- 1 bay leaf

## INSTRUCTIONS:

**ONE:** Preheat oven to 400°F. Lightly mist an 11-cup (2.6 L) casserole dish with cooking spray; set aside. Cook spaghetti to al dente according to package directions. Drain pasta, rinse under cold water and drain again; set aside.

**TWO:** In a food processor fitted with a chopping blade, add garlic and pulse until finely chopped. Add basil and pulse again until finely chopped. Add oil and half of Parmigiano-Reggiano and pulse until well blended. Remove 1 Tbsp basil mixture and reserve in a medium bowl. Add cottage cheese to food processor and process until smooth and blended.

**THREE:** Add beef, wheat germ and milk to bowl with reserved basil mixture and mix gently until blended. Form mixture into rounded teaspoon-sized meatballs (about 24 in total). Heat a large, heavy nonstick skillet over medium-high. Mist skillet with cooking spray and add meatballs and onion. Cook, turning occasionally, until meatballs are browned and onions are translucent, about 2 minutes. Add tomatoes and bay leaf to skillet, reduce heat to medium and simmer until meatballs are cooked through and sauce is beginning to thicken, about 8 minutes. Discard bay leaf.

**FOUR:** Spoon ¼ cup tomato-meatball mixture into bottom of prepared casserole dish. Toss spaghetti with remaining tomato-meatball mixture and transfer half of spaghetti mixture to casserole dish. Dot tops of noodles in dish with half of basil mixture then cover with remaining spaghetti mixture. Dot top layer of noodles with remaining basil mixture and sprinkle with remaining Parmigiano-Reggiano. Cover with aluminum foil and bake in oven until bubbling, about 10 minutes. Then remove foil and continue to cook until top is browned, about 10 minutes. Let rest for 5 minutes before serving.

**MAKE AHEAD: Assemble your casserole the night before and chill, tightly wrapped in the refrigerator, until needed. Bake, covered, for 10 minutes longer than indicated in the recipe when baking straight from the refrigerator.**

*Nutrients per 6-oz serving: Calories: 263, Total Fat: 7 g, Sat. Fat: 1 g, Carbs: 38 g, Fiber: 7 g, Sugars: 2 g, Protein: 15 g, Sodium: 157 mg, Cholesterol: 16 mg*

# How to Prepare Spaghetti & Meatball Casserole

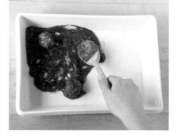

**ONE:** Spoon ¼ cup tomato-meatball mixture into bottom of prepared casserole dish.

**TWO:** Toss spaghetti with remaining tomato-meatball mixture and transfer half of spaghetti mixture to casserole dish.

**THREE:** Dot tops of noodles in dish with half of basil mixture then cover with remaining spaghetti mixture.

**FOUR:** Dot top layer of noodles with remaining basil mixture and sprinkle with Parmigiano-Reggiano. Bake.

**Nutritional Bonus:**
An often overlooked nutrient, manganese performs a bevy of functions. The mini but mighty mineral not only helps form connective tissue and bones, but is also involved in fat and carb metabolism, and is essential for brain and nerve function and calcium absorption. Enjoy a single serving of our baked spaghetti and meatballs for over 70% of your daily requirement of the trace mineral.

140

Steak & Farfalle Pasta

# Steak & Farfalle Pasta
## WITH CREAMY TOMATO SAUCE

*Serves 8. **Hands-on time:** 30 minutes.*
***Total time:** 1 hour, 30 minutes (includes 1 hour for marinating).*

**While most creamy sauces are so laden with butter and oil that you can actually see the fat glistening off the pasta, we've chosen to keep it light with a tomato-based sauce smoothed with low-fat sour cream. Top that off with lean steak and lesser-known whole-wheat farfalle pasta and you've got yourself a deliciously clean dinner sure to please any pasta lover in your family.**

### INGREDIENTS:

- 5 cloves garlic, finely minced, divided
- ¼ cup red wine vinegar
- 1 tsp Dijon mustard
- ½ tsp ground cinnamon
- ½ tsp fresh ground black pepper
- 1 lb lean eye round steak, cubed
- 16 oz whole-wheat farfalle pasta
- Olive oil cooking spray
- 1 medium yellow onion, finely diced
- 1 28-oz jar or can no-salt-added crushed tomatoes
- 1½ tsp Italian seasoning
- 1 tsp dried basil
- 8 oz low-fat sour cream

### INSTRUCTIONS:

ONE: Prepare marinade: In a bowl, whisk together 3 cloves garlic, vinegar, Dijon, cinnamon and pepper. Pour marinade over steak cubes in another container, cover and refrigerate for at least 1 hour. (You can also leave steak to marinate overnight.)

TWO: Cook farfalle according to package directions. Drain and set aside.

THREE: Drain steak cubes and discard marinade. Heat a large cast-iron or nonstick skillet on high for 1 minute. Reduce heat to medium-high, mist with cooking spray and sauté steak until browned on each side, about 4 minutes total. Remove steak from skillet and set aside.

FOUR: Mist same skillet with cooking spray again, add onion and remaining 2 cloves garlic and sauté until brown, about 2 to 3 minutes. Add tomatoes and reduce heat to medium-low. Add seasoning, basil and sour cream and combine. Cook for an additional 2 to 3 minutes, then mix in reserved steak and cook for 2 more minutes, until meat and sauce are completely warmed.

FIVE: Serve 1 cup farfalle with ¾ cup steak sauce. Garnish with an additional sprinkling of Italian seasoning, if desired.

*Nutrients per serving (1 cup pasta and ¾ cup steak sauce): Calories: 380, Total Fat: 7 g, Sat. Fat: 3 g, Carbs: 52 g, Fiber: 4 g, Sugars: 9 g, Protein: 28 g, Sodium: 350 mg, Cholesterol: 45 mg*

# Bolognese Sauce

***Makes** about 4 cups. **Hands-on time:** 40 minutes. **Total time:** 1 hour, 30 minutes.*

**Also known as *ragù* or *ragù alla bolognese*, this northern Italian meat sauce is thick, rich and full flavored. To keep it clean, we've omitted the traditional pancetta (cured meat similar to bacon), but otherwise it's just like Mama's.**

### INGREDIENTS:

- 1 carrot, peeled and cut into chunks
- 1 celery rib, cut into chunks
- 1 small onion, cut into chunks
- 2 tsp olive oil
- 8 oz 90% lean ground beef
- 1 tsp low-sodium soy sauce
- ¼ tsp fine sea salt, or more to taste
- ¼ tsp fresh ground black pepper, or more to taste
- 1 cup low-fat (skim or 1%) milk
- 1 cup low-sodium beef broth
- 2 lb tomatoes, preferably Roma, peeled, halved and seeded

### INSTRUCTIONS:

ONE: In a food processor, combine carrot, celery and onion; pulse to finely chop.

TWO: In a large saucepan, heat oil over medium-high. Add carrot mixture and cook for 2 minutes, stirring occasionally. Add beef, soy sauce, salt and pepper and cook, stirring occasionally and breaking up meat, until meat is no longer pink, 2 to 3 minutes. Add milk and cook, stirring occasionally, until most of milk has evaporated, 10 to 12 minutes. Add broth and cook, stirring occasionally, until most of broth has evaporated, 10 to 12 minutes.

THREE: Meanwhile, in a blender or food processor, purée tomatoes (you should have about 3⅓ cups purée).

FOUR: When broth has evaporated from beef mixture, stir in tomato purée. Bring to a boil, then reduce to low and simmer, uncovered and stirring occasionally, until thick, about 45 minutes. Remove from heat, taste and season with more salt and/or pepper, if desired. Cover and set aside until ready to serve.

**TIP: If you've made a bounty of Bolognese Sauce and are looking to liven up the leftovers, try this: Sauté 2 diced carrots and 1 Tbsp smoked paprika. Stir in 2½ cups Bolognese Sauce and 1 Tbsp sriracha or chile sauce, or to taste. Spoon over 8 oz pasta, cooked. We call it super-easy and exotic, but you can call it Smoky, Spicy Rotini.**

*Nutrients per ½-cup serving: Calories: 90, Total Fat: 3 g, Sat. Fat: 1 g, Monounsaturated Fat: 1.5 g, Polyunsaturated Fat: 0.25 g, Carbs: 9 g, Fiber: 2 g, Sugars: 6.5 g, Protein: 8.5 g, Sodium: 147 mg, Cholesterol: 18 mg*

**For step-by-step instructions on how to peel and seed tomatoes for sauce, see page 133.**

# Vegetable & Beef Alfredo

*Serves* 4. ***Hands-on time:*** *20 minutes.* ***Total time:*** *35 minutes.*

Thanks to crave-worthy components such as creamy cheese sauce and carb-rich pasta, traditional alfredo is a king among comfort foods. In cleaning up this fat-filled classic, we not only kept its mouth-watering qualities intact but added even more appeal to the mix. Steak offers a meaty flavor and protein boost, while leafy greens, squash and peas provide varying textures and increased nutrition.

## INGREDIENTS:

- 8 oz whole-grain linguine
  (TIP: Half a box of pasta usually totals 8 oz)
- 2 tsp olive oil
- 3 cloves garlic, minced
- 2 tsp whole-wheat flour
- 1 cup skim milk
- 2 oz low-fat Swiss cheese, grated (about 1 cup)
- Olive oil cooking spray
- 6 oz lean flank steak, thinly sliced
- ¼ tsp sea salt
- 1 tsp lemon zest (from 1 medium lemon)
- 2 packed cups baby spinach leaves
- 1 small zucchini, cut into matchsticks
- 2 cups frozen peas, thawed
- Fresh basil for garnish, optional

## INSTRUCTIONS:

**ONE:** Cook linguine according to package directions; drain and set aside.

**TWO:** Add oil and garlic to stockpot where linguine was cooked and heat over medium for 1 to 2 minutes, until garlic turns golden and is fragrant. Add flour and cook for 2 more minutes, then mash garlic with the back of a spoon until a thick paste forms. Add milk and whisk well. Bring mixture to a slow simmer over low heat and cook for 2 to 3 minutes, until mixture thickens. Stir in cheese, remove mixture from heat and set aside.

**THREE:** Coat a large skillet with cooking spray and set over high heat. Season steak with salt and lemon zest and add to skillet. Cook for 1 to 2 minutes, stirring once or twice, until steak begins to brown. Add spinach, zucchini and peas, cover and cook for 2 minutes, until spinach wilts and steak is cooked through. Toss steak-vegetable mixture with linguine and cheese sauce. Serve immediately, garnishing with basil, if desired.

**Nutrients per 1½-cup serving:** *Calories: 380, Total Fat: 6.5 g, Sat. Fat: 2 g, Monounsaturated Fat: 2.5 g, Polyunsaturated Fat: 0.5 g, Carbs: 58 g, Fiber: 10 g, Sugars: 5 g, Protein: 25 g, Sodium: 235 mg, Cholesterol: 20 mg*

# Summertime Carbonara
## WITH BELL PEPPER, HAM & RADISH

*Serves* 4. ***Hands-on time:*** *20 minutes.* ***Total time:*** *20 minutes.*

Be sure to buy radishes with the tops still attached – not only are they more cost effective, but they're also a two-for-one deal in terms of culinary uses. Minced radish tops can be used as a garnish à la sprinkled chopped parsley, or you can wilt the tops in a sauté as you would other hearty greens.

## INGREDIENTS:

- 1 tsp extra-virgin olive oil
- 1 large yellow onion, chopped
- 1 orange bell pepper, chopped
- ½ lb low-sodium, nitrate-free, lean ham, cut into ½-inch cubes
- 8 oz whole-wheat linguine
- 1 egg
- ¼ cup 2% plain Greek yogurt
- 6 radishes, halved and thinly sliced
- ¼ cup minced radish tops, rinsed well and patted dry, optional

## INSTRUCTIONS:

**ONE:** In a large nonstick pan, heat oil on medium for 1 minute. Add onion and sauté for 3 minutes, stirring occasionally. Add pepper and ham and continue cooking for another 2 minutes. Remove mixture from heat and set aside.

**TWO:** Fill a large pot halfway with water and bring to a boil. Prepare linguine until al dente according to package directions. Drain quickly, then immediately return linguine to hot pot. Crack egg over top of linguine and use a pasta fork to gently fold and stir egg into pasta, about 1 minute. When egg has turned opaque and thick, add reserved pepper-ham mixture to linguine. Gently toss to combine. Add yogurt and radishes and gently toss to combine. Serve hot, garnishing with radish tops, if desired.

**Nutrients per 2-cup serving:** *Calories: 299, Total Fat: 5 g, Sat. Fat: 1 g, Carbs: 49 g, Fiber: 7 g, Sugars: 4 g, Protein: 20 g, Sodium: 558 mg, Cholesterol: 87 mg*

**Nutritional Bonus:**
They make for a pretty garnish,
but the benefits of radish tops
don't end there: They contain
about 6 times more vitamin
C than their roots! Both roots
and leaves are rich in vitamin
C and fiber – especially when
eaten raw – and lend a slight
peppery zing to recipes.

# Poultry

If poultry's your passion (and why shouldn't it be? When properly prepared, this lean protein is the perfect clean food), then you're in for a treat with the recipes in this chapter. We've got a show-stopping Stuffed Chicken, a no-fuss Breaded Tandoori Chicken and a twist on your typical quesadilla (shh... it's made with turkey and green salsa!). And, before you can cry fowl, yes we've spared you the fat, but not the flavor.

# Curried Chicken
## WITH PEAS

*Serves* 4. ***Hands-on time:*** *10 minutes.* ***Total time:*** *30 minutes.*

**This colorful dish combines the perfect blend of Indian flavors, boasting a richness you typically don't find in simple stir-fry cooking. Scallions and garlic season lean chicken while it's being seared to golden brown, then everything is simmered in a thick curry sauce until tender. And, when added just before serving, bright green peas and cilantro offer a vibrant hue and fresh flavor.**

**INGREDIENTS:**

- 1 cup brown rice
- 1 Tbsp olive oil
- ½ cup chopped scallions
- 2 cloves garlic, minced
- 1 lb boneless, skinless chicken breast, cubed
- 2 Tbsp mild or hot curry paste
- 1 cup low-sodium chicken broth
- ½ cup frozen green peas (do not thaw)
- 2 Tbsp chopped fresh cilantro
- Sea salt and fresh ground black pepper, to taste

**INSTRUCTIONS:**

**ONE:** Cook rice according to package directions.

**TWO:** Meanwhile, heat oil in a wok or large skillet on medium-high. Add scallions and garlic and cook for 1 minute, stirring frequently. Add chicken and cook for 2 minutes, stirring frequently, until golden brown on all sides.

**THREE:** In a small bowl, whisk curry paste into broth. Add curry mixture to wok and bring to a simmer over same heat. Simmer for 2 minutes, until chicken is cooked through. Add peas and cook for 30 seconds, until just tender. Remove from heat, stir in cilantro and season with salt and pepper. Serve chicken mixture over rice.

**Nutrients per serving (1 cup chicken mixture and ½ cup rice):** *Calories: 337, Total Fat: 7 g, Sat. Fat: 1 g, Carbs: 37 g, Fiber: 3 g, Sugars: 2 g, Protein: 32 g, Sodium: 393 mg, Cholesterol: 66 mg*

**Nutritional Bonus:**
Cremini mushrooms are a good source of iron, which aids in transporting oxygen throughout the body. However, iron needs copper to function properly. Cremini mushrooms are a perfect little package containing both minerals!

Chicken & Mushroom Ragu

**NEW!**

# Chicken & Mushroom Ragu

*Serves 6. Hands-on time: 15 minutes. Total time: 45 minutes.*

**Using fresh lasagna sheets cut into strips is a great trick; they look like homemade pasta! If you can't find fresh lasagna sheets, simply use your favorite whole-grain pasta, cooked as per package directions.**

## INGREDIENTS:

- 1 oz dried porcini mushrooms (about 1½ cups)
- 1 12-oz pkg fresh whole-wheat lasagna sheets
- 2 Tbsp olive oil
- 2 cloves garlic, minced
- 4 cups thinly sliced cremini mushrooms
- 2 4-oz boneless, skinless chicken breasts, cooked, cooled and shredded
- Pinch red chile flakes
- ⅓ cup low-sodium chicken broth
- 1 28-oz box diced tomatoes, drained (reserve liquid for future use)
- Sea salt, to taste
- ½ cup crushed toasted, unsalted walnuts
- 2 cups baby arugula
- Fresh ground black pepper, to taste

## INSTRUCTIONS:

**ONE:** In small bowl, soak porcini mushrooms with enough warm water to cover for 30 minutes or until softened. Drain through fine mesh sieve, reserving soaking liquid.

**TWO:** With long side of lasagna sheet parallel to bottom edge of your work surface, slice each sheet vertically (knife parallel to pasta's short side) into 12 equal strips.

**THREE:** Prepare ragu: In a large skillet, heat oil on medium-high. Add garlic and then cremini mushrooms, cooking in batches if necessary so pan is not crowded, stirring occasionally, about 2 to 3 minutes or until mushrooms are golden brown. Add porcini mushrooms, chicken and chile flakes and cook, stirring frequently, for 1 minute. Add reserved mushroom soaking liquid, broth and tomatoes to skillet and stir until reduced by half, about 6 to 8 minutes. Reduce heat to medium-low and simmer until most of liquid has evaporated, about 6 to 8 minutes.

**FOUR:** Meanwhile, bring a large pot of salted water to a boil. Cook lasagna strips for about 5 minutes. Drain noodles, reserving ½ cup cooking liquid.

**FIVE:** Add lasagna strips, walnuts and arugula to skillet with ragu and gently toss until combined. If mixture is dry, add reserved lasagna cooking liquid, 1 Tbsp at a time, as needed. Season with salt and pepper. Divide mixture among 6 serving bowls and serve immediately.

*Nutrients per 1¼-cup serving: Calories: 397, Total Fat: 12 g, Sat. Fat: 4.5 g, Monounsaturated Fat: 4.5 g, Polyunsaturated Fat: 4 g, Carbs: 49 g, Fiber: 11 g, Sugars: 5.5 g, Protein: 22 g, Sodium: 103.5 mg, Cholesterol: 21 mg*

# Buffalo Chicken

## WITH BUTTERMILK-FETA SAUCE & SPICY ESCAROLE

*Serves 6. Hands-on time: 20 minutes. Total time: 1 hour.*

**This thinned-out version of the classic is easy to prepare and will inject a little life into your weeknight chicken dinner.**

## INGREDIENTS:

- ½ cup nonfat plain Greek yogurt
- 2 Tbsp nonfat buttermilk
- 2 Tbsp white wine vinegar
- ⅓ cup low-fat feta cheese, crumbled
- 3 green onions, chopped (about ¼ cup)
- ¼ tsp sea salt
- 4 Tbsp hot sauce
- 1 Tbsp olive oil
- 1 Tbsp paprika
- 4 boneless, skinless chicken breasts (about 1½ lb), each cut into 2 3-inch pieces
- Olive oil cooking spray

### ESCAROLE
- 2 tsp olive oil
- 1 head escarole (about 1 lb), cored and coarsely chopped
- 2 cloves garlic, minced
- 1 tsp hot sauce
- ¼ tsp crushed red pepper flakes
- 2 Tbsp sesame seeds, toasted

## INSTRUCTIONS:

**ONE:** In a medium bowl, whisk together yogurt, buttermilk, vinegar, feta, onions and salt. Cover and refrigerate until ready to serve (or up to 2 days).

**TWO:** In a small bowl, combine hot sauce, oil and paprika. Place chicken in a large shallow dish. Pour hot sauce mixture over chicken, tossing to coat. Cover and marinate in refrigerator for at least 30 minutes or up to 8 hours.

**THREE:** Preheat oven to 400°F. Mist a large baking sheet with cooking spray. Remove chicken from hot sauce marinade, discarding marinade, and place chicken on baking sheet. Bake for 8 to 10 minutes or until chicken is cooked through (no need to flip). Top with buttermilk-feta sauce, dividing evenly, or pour sauce into a separate bowl for dipping.

**FOUR:** Prepare escarole: Heat oil in a large nonstick skillet over medium-high. Add escarole and sauté for 5 minutes or until slightly wilted. Add garlic and hot sauce, stirring occasionally, and cook for 5 to 7 minutes or until escarole is completely wilted. Sprinkle pepper flakes and sesame seeds over top. Divide escarole evenly among 6 plates and top with Buffalo Chicken.

*Nutrients per serving (4 oz chicken [about 2 pieces], 2 Tbsp sauce, 1 cup Spicy Escarole): Calories: 274, Total Fat: 10 g, Sat. Fat: 2 g, Monounsaturated Fat: 4 g, Polyunsaturated Fat: 1 g, Carbs: 11 g, Fiber: 8 g, Sugars: 1 g, Protein: 34 g, Sodium: 605 mg, Cholesterol: 68 mg*

# Turkey Quesadillas
## WITH GREEN SALSA

*Serves 2. Hands-on time: 25 minutes. Total time: 30 minutes.*

Put a Mexican spin on your all-American turkey sandwich with this easy, satisfying recipe for two. If you're left with extra salsa, try it alongside chicken, steak or salmon, or stir it into low-fat sour cream or yogurt for a Latin-inspired salad dressing.

### INGREDIENTS:

- 10 oz tomatillos (4 to 6), husked and rinsed
- ½ jalapeño pepper, stemmed, halved lengthwise and seeded
- ¼ white onion
- 15 small tender sprigs fresh cilantro
- 2 cloves garlic
- Fine sea salt, to taste
- 2 whole-wheat tortillas (9 or 10 inches each)
- 2 oz shredded low-fat Colby and Monterey Jack cheese blend or Mexican cheese blend (about ½ cup)
- 2 oz cooked skinless turkey breast, shredded (about ½ cup)

**TIP: Look for tomatillos with dry, tight-fitting husks in your supermarket's produce section and at Latin markets.**

### INSTRUCTIONS:

**ONE:** In a medium saucepan, bring 3 cups water to a boil over medium-high heat. Add tomatillos and cook for 5 minutes. Add jalapeño and cook until tomatillos and jalapeño are tender, about 2 minutes. Using a slotted spoon, transfer mixture to a blender. Add ¼ cup cooking liquid, onion, cilantro and garlic and purée until smooth. Season with salt and set mixture aside to cool.

**TWO:** Arrange tortillas on a work surface. Sprinkle cheese on half of each tortilla, leaving a 1-inch border at the edges. Arrange turkey over top, dividing evenly, then fold tortillas in half over filling.

**THREE:** In a large nonstick skillet, cook quesadillas over medium heat, covered, until golden brown on the bottoms, 3 to 4 minutes. Carefully turn over and cook, uncovered, until golden brown and cheese is melted, 2 to 3 minutes.

**FOUR:** Cut each quesadilla into 4 or 6 wedges and serve with salsa.

**Nutrients per serving (1 quesadilla and ⅓ cup salsa):** *Calories: 314, Total Fat: 6 g, Sat. Fat: 1.5 g, Carbs: 40 g, Fiber: 4 g, Sugars: 8 g, Protein: 21 g, Sodium: 469 mg, Cholesterol: 20 mg*

**NUTRITIONAL BONUS: Tomatillos – found in our Green Salsa – look like small green tomatoes, except they have papery husks, which can easily be peeled off. Like tomatoes, tomatillos are a great source of vitamins C and K, potassium and manganese, plus they have almost 3 times the niacin of their ruby-hued cousins.**

# Chicken & Fresh Apricot Tagine

*Serves 4. Hands-on time: 40 minutes. Total time: 1 hour.*

**A tagine is a Moroccan stew that often includes fresh or dried fruit. In our version, apricots and dried dates contrast nicely with salty olives.**

### INGREDIENTS:

- 1 Tbsp safflower oil
- 1½ lb boneless, skinless chicken breasts (about 4), cut into 2-inch pieces
- Sea salt and fresh ground black pepper, to taste
- Olive oil cooking spray
- ½ large white onion, chopped
- 1 cup chopped carrots
- 1 tsp ground ginger
- ½ tsp ground cinnamon
- ¼ tsp ground cardamom
- ¼ tsp red chile flakes, or to taste
- 1 Tbsp white whole-wheat flour
- 3 cloves garlic, chopped
- 2½ cups low-sodium chicken broth
- 4 dried Medjool dates, chopped (about ⅓ cup)
- 5 apricots, pitted and quartered
- 8 large green olives, pitted and quartered
- 1 Tbsp fresh lemon juice
- ¾ cup whole-wheat couscous
- 1 Tbsp pine nuts, toasted
- 2 Tbsp chopped fresh mint

### INSTRUCTIONS:

**ONE:** Heat oil in a heavy pot or Dutch oven on medium-high. Season chicken with salt and pepper. Add to pot and cook, without moving, until browned on bottom, 1 to 2 minutes. Flip over and repeat on opposite side. Transfer to a large bowl (chicken will not be cooked through at this point). If bits of chicken are stuck to pot, add ¼ cup water and scrape pot with a spatula as water boils; add to chicken.

**TWO:** Coat pot with cooking spray and decrease heat to medium. Add onion and carrots. Sprinkle with a pinch each salt and pepper and cook until soft and lightly browned, 6 to 7 minutes. Add ginger, cinnamon, cardamom, chile flakes and flour. Cook for 1 minute, stirring often. Add garlic and cook for 1 more minute. Add broth and dates and bring to a steady simmer.

**THREE:** Add chicken and any juices back to pot. Reduce heat to maintain a slow, gentle simmer (low to medium-low; you should see just a few bubbles slowly surfacing at a time). Cook for 10 minutes, uncovered and stirring occasionally. Add apricots and simmer gently until soft, but not falling apart, about 10 minutes. Check chicken to ensure doneness. Stir in olives and lemon juice. Taste and adjust seasoning, if desired.

**FOUR:** Meanwhile, prepare couscous according to package directions.

**FIVE:** To serve, add ½ cup couscous to each of 4 bowls. Divide stew evenly among bowls and top each with pine nuts and mint. (Stew may be made up to 2 days in advance; cover and refrigerate. Reheat gently on low heat. Add pine nuts and mint, and prepare couscous just before serving.)

**Nutrients per serving (2 cups stew, 1 scant tsp pine nuts, ½ cup couscous):** *Calories: 454, Total Fat: 8 g, Sat. Fat: 1 g, Monounsaturated Fat: 4 g, Polyunsaturated Fat: 2 g, Carbs: 49 g, Fiber: 7 g, Sugars: 22 g, Protein: 48 g, Sodium: 369 mg, Cholesterol: 99 mg*

Chicken & Fresh Apricot Tagine

# Artichoke Stuffed

## WITH ITALIAN TURKEY SAUSAGE, ROASTED PEPPERS & WHOLE-WHEAT BREAD CRUMBS

*Serves 6.* **Hands-on time:** *30 minutes.* **Total time:** *1 hour, 15 minutes.*

**Don't underestimate the power of these edible flower buds. A single artichoke can make a savory and satisfying fiber-rich meal, especially when stuffed and baked.**

### INGREDIENTS:

- 1 lemon, juiced and zested, divided
- 6 medium fresh artichokes
- 2 bay leaves
- Kosher salt, to taste
- Fresh ground black pepper, to taste
- 3 Tbsp olive oil, divided
- ½ cup diced red onion
- ½ cup diced celery
- 2 cloves garlic, crushed, optional
- 2 cups whole-wheat bread crumbs
- 2 roasted peppers, drained and diced
- 3 Tbsp chopped Italian parsley
- 2 tsp dried oregano or Italian seasoning
- ½ lb mild Italian turkey sausage, removed from casing
- 1 cup low-sodium vegetable stock, chicken stock or water

### INSTRUCTIONS:

**ONE:** Prepare artichokes (see "Prepping Your Artichokes," p. 151).

**TWO:** Chop reserved artichoke stems into small bits. Heat 2 Tbsp oil in a medium skillet. Add onion, celery, artichoke stems and garlic, if desired, and sauté over medium heat until crisp-tender, 2 to 3 minutes.

**THREE:** In a medium bowl, combine bread crumbs, roasted peppers, onion-celery mixture, parsley, oregano and lemon zest.

**FOUR:** Using a knife, kitchen shears or your hands, break up sausage into small bits and add to bread crumb mixture. Season with salt and pepper.

**FIVE:** Preheat oven to 375°F. Spoon a portion of bread crumb mixture into each artichoke (in center and in between leaves). Combine remaining 1 Tbsp oil with stock and pour into a baking dish just large enough to hold artichokes. Arrange artichokes, stuffing side up, in dish.

**SIX:** Bake for 45 minutes or until filling is browned. Remove artichokes from oven, drizzle a little cooking liquid from baking dish over top and serve.

**Nutrients per stuffed artichoke:** *Calories: 257, Total Fat: 11 g, Sat. Fat: 1 g, Monounsaturated Fat: 6 g, Polyunsaturated Fat: 1.5 g, Carbs: 54 g, Fiber: 15 g, Sugars: 8 g, Protein: 20 g, Sodium: 648 mg, Cholesterol: 28 mg*

# HOW TO PICK & PREP Artichokes

## What You'll Need:

- Large bowl, for prepped artichokes
- 6-qt pot (not aluminum) for cooking artichokes
- Stainless steel chef's knife, for trimming artichokes
- Paring knife, for trimming stems
- Kitchen shears, for trimming artichoke leaves
- Stainless steel spoon, for removing choke
- Medium bowl, for mixing stuffing
- Medium skillet, for cooking filling
- Colander, for draining artichokes
- Baking dish, preferably ceramic

## HOW TO CHOOSE THE BEST ARTICHOKE:

- Choose an artichoke that is heavy for its size, with no wrinkles running from the inside tip of the petals to the base.
- Check the cut end of the stem: a blackened cut indicates an artichoke that has been stored for too long.
- Avoid artichokes with brown spongy areas, usually near the stem. (However, you may cut the brown parts away using a stainless steel knife.)

NOTE: Fall and winter artichokes may have bronze-tipped leaves or a whitish blistered appearance if exposed to light frost. Artichoke lovers seek out these "frosted" artichokes because they are the most tender and sweet.

## Prepping Your Artichokes

**ONE:** Fill a bowl with cold water and add half of lemon juice (see recipe, left). Using a stainless steel chef's knife, slice off the stems of the artichokes flush with the base so artichokes sit up.

**TWO:** Slice off the top quarter of the artichokes, about 2 to 3 inches. Turn artichokes upside down.

**THREE:** Trim off the dark end from the stems, then carefully pare off the outer dark green layer, leaving behind the tender pale green cores. Add stems to lemon water.

**FOUR:** Working in a spiral, pull 1 leaf at a time, breaking it back at the point where it meets the artichoke bottom. Keep breaking off leaves, going in order around the artichoke until just the outer layer of tough dark green leaves has been removed (about 4 or 5).

**FIVE:** Using kitchen shears or scissors, snip off the thorny tips of the remaining artichoke leaves.

**SIX:** Bring a 6-qt (non-aluminum) pot of water to a boil. Add the remaining lemon juice, bay leaves, salt, pepper and artichokes. Bring water back to a boil, reduce heat, cover and simmer for 25 minutes or until artichokes are tender when pierced easily with a fork. Drain artichokes in a colander and cool to room temperature.

**SEVEN:** Pull open artichokes from the center, spread out the leaves and pull out centers to gain access to the hairy choke in the middle.

**EIGHT:** Using a stainless steel spoon, scrape out the choke, avoiding cutting into the artichoke heart below (this may be done up to 2 days ahead of time).

# Stuffed Chicken
## WITH SPICY ROASTED RED PEPPER SAUCE

*Serves 2. **Hands-on time:** 30 minutes. **Total time:** 1 hour 50 minutes*

*Clean Eating* Food Editor Sandy Cordeiro got the inspiration for this recipe from her cousin, who cooked up a savory yet far-from-clean version at a girls' night dinner. To lighten things up, Sandy reduced the amount of goat cheese, nixed the store-bought cream-based sauce and added one of her favorite foods: roasted red peppers.

### INGREDIENTS:
- 3 red bell peppers
- 1 Tbsp olive oil
- 1 Tbsp balsamic vinegar
- 1 cup low-sodium chicken broth
- 2 to 3 cloves garlic, chopped
- ¼ to ½ jalapeño pepper, seeded and minced
- ½ tsp dried Italian seasoning
- Sea salt and fresh ground black pepper, to taste
- 2 boneless, skinless chicken breasts (4 to 6 oz each)
- 2 Tbsp goat cheese
- 6 to 8 asparagus spears, trimmed (if large, halve lengthwise)

**TIP: If you tend to stay away from spicy fare, reduce the amount of jalapeño or omit it completely.**

### INSTRUCTIONS:

ONE: Preheat oven to 400°F. Roast bell peppers on a baking sheet for 20 minutes. Then turn and roast for another 30 minutes. Remove bell peppers and place under an inverted glass bowl to steam for about 10 minutes (be careful when transferring bell peppers, as they will be very hot and may have hot juices flowing). With a paring knife, scrape off browned skin, then halve, remove stems and seed. Slice 1 bell pepper into strips, reserve strips and set aside.

TWO: Place remaining roasted peppers, minus any juices, into a blender with oil, vinegar, broth, garlic and jalapeño. Blend until smooth. Pour roasted pepper sauce into saucepan over medium-low to medium heat. Add Italian seasoning, salt and pepper and cook for 10 minutes.

THREE: Meanwhile, lay chicken on a cutting board. With the palm of 1 hand holding the chicken, cut each breast almost in half horizontally (knife should be parallel to cutting board). Open each breast like a book and spread 1 Tbsp goat cheese on half of each breast. Add 3 to 4 asparagus spears to each, then half of reserved bell pepper strips. Close chicken by folding top half back over, sandwiching filling.

FOUR: Carefully transfer stuffed chicken breasts to casserole dish. Pour about ½ cup roasted red pepper sauce over chicken breasts and bake for 35 to 40 minutes, until chicken is cooked through but cheese is still soft and sauce is still moist. Pour additional warmed roasted red pepper sauce over stuffed chicken breasts before serving, if desired. You may store additional sauce for other use in a resealable container in the refrigerator for 2 days; purée and reheat prior to use.

*Nutrients per serving (1 stuffed chicken breast and ¼ cup sauce): Calories: 323, Total Fat: 13 g, Sat. Fat: 4 g, Carbs: 16 g, Fiber: 5 g, Sugars: 10 g, Protein: 34 g, Sodium: 512 mg, Cholesterol: 77 mg*

# Piri Piri Roast Chicken
## WITH OLIVES & LEMON-THYME BABY POTATOES

*Serves 6. **Hands-on time:** 15 minutes. **Total time:** 1 hour, 50 minutes.*

**Portuguese chicken is marinated in a spicy and lemony sauce made from the Piri Piri pepper, a fiery hot little pepper native to Mozambique and transported to Portugal aboard merchant ships. Since Piri Piri peppers are virtually impossible to find in North America, we've opted for a simple sauce of lemon juice, oil, paprika and cayenne. Or, you can simply use your favorite dried hot pepper, hot sauce or fresh hot pepper.**

### INGREDIENTS:
- ⅓ cup fresh lemon juice, divided
- 10 cloves garlic, minced, divided
- 3 Tbsp olive oil, divided
- 2 Tbsp red wine vinegar
- 1 Tbsp paprika
- ½ tsp ground cayenne pepper (or ¼ tsp for less heat)
- 1 whole chicken (3 to 4 lb), skin removed
- 2 lb mini Yukon gold potatoes
- ⅓ cup whole pitted black olives, halved
- 2 Tbsp chopped fresh thyme
- 2 tsp lemon zest
- Sea salt and fresh ground black pepper, to taste

### INSTRUCTIONS:

ONE: In a small bowl, whisk together ¼ cup lemon juice, 8 cloves garlic, 2 Tbsp oil, vinegar, paprika and cayenne. Place chicken in a large sealable plastic bag. Pour in marinade, turning to coat inside and out. Seal bag, removing all of the air, and refrigerate for a minimum of 1 hour or overnight.

TWO: Preheat oven to 375°F. Place a rack in center position.

THREE: In a large bowl, toss potatoes and olives with remaining 1 Tbsp oil, thyme, lemon zest, remaining garlic, salt and pepper. Remove chicken from marinade and place into a 9 x 13-inch roasting pan (**NOTE:** If you have a similar sized cast-iron pan, use it instead), breast side down, and arrange potato mixture around chicken. Roast in oven for 40 minutes. Remove pan carefully, turn chicken breast side up and baste with pan juices. Gently stir potatoes to brown evenly. Place back in oven and continue to roast for another 40 to 45 minutes, until a thermometer inserted into thickest part of chicken reads 165°F. Remove from oven, cover loosely with foil and let rest for 5 minutes. Cut chicken into 6 pieces (each breast into 3 pieces, both legs in half) and serve each with ¾ cup potato mixture, drizzled with pan juices.

*Nutrients per serving (4½ oz chicken and ¾ cup potato mixture): Calories: 533, Total Fat: 17 g, Sat. Fat: 3 g, Monounsaturated Fat: 8 g, Polyunsaturated Fat: 3 g, Carbs: 31 g, Fiber: 2.5 g, Sugars: 0.5 g, Protein: 61 g, Sodium: 289 mg, Cholesterol: 185 mg*

**Piri Piri Roast Chicken**

## Nutritional Bonus:
Ever wonder why a bowl of spicy soup seems to help relieve congestion when you have the sniffles? Thank capsaicin, the spicy compound found in all hot peppers. Capsaicin stimulates your circulatory system and mucus membranes to help clear congestion from a stuffed-up nose. A similar ingredient is found in many cold remedies.

**Nutritional Bonus:**
Quinoa was prized by the ancient Aztecs as a superfood that made them fit for battle. These mineral-rich seeds deliver high doses of nutrients responsible for healthy, strong muscles, including iron, magnesium and manganese. But remember, for the tastiest quinoa, always rinse it first in a fine-meshed strainer before cooking. Rinsing removes the saponin from the seeds, a natural plant insect repellant that can impart a bitter flavor.

Shrimp & Chicken Gumbo

# Shrimp & Chicken Gumbo

## WITH COLLARDS & OKRA

*Serves 8. **Hands-on time:** 40 minutes. **Total time:** 1 hour, 30 minutes.*

**There are as many varieties of gumbo as there are families in Louisi-ana – think chicken and sausage, seafood, catfish, vegetarian and so many more. Our clean stab at the southern favorite – using our Every-day Marinara – makes up a large batch, which is perfect for freezing!**

## INGREDIENTS:

- ½ cup whole-wheat flour
- 2 Tbsp olive oil
- 1 lb boneless, skinless chicken breast, diced
- 2 medium white onions, diced
- 2 celery ribs, diced
- 4 cloves garlic, minced
- 1 tsp paprika
- 8 cups low-sodium chicken broth
- 2 cups Everyday Marinara Sauce (see recipe, p. 133)
- 2 sprigs fresh thyme
- 1 lb collard greens (about ½ bunch), stems trimmed and discarded, leaves roughly chopped
- 8 oz fresh okra, stems removed, chopped into ½-inch pieces
- 1 lb shrimp (about ¾ oz each or 1-inch diameter), peeled and deveined, tails on (21 to 25 per lb)
- Sea salt and fresh ground black pepper, to taste
- 4 cups steamed quinoa
- 3 green onions, thinly sliced
- Hot sauce, to taste, optional

## INSTRUCTIONS:

**ONE:** Preheat oven to 375°F. Spread flour onto a small baking sheet in a ¼-inch-thick layer and brown in oven for 30 to 35 minutes, stirring occasionally, until flour is a dark nutty-brown color. Remove from oven and set aside. (**NOTE:** Browned flour can be prepared ahead of time in a larger batch. Refrigerate in a resealable container until ready to use as a robust-flavored thickener in any stew or sauce.)

**TWO:** Heat oil in a large stockpot over medium-high. Add chicken and cook for 3 to 4 minutes, until opaque and light golden brown. Add white onions, celery and garlic to pot with chicken. Cook for 8 to 10 minutes, until onions are soft and translucent. Add flour and stir until vegetables are coated. Add paprika and stir, then add broth, Everyday Marinara Sauce and thyme.

**THREE:** Increase heat to high and bring gumbo to a boil. Reduce heat to medium-low, stir in collards and let simmer for 45 minutes. Add okra and shrimp and continue to simmer for 10 minutes. Season gumbo with salt and pepper.

**FOUR:** To serve, scoop ½ cup quinoa into a soup bowl. Top with 2 cups gumbo and 1 tsp green onions. Serve with a dash or two of your favorite hot sauce, if desired.

**Nutrients per 2½-cup serving (2 cups gumbo and ½ cup quinoa):** *Calories: 445, Total Fat: 10 g, Sat. Fat: 2 g, Monounsaturated Fat: 4 g, Polyunsaturated Fat: 1.5 g, Carbs: 40 g, Fiber: 7 g, Sugars: 5 g, Protein: 50 g, Sodium: 281 mg, Cholesterol: 152 mg*

# Clean Chicken & Waffles

*Serves 4. **Hands-on time:** 15 minutes. **Total time:** 1 hour.*

**Chicken and waffles come in many variations – from golden and crisp, topped with deep-fried chicken, to soft and tender with a cream-drenched chicken stew. Our velvety chicken topping, made with Greek yogurt, soaks into a freshly prepared waffle for a skinnier remake that's just as satisfying as any classic.**

## INGREDIENTS:

- 1½ cups plus 1 Tbsp whole-wheat pastry flour, divided
- 3 Tbsp ground flaxseeds
- 1 tsp baking powder
- 6 egg whites
- 1½ cups skim milk
- 1 medium zucchini (about 6 oz), grated (1½ cups)
- ½ lb boneless, skinless chicken breast, cubed
- 1 tsp paprika
- 1 Tbsp olive oil
- 2 stalks celery, thinly sliced
- 8 oz white or cremini mush-rooms, quartered
- 1 pint Brussels sprouts, trimmed and quartered
- 1 small bunch broccoli rabe (about 8 oz), trimmed and thinly sliced
- ½ cup low-sodium chicken broth
- 1 cup nonfat plain Greek yogurt
- 1 Tbsp Dijon mustard
- ½ cup tarragon leaves, optional

## INSTRUCTIONS:

**ONE:** Preheat a waffle iron. In a large bowl, whisk together 1½ cups flour, flaxseeds and baking powder until smooth. Make a well in the center of the mixture and add egg whites, milk and zucchini. Stir wet ingredients in center carefully until combined, then slowly mix into flour mixture until just combined, about 15 turns. Pour a heaping ¼ cup batter into the center of the waffle iron, spread batter out over iron surface with a spatula and close. Bake until waffle is golden and cooked through, about 4 minutes. Repeat with remaining batter to make a total of 4 waffles, setting cooked waffles on a cooling rack.

**TWO:** Sprinkle chicken with paprika and remaining 1 Tbsp flour. Heat a large stockpot with oil over medium heat. Add chicken and cook for 3 to 4 minutes, turning once, until chicken begins to brown. Transfer chicken to a plate. Add celery, mushrooms, Brussels sprouts and broccoli rabe to same pot over medium heat and cook for 2 to 3 minutes, stirring occasionally, until mushrooms soften or begin to brown and give off their liquid. Return chicken to pot and add broth. Cover and simmer for about 5 minutes, until chicken is cooked through and no longer pink inside.

**THREE:** Turn off heat (leave pot on burner). Transfer 1 cup chicken mixture to a medium bowl. Stir in yogurt and Dijon. Add mixture back to pot and stir. To serve, spoon 1½ cups chicken mixture over each waffle. Garnish with tarragon, if desired.

**Nutrients per serving (1 waffle and 1½ cups chicken mixture):** *Calories: 399, Total Fat: 8 g, Sat. Fat: 1 g, Monounsaturated Fat: 3 g, Polyunsaturated Fat: 2.5 g, Carbs: 48 g, Fiber: 8 g, Sugars: 10 g, Protein: 36 g, Sodium: 343 mg, Cholesterol: 35 mg*

# Breaded Tandoori Chicken

WITH FETA PITA CRISPS

*Serves 4. **Hands-on time:** 35 minutes. **Total time:** 40 minutes.*

**Traditional tandoori dishes are usually left to marinate overnight, but we've cut down on time by opting for a seasoned breading instead.**

## INGREDIENTS:

- 3 whole-wheat pitas, divided
- 4 oz low-fat feta cheese
- 1½ tsp curry powder, divided
- 2 egg whites
- ½ lb fresh green beans, trimmed
- 2 large carrots, cut into 1-inch-long matchsticks
- 3 tsp extra-virgin olive oil, divided
- ½ tsp ground ginger
- 1 small yellow onion, diced
- 4 cloves garlic, minced
- 4 oz nonfat plain Greek yogurt
- 1 1-lb boneless, skinless, untrimmed chicken breast
- ¼ cup fresh minced cilantro for garnish, optional

## INSTRUCTIONS:

**ONE:** Preheat oven to 350°F. Cut along the edges of 2 pitas, separating each into 2 circular halves. Lay 4 pita halves on 2 baking sheets and crumble 1 oz feta onto each. Bake for 15 minutes and set aside.

**TWO:** Rip remaining pita into pieces and, in a food processor, process until pieces have become medium-fine bread crumbs. In a flat-bottomed bowl, combine ½ cup bread crumbs with ½ tsp curry powder. Mix well and set aside. Place egg whites in another flat-bottomed bowl and set aside.

**THREE:** Fill a medium pot halfway with water and bring to a boil on high heat. Add beans and carrots, reduce heat to medium-high and simmer for 5 minutes; drain. Stir in 1 tsp oil and ginger. Set aside.

**FOUR:** Prepare tandoori sauce: Heat 1 tsp oil in a large nonstick pan on medium for 1 minute. Add onion and cook for 3 minutes. Stir in garlic and remaining 1 tsp curry powder and cook for 2 more minutes, stirring often. Remove from heat, stir in yogurt and set aside.

**FIVE:** Trim visible fat from chicken; discard fat. Butterfly chicken: Place breast on a cutting board and press down firmly. Holding a sharp knife parallel to the cutting board and positioned along 1 of the longer sides, carefully cut breast in half (about ½ inch thick). Then cut each half into 2 4-oz "wings" (for a total of 4 4-oz portions).

**SIX:** Dip "wings" in egg whites, then press both sides firmly into bread-crumb mixture.

**SEVEN:** Remove tandoori sauce from pan and heat remaining 1 tsp oil in same pan for 1 minute. Add chicken and cook for 3 minutes. Carefully turn "wings" over and cook for 2 minutes. If flesh is not cooked through, cook for 2 more minutes and check again. Serve each "wing" with 2 Tbsp tandoori sauce, 1 pita half and about ½ cup bean-carrot mixture. Garnish with cilantro, if desired.

**Nutrients per serving (4 oz chicken, 2 Tbsp sauce, 1 pita half, ½ cup bean-carrot mixture):** *Calories: 333, Total Fat: 9 g, Sat. Fat: 3 g, Monounsaturated Fat: 3 g, Polyunsaturated Fat: 1 g, Carbs: 38 g, Fiber: 5 g, Sugars: 4 g, Protein: 40 g, Sodium: 612 mg, Cholesterol: 75 mg*

# New Potato & Turkey Skillet Supper

*Serves 4. **Hands-on time:** 15 minutes. **Total time:** 45 minutes.*

**New potatoes, or baby potatoes, come in shades of rose and gold. They are simply young potatoes harvested before they can grow to their full maturity. Thanks to their small size, fine texture and thin skin, these young'uns are especially quick-cooking and easy to work with.**

## INGREDIENTS:

- Olive oil cooking spray
- 1 lb ground turkey breast
- Sea salt and fresh ground black pepper, to taste
- 1 lb new potatoes, scrubbed and quartered
- Pinch dried thyme
- ¾ cup low-sodium chicken broth
- 1 lb Swiss chard, thick stems removed, leaves chopped
- 1 pint grape tomatoes
- 1 tsp chopped fresh rosemary
- Pinch red chile flakes, or to taste
- Juice ½ lemon, plus 4 wedges for serving
- ½ cup crumbled feta cheese (about 2 oz)

## INSTRUCTIONS:

**ONE:** Preheat oven to 425°F.

**TWO:** Coat a large (at least 12-inch) ovenproof skillet with cooking spray and heat on medium. Add turkey, season with salt and pepper and cook, breaking up meat with a spoon, until no pink is visible, 5 to 6 minutes. Transfer turkey to a bowl and return skillet to heat.

**THREE:** Add potatoes and thyme to hot skillet and season with salt and pepper. Transfer skillet to oven and cook until lightly browned and tender, about 20 minutes, stirring once. Carefully return skillet to stovetop on medium-high heat (leave oven at same temperature). Add broth and bring to a simmer. Add chard and stir just until wilted. Stir in tomatoes, rosemary, chile flakes, lemon juice and reserved turkey. Ensure broth is simmering and transfer skillet back to oven. Cook until tomato skins burst, about 10 minutes, stirring halfway through. Divide mixture among four bowls and top evenly with feta. Serve immediately with lemon wedges on the side.

**Nutrients per serving (1¼ cups potato mixture and 2 Tbsp feta):** *Calories: 271, Total Fat: 4 g, Sat. Fat: 1.5 g, Carbs: 24 g, Fiber: 5 g, Sugars: 4 g, Protein: 35 g, Sodium: 559 mg, Cholesterol: 59 mg*

New
Potato &
Turkey Skillet
Supper

**Nutritional Bonus:**
Both basil and cilantro brim with vitamin K. Just a 2-Tbsp serving of basil provides 27% of your daily-recommended intake while a 4-Tbsp serving of cilantro offers 16%. Vitamin K is essential for bone growth and blood coagulation by helping the body transport calcium.

Thai Green Chicken Curry

# Thai Green Chicken Curry

## WITH SNAP PEAS & CARROTS

*Serves 4. **Hands-on time:** 25 minutes. **Total time:** 55 minutes.*

We've paired our curry with bright, vernal vegetables – snap peas and carrots – but feel free to switch things up and use whatever is in season.

### INGREDIENTS:

- 1 cup brown jasmine rice
- 2 tsp sunflower, safflower or peanut oil (or any other high-heat cooking oil)
- 2 Tbsp Thai Green Curry Paste, (see recipe, right; or store-bought)
- 1 cup low-fat coconut milk
- ½ cup low-sodium chicken broth
- 1 lb boneless, skinless chicken breasts, cut into ½-inch strips, longer strips halved
- 1½ cups snap peas, halved on a diagonal
- 1 large carrot, thinly sliced on a diagonal
- 2 Kaffir lime leaves, optional
- 2 Tbsp thinly sliced fresh basil leaves (ideally Thai basil)
- 2 tsp fish sauce, or more to taste
- 1 tsp Sucanat
- 2 green onions, thinly sliced on a diagonal

### INSTRUCTIONS:

**ONE:** Prepare rice according to package directions.

**TWO:** When rice is about 20 minutes from being done, heat oil in a large wok or skillet on medium-high. Add curry paste and cook, stirring, until fragrant, about 1 minute. Stir in coconut milk and broth and bring to a boil. Add chicken and return to a boil. Reduce heat to low and simmer for 2 minutes. Add snap peas, carrot and, if desired, Kaffir lime leaves. Cover and simmer until chicken is cooked through and vegetables are tender, about 6 minutes. Stir in basil and simmer for 1 minute. Stir in fish sauce and Sucanat.

**THREE:** Serve curry mixture over rice, sprinkled with green onions.

**NOTE: Thai Green Curry Paste and fish sauce are available in the ethnic or Asian section of most major supermarkets. Look for Kaffir lime leaves at your local Asian market.**

*Nutrients per serving (1 cup curry and ¾ cup rice): Calories: 289, Total Fat: 6 g, Sat. Fat: 2 g, Monounsaturated Fat: 2 g, Polyunsaturated Fat: 1 g, Carbs: 27 g, Fiber: 3 g, Sugars: 5 g, Protein: 31 g, Sodium: 283 mg, Cholesterol: 66 mg*

# Thai Green Curry Paste

*Makes about ¾ cup. **Hands-on time:** 20 minutes. **Total time:** 20 minutes.*

Most green curry pastes include a blend of these basic ingredients, but the amounts of each may vary. Use this as a starting point and experiment to create your own blend. Also, traditionalists will tell you that it isn't authentic if it doesn't have galangal, shrimp paste and Kaffir lime – but those can be hard to find, so we've offered substitutions.

### INGREDIENTS:

- 2 stalks lemongrass
- 2 to 3 green Thai chiles, serrano chiles or jalapeño peppers, stemmed, halved lengthwise, seeds and veins removed, and roughly sliced
- 1 shallot, roughly sliced
- 1 2-inch piece fresh galangal or ginger root, peeled and roughly sliced
- 4 cloves garlic
- 1 cup roughly chopped cilantro stems
- 1½ tsp ground coriander
- 1 tsp ground cumin
- 1 tsp shrimp paste or ½ tsp fine sea salt
- ½ tsp Kaffir lime zest or regular lime zest
- ½ tsp fresh ground white pepper
- 2 to 4 Tbsp low-fat coconut milk, if using a food processor

### INSTRUCTIONS:

**ONE:** Remove tough outer leaves from lemongrass revealing softer, fleshier, pale yellow "heart." Cut 2 inches from base of lemongrass and discard. Thinly slice remaining stalk about two-thirds from base to tip, or until stalk becomes woody and is no longer pale yellow. Place sliced lemongrass in a mortar and pestle or food processor and grind or process until finely minced.

**TWO:** Add chiles, shallot, galangal, garlic, cilantro, coriander, cumin, shrimp paste, Kaffir lime zest and white pepper. If using a food processor, also add 2 Tbsp coconut milk. Grind or process to make a thick paste, scraping down the bowl of the food processor and adding more coconut milk as necessary.

**THREE:** If not using immediately, store paste in refrigerator for up to 2 weeks or in the freezer for several months.

**NOTE: Lemongrass and galangal are available in Asian markets and often in the produce section of major supermarkets. Shrimp paste and Kaffir limes are available at Asian markets.**

*Nutrients per 2-Tbsp serving: Calories: 15, Total Fat: 0.5 g, Sat. Fat: 0.25 g, Carbs: 3 g, Fiber: 0.5 g, Sugars: 1 g, Protein: 1 g, Sodium: 123 mg, Cholesterol: 0 mg*

# Wild Rice Stuffed Chicken Breast
## WITH ZUCCHINI RIBBONS

*Serves* 4. ***Hands-on time:*** *25 minutes.* ***Total time:*** *1 hour, 25 minutes.*

**Wild rice is actually not rice at all; it is a type of grass called "water oat." Its nutty flavor and chewy texture make it a superb choice for stuffing meats.**

## INGREDIENTS:

- ¼ cup wild rice
- ⅛ tsp sea salt, plus additional to taste
- 2 oz low-fat feta cheese, crumbled (½ cup)
- ¼ cup pitted Kalamata olives, coarsely chopped
- 6 sun-dried tomatoes, thinly sliced, softened in warm water for 30 minutes
- 2 Tbsp chopped fresh basil
- 3 Tbsp chopped fresh flat-leaf parsley, divided
- 2 Tbsp fresh lemon juice, divided
- Fresh ground black pepper, to taste
- 4 tsp olive oil, divided
- 2 cloves garlic, minced
- 2 tsp chopped fresh thyme
- 2 medium yellow zucchini, trimmed
- 1 medium green zucchini, trimmed
- 4 5-oz boneless, skinless chicken breasts
- 3 Tbsp whole-wheat flour
- 1½ cups low-sodium chicken broth, divided

## INSTRUCTIONS:

ONE: In a small pot, bring 2 cups water to a boil on high heat. Add salt and stir in rice. Return water to a boil, then reduce heat to low. Cover pot with a lid and simmer for 35 minutes, until rice is tender. Drain through a fine mesh strainer and let rice cool to room temperature. Transfer to a bowl and stir in feta, olives, tomatoes, basil, 2 Tbsp parsley and 1 Tbsp lemon juice. Season with salt and pepper; set aside.

TWO: Prepare zucchini ribbons: Preheat oven to 375°F. In a small bowl, combine remaining 1 Tbsp lemon juice, 2 tsp oil, garlic and thyme. Thinly slice zucchini lengthwise into ¼-inch-thick strips and arrange in a single layer on two parchment-lined baking sheets. Brush strips with lemon juice mixture and season with salt and pepper. Roast in oven for 15 minutes or until light golden brown and softened. Remove from oven and keep warm. Keep oven on at same temperature.

THREE: Lay chicken breasts between two sheets of plastic wrap and pound with flat side of a meat mallet until ¼ inch thick. Season both sides of chicken with salt and pepper.

FOUR: Place ¼ cup rice mixture onto the center of each chicken breast. Roll up breast to enclose filling, tucking in ends and securing with a toothpick or kitchen twine.

FIVE: In a nonstick sauté pan, heat remaining 2 tsp oil on medium-high. Place chicken breasts into pan, seam side down, and cook 2 minutes per side, until chicken is golden brown on all sides. Remove pan from heat and transfer chicken to a parchment-lined baking sheet and roast in oven for 10 minutes, until chicken is fully cooked and stuffing is hot throughout.

SIX: In a small bowl, combine flour and ½ cup broth. Whisk to combine, making sure there are no lumps. Return sauté pan to medium-high heat and add flour mixture to pan. Cook, stirring constantly with a wooden spoon, for about 3 minutes. Add remaining 1 cup broth to pan and stir to combine. Bring mixture to a boil on medium-high heat. Reduce heat to medium, stir and allow sauce to simmer until thickened and reduced by one-third, about 6 to 8 minutes. Season with salt and pepper and stir in remaining 1 Tbsp parsley.

SEVEN: To serve, mound zucchini ribbons onto 4 plates, dividing evenly. Remove toothpick or twine from chicken breasts and cut each in half on the diagonal. Place one chicken breast on each plate, drizzle with parsley-broth sauce and serve immediately.

Nutrients per serving (1 breast, ¼ cup stuffing, ½ cup sauce, ¾ cup zucchini): *Calories: 367, Total Fat: 15 g, Sat. Fat: 3.5 g, Monounsaturated Fat: 7.5 g, Polyunsaturated Fat: 2 g, Carbs: 22.5 g, Fiber: 4 g, Sugars: 4.5 g, Protein: 38.5 g, Sodium: 663 mg, Cholesterol: 82.5 mg*

**This recipe also appears on the front cover.**

## Nutritional Bonus:
**Wild rice is easily digestible, gluten free and high in fiber. If you're looking to boost your protein intake, wild rice is a great choice. It contains 6 g of protein in ¼ cup uncooked – double the protein of brown rice!**

**Garlic Rapini**

**Spatchcock Chicken**

**Nutritional Bonus:**
Porcini mushrooms are high in niacin, containing 4.5 mg per 100-g serving. Niacin, or vitamin B3, helps turn carbohydrates into energy and also promotes healthy skin, hair and liver.

# Spatchcock Chicken
### WITH PORCINI PARMESAN BREAD CRUMBS & GARLIC RAPINI

*Serves 6. Hands-on time: 25 minutes. Total time: 1 hour, 15 minutes.*

**The term "spatchcock," originating in 18th century Ireland, refers to a method of cooking where the backbone of the bird is removed, halves are spread apart and the chicken is flattened out for grilling or roasting. Spatchcock cooking reduces cooking time by about 30% and is a perfect way to grill a whole chicken evenly and quickly.**

## INGREDIENTS:

- ¼ cup dried porcini mushrooms
- 1 cup whole-wheat bread crumbs
- ¼ cup fresh grated Parmesan cheese
- 2 Tbsp olive oil, divided
- 2 Tbsp chopped fresh flat-leaf parsley
- ⅓ cup low-fat buttermilk
- ½ tsp paprika
- 4 cloves garlic, minced, divided
- 1 whole chicken (3 to 4 lb)
- Sea salt, to taste
- 1 bunch rapini, trimmed
- ¼ tsp red chile flakes
- 1 anchovy fillet, rinsed and minced, optional
- 1 Tbsp fresh lemon juice
- Fresh ground black pepper, to taste

**NOTE: Save time by asking your butcher to spatchcock your chicken for you!**

## INSTRUCTIONS:

ONE: Preheat oven to 350°F.

TWO: In a spice grinder or small food processor, grind mushrooms into a fine powder. Transfer to a medium bowl and add bread crumbs, Parmesan, 1 Tbsp oil and parsley, stirring to combine. Set aside. In a small bowl, whisk together buttermilk, paprika and half of garlic. Set aside.

THREE: Using kitchen shears, cut along both sides of chicken's backbone, remove and discard. Turn breast side up and press down on center of breast to flatten. Tuck wing tips in behind top of breast. Using your fingertips, start at one of the cuts in the backbone and remove and discard skin from chicken breast and legs.

FOUR: Brush chicken with buttermilk mixture. Sprinkle top of chicken with bread crumb mixture, pressing seasoning into meat. Transfer chicken, breast and meat facing up, to a large casserole dish or roasting pan with a wire rack. Roast in oven for about 50 minutes or until a thermometer inserted in thickest part of meat reads 165°F.

FIVE: Meanwhile, bring a large saucepan of salted water to a boil. Prepare a bowl with ice water. Plunge rapini into pot of boiling water and cook for 2 minutes, until stems are tender-crisp. Remove and immerse immediately into ice bath to halt cooking process.

SIX: Remove chicken from oven, cover loosely with aluminum foil and let rest for 5 minutes before carving.

SEVEN: While chicken is resting, heat remaining 1 Tbsp oil in a large skillet on medium-high. Add remaining garlic, chile flakes and anchovy,

if desired. Add rapini and sauté, stirring frequently, for 3 to 4 minutes, until hot. Season with lemon juice, salt and pepper. Serve alongside chicken.

TIP: Don't try to rehydrate dry porcini and toss them onto your salad. Porcini should always be cooked, as they may cause stomach upset when eaten raw.

*Nutrients per serving (4½ oz chicken and ½ cup rapini): Calories: 312, Total Fat: 8 g, Sat. Fat: 2g, Monounsaturated Fat: 4 g, Polyunsaturated Fat: 1 g, Carbs: 17 g, Fiber: 2 g, Sugars: 4 g, Protein: 37 g, Sodium: 623 mg, Cholesterol: 81 mg*

# Sweet & Sour Chicken

*Serves 6. Hands-on time: 20 minutes. Total time: 1 hour.*

**To save time and make this Asian-inspired meal even simpler than it already is, pre-chop your vegetables and let your chicken marinate in the fridge up to eight hours ahead of time. Then, when you and your loved ones are ready to eat, it'll take just 10 minutes to get dinner on the table!**

## INGREDIENTS:

- ⅓ cup low-sodium soy sauce
- 2 Tbsp raw honey
- 2 cloves garlic, minced
- 1 tsp fresh ginger, grated
- ¼ tsp crushed red pepper flakes
- 1¼ lb boneless, skinless chicken breasts (about 4 breasts), chopped into 1-inch pieces
- 1 medium red bell pepper, cut into 1-inch chunks (about 1 cup)
- 1 medium green bell pepper, cut into 1-inch chunks (about 1 cup)
- 1 small yellow onion, chopped (about ¾ cup)
- ½ fresh pineapple, cut into 1-inch cubes (about 1¾ cups)
- 12 sprigs fresh cilantro, chopped (about ¼ cup)
- 1½ cups cooked brown rice, optional

## INSTRUCTIONS:

ONE: In a small bowl, whisk together soy sauce, honey, garlic, ginger and pepper flakes. Place chicken in a large shallow dish. Pour soy sauce mixture over chicken, tossing gently. Cover and refrigerate for at least 30 minutes or up to 8 hours.

TWO: Heat a large nonstick skillet over medium-high. Add chicken and marinade and sauté for 5 minutes or until chicken is cooked through. Add bell peppers and onion and cook for 5 minutes or until vegetables are slightly tender. Add pineapple and cook for 2 more minutes. Sprinkle with cilantro and serve immediately over rice for a complete meal, if desired.

*Nutrients per serving (1¼ cups chicken mixture; not including rice): Calories: 161, Total Fat: 1.5 g, Sat. Fat 0.25 g, Monounsaturated Fat: 0.25 g, Polyunsaturated Fat: 0.5 g, Carbs: 17 g, Fiber: 2 g, Sugars: 13 g, Protein: 21 g, Sodium: 404 mg, Cholesterol: 48 mg*

# Seafood

Surprisingly easy to prepare, seafood is the busy cook's best friend. And with fresh and nutritious recipes in this chapter, you'll be able to transform your fillet or shellfish of choice into an uncomplicated yet elegant dish that will impress your friends and delight your family. Whether you want to let them know their meal is also low in saturated fat and high in omega-3s is up to you!

# Vanilla-Scented Scallops
## WITH QUINOA CREAMED CORN

*Serves 4. **Hands-on time:** 10 minutes. **Total time:** 25 minutes.*

**Sweet meat from the ocean floor, scallops pair extremely well with other naturally mild or sweet flavors such as corn and vanilla. To get the most out of your dishes, pick scallops that are rosy in hue, as they have a richer flavor.**

INGREDIENTS:

- 1 vanilla bean
- 3 tsp olive oil, divided
- 1 clove garlic, crushed
- 1 cup uncooked quinoa, rinsed under cold running water
- 2 cups low-sodium chicken broth
- 4 cobs of corn, kernels removed, reserve 1 de-kernelled cob for broth, divided
- 1 cup baby spinach leaves
- 1 lb sea scallops (about 20)
- 2 Tbsp white whole-wheat flour or whole-wheat pastry flour
- ¼ cup nonfat plain Greek yogurt

INSTRUCTIONS:

ONE: Cut vanilla bean in half lengthwise. With a knife, scrape out seeds from vanilla bean and set aside; reserve bean casing. Heat a medium saucepan over medium-high. Add 1 tsp oil and garlic. Cook for 1 minute until garlic is fragrant and golden. Add quinoa and heat for 1 to 2 minutes, stirring often until quinoa is dry. Add empty vanilla bean casing, broth and reserved corncob. Bring to a boil and cover. Reduce heat to low and simmer for 10 to 12 minutes, until quinoa is soft and centers of grains are translucent. Remove corncob and vanilla bean casing; discard both. Turn off heat, stir in corn kernels and spinach and cover.

TWO: Rub scallops with vanilla seeds. Place flour on a sheet of wax paper and press both sides of scallops into flour. Heat a large skillet over high and add remaining 2 tsp oil. Add scallops and cook for about 2 minutes per side, turning once, until scallops have a golden crust and are just cooked through.

THREE: Stir yogurt into quinoa mixture and distribute between 4 plates or soup bowls. Top each with about 5 scallops and serve immediately.

**Nutrients per serving (5 scallops and 1 cup quinoa mixture):** *Calories: 456, Total Fat: 9.5 g, Sat. Fat: 1 g, Carbs: 63 g, Fiber: 7.5 g, Sugars: 5 g, Protein: 34 g, Sodium: 258 mg, Cholesterol: 37 mg*

# Szechuan Shrimp
## WITH BROCCOLI, PEPPERS & MUSHROOMS

*Serves 1.* **Hands-on time:** *10 minutes.* **Total time:** *18 to 20 minutes.*

**The distinctive flavor of Szechuan pepper – also sold as Sichuan pepper or Chinese pepper – adds heat and citrus undertones. While the pepper has a unique flavor and can be widely found in larger grocery stores and Asian markets, you can substitute it with one teaspoon lemon pepper. Or try the following combination in its place: one teaspoon fresh ground black pepper and a half-teaspoon lemon zest.**

**OPTION: White sesame seeds can be used in place of black for a similar flavor but less dramatic presentation.**

### INGREDIENTS:

- 1 tsp sesame oil
- 3 green onions, thinly sliced
- 1¾ cups shiitake mushrooms, stems removed and discarded, caps thinly sliced (1 cup)
- 1 cup broccolini florets or small broccoli florets
- 1 small red bell pepper, cut into thin strips, or ½ cup thawed-from-frozen pepper strips
- 2 medium cloves garlic, minced
- ¼ lb fresh large raw shrimp, peeled and deveined, tails off
- 1 tsp ground Szechuan pepper
- ¼ tsp red pepper flakes
- 1 2-inch knob fresh ginger, peeled and grated
- 2 tsp low-sodium tamari or soy sauce
- 1½ oz cooked soba (buckwheat) noodles, brown rice or brown jasmine rice, optional
- 2 tsp black sesame seeds
- Chopped fresh cilantro, for garnish

### INSTRUCTIONS:

**ONE:** Heat oil in a medium skillet over medium-high. Add onions, mushrooms, broccolini, bell pepper and garlic. Stir to coat with oil and cook for 3 to 4 minutes, stirring frequently, until broccolini is bright green.

**TWO:** Stir in shrimp, Szechuan pepper and red pepper flakes; cook for 1 minute. Holding grated ginger over skillet, squeeze ginger to extract juice; discard solids. Stir in tamari and 2 tsp water, and cook for 3 to 4 more minutes, stirring frequently, until shrimp is opaque and vegetables are tender-crisp. Add up to 2 Tbsp water, if needed, to prevent sticking.

**THREE:** Serve mixture over noodles or rice, if desired, and garnish with sesame seeds and cilantro. Enjoy immediately.

**Nutrients per serving (¼ lb shrimp, 1½ cups mixed vegetables, 1½ oz noodles):**
*Calories: 385, Total Fat: 15 g, Sat. Fat: 2 g, Monounsaturated Fat: 4 g, Polyunsaturated Fat: 5 g, Carbs: 32 g, Fiber: 8 g, Sugars: 6 g, Protein: 34 g, Sodium: 505 mg, Cholesterol: 172 mg*

# Crispy Calamari
## WITH ROASTED PEPPER & GARLIC SAUCE

*Serves 4. **Hands-on time:** 35 minutes. **Total time:** 1 hour, 20 minutes.*

**This cleaned-up version of the restaurant favorite has all of the good stuff – crunchy coating, protein-rich seafood – and none of the fat.**

### INGREDIENTS:

- Olive oil cooking spray
- 2 red bell peppers
- 7 cloves garlic, unpeeled
- 1 habanero chile, seeded and chopped
- ½ tsp sea salt, plus additional to taste, divided
- ¾ cup whole-wheat panko
- ¼ cup medium stone-ground cornmeal
- ½ tsp garlic powder
- Fresh ground black pepper, to taste
- 1 egg
- 1 lb cleaned squid, tentacles and bodies
- 2 Tbsp chopped fresh cilantro
- Lime wedges, for garnish

### INSTRUCTIONS:

**ONE:** Turn broiler on to high and place oven rack about 8 inches from heat source. Line a rimmed baking sheet with foil and coat with cooking spray. Cut sides of bell peppers away from cores so you have 8 flat pieces; discard core and seeds. Place on baking sheet, skin side up, and broil until skin is completely black, 10 to 12 minutes. Transfer bell peppers to a bowl and cover tightly for about 10 minutes. When cool enough to handle, peel all black skin away from peppers and discard. Chop peppers.

**TWO:** Turn off broiler and preheat oven to 400°F. Place garlic on a piece of foil and mist with cooking spray. Gather up edges of foil and pinch together at top, enclosing garlic in a loose pouch. Place on a baking sheet and roast for 15 minutes. Open foil packet and let cool for 5 to 10 minutes.

**THREE:** Squeeze garlic cloves out of their skins and add cloves to a blender; discard skins. Add bell peppers and habanero, and purée until smooth. Transfer mixture to a small bowl and season with salt to taste.

**FOUR:** Preheat oven to 400°F. Line a rimmed baking sheet with foil and coat thoroughly with cooking spray. In a gallon-size zip-top bag, combine panko, cornmeal, garlic powder, ½ tsp salt and pepper. In a medium bowl, beat egg. Slice squid bodies into about ½-inch-thick pieces. Including tentacles, pat squid dry with paper towels. Dip quarter of squid in egg, shaking off excess, and add to bag with panko mixture. Seal bag and shake well to coat squid. Spread squid on baking sheet in a single layer. Repeat steps with remaining squid. Bake for 13 to 15 minutes, until squid is opaque and slightly firm. Transfer to a large plate and sprinkle with cilantro. Serve immediately with lime wedges and dipping sauce.

**Nutrients per serving (1 cup calamari and 3 Tbsp sauce):** *Calories: 215, Total Fat: 2 g, Sat. Fat: 0.5 g, Carbs: 25 g, Fiber: 3 g, Protein: 24 g, Sodium: 326 mg, Cholesterol: 264 mg*

# How to Prepare Calamari

**ONE:** Slice squid bodies into about ½-inch-thick pieces. Including tentacles, pat squid dry as well as you can with paper towels.

**TWO:** Dip quarter of squid in egg, shaking off excess.

**THREE:** Add to bag with panko mixture.

**FOUR:** Seal bag and shake well to coat squid pieces. (Shaking in batches ensures that squid will be well coated.)

**FIVE:** Spread squid on prepared baking sheet in a single layer with pieces touching as little as possible. Repeat steps with remaining squid. Bake.

# Catfish Fillets
## WITH WARM CORN RELISH

*Serves 4.* ***Hands-on time:*** *18 minutes.* ***Total time:*** *24 minutes.*

**In the Deep South, catfish is a staple on restaurant menus. With this clean recipe, you can easily create a restaurant experience at home without losing any of the full flavor you expect when dining out.**

## INGREDIENTS:

### RELISH

- Olive oil cooking spray
- ½ cup diced red onion
- ½ medium green bell pepper, diced
- ¼ tsp dried thyme
- 1 cup frozen whole-kernel corn, thawed and patted dry
- 2 Tbsp finely chopped fresh parsley
- 1 tsp safflower oil
- ¾ tsp balsamic vinegar
- ⅛ tsp ground cayenne pepper
- ⅛ tsp sea salt

### CATFISH

- 2 8-oz catfish fillets, rinsed and patted dry, each halved lengthwise
- 2 egg whites
- ⅔ cup plain yellow cornmeal
- 1 tsp paprika
- ¼ tsp garlic powder
- ¼ tsp ground cayenne pepper
- ⅛ tsp fresh ground black pepper
- 1 Tbsp safflower oil
- ¼ tsp sea salt
- 1 lime, quartered

## INSTRUCTIONS:

**ONE:** Prepare relish: Heat a large nonstick skillet on medium-high. Coat skillet with cooking spray. Add onion, bell pepper and thyme and cook for 3 minutes or until vegetables are tender-crisp. Add corn and cook for 1 minute, stirring frequently. Remove from heat, place mixture in a small bowl and cover to keep warm.

**TWO:** Prepare catfish: Place catfish and egg whites in a shallow pan, turning fillets several times to coat. In another shallow pan, combine cornmeal, paprika, garlic powder, cayenne and black pepper. Use one hand to pick up a piece of fish and place it in cornmeal mixture. Use other hand to toss gently yet thoroughly to coat fillet completely and set aside on separate plate. Repeat with remaining fillet. (Discard any remaining egg white and cornmeal mixture.) Heat 1 Tbsp oil in a large nonstick skillet on medium. Add fish and cook for 3 minutes, then flip over and cook for 3 more minutes or until opaque in center. Place fish on a serving plate and sprinkle evenly with salt. Slice each fillet in half lengthwise before serving, equalling 4 pieces.

**THREE:** Combine corn mixture with remaining relish ingredients. Serve alongside or over top of fish and accompany with lime wedges.

*Nutrients per serving (4 oz catfish and ⅓ cup relish): Calories: 288, Total Fat: 9 g, Sat. Fat: 1 g, Monounsaturated Fat: 4 g, Polyunsaturated Fat: 2 g, Omega-3s: 510 mg, Omega-6s: 670 mg, Carbs: 28 g, Fiber: 3 g, Sugars: 2 g, Protein: 24 g, Sodium: 266 mg, Cholesterol: 65 mg*

**For a photo of this recipe, see page 120.**

# Green Tea Poached Salmon
## WITH GINGER LIME SAUCE

*Serves 4.*

This simple salmon recipe (five ingredients!) from Food Network chef Claire Robinson will make you realize tea isn't just for sipping anymore.

### INGREDIENTS:

- 2 limes, halved, divided
- 4 Tbsp raw honey, divided
- 1 4-inch piece fresh ginger, peeled and chopped (TIP: Easily chop ginger in a food processor)
- 4 Tbsp loose-leaf green tea, spooned into an infuser ball or piece of cheesecloth tied with twine, or 6 green tea bags
- 4 6-oz wild-caught salmon fillets, skin and bones removed

### PANTRY STAPLES:

- 1 tsp sea salt
- 1 tsp whole black peppercorns
- Fresh ground black pepper, to taste (optional)

### INSTRUCTIONS:

**ONE:** Put 6 cups water into a straight-sided skillet or pot with a lid. Add 3 lime halves (squeezing juice into the water before adding), 3 Tbsp honey, ginger, salt and peppercorns and bring to a boil over medium-high heat. Reduce to a simmer, cover and cook for 10 minutes to infuse water with flavor. Remove ½ cup poaching liquid and set aside.

**TWO:** Remove skillet or pot from heat and add tea, allowing to steep for 3 to 5 minutes. Remove tea and place skillet or pot over heat again at the lowest heat setting before carefully sliding salmon into water. Cover and poach until fish is just cooked through and firm to the touch, 6 to 7 minutes.

**THREE:** Meanwhile, in a small pot, simmer reserved ½ cup poaching liquid along with juice and zest of remaining lime half and remaining 1 Tbsp honey until liquid reduces by two-thirds and thickens, about 7 to 10 minutes.

**FOUR:** Remove salmon with a slotted spoon and plate. Drizzle a bit of reduced sauce over each fillet. Season with black pepper, if desired.

**TIP FROM CLAIRE: "This poached salmon is even better cold the next day. Reserve some of the poaching liquid and put it right over top of any leftover salmon before popping it into the fridge."**

**Nutrients per 6-oz serving:** *Calories: 364, Total Fat: 11.5 g, Sat. Fat: 2 g, Omega-3s: 2,950 mg, Omega-6s: 760 mg, Carbs: 28 g, Fiber: 1 g, Sugars: 17 g, Protein: 38 g, Sodium: 565 mg, Cholesterol: 93.5 mg*

# Apricot-Glazed Scallops
## WITH SNOW PEAS

*Serves 4. **Hands-on time:** 10 to 15 minutes. **Total time:** 10 to 15 minutes.*

For the perfect balance of flavors, this stir-fry marries sweet apricot preserves with tangy soy sauce. But what really takes the dish over the top is the addition of tender, slightly rich scallops and zesty ginger. Nestle the scallop mixture into clear cellophane noodles for a unique dish the entire family (and guests!) will love.

### INGREDIENTS:

- 6 oz cellophane noodles (aka bean thread noodles)
- 1 Tbsp safflower oil
- ½ cup minced white onion
- 1 Tbsp minced fresh ginger
- 2 cloves garlic, minced
- 2 lb fresh or frozen large sea scallops (thawed if frozen)
- 1½ Tbsp low-sodium soy sauce
- ½ cup all-natural apricot preserves
- 2 cups fresh or frozen snow peas (do not thaw, if frozen)
- Sea salt and fresh ground black pepper, to taste

### INSTRUCTIONS:

**ONE:** Soak noodles in very hot water for 10 minutes (hot water from the tap is fine; no need to simmer or boil over the stovetop); drain and set aside.

**TWO:** Meanwhile, heat oil in a wok or large skillet on medium-high. Add onion, ginger and garlic and cook for 2 minutes, until tender, stirring frequently. Add scallops and cook for 2 minutes, until opaque. In a small bowl, whisk soy sauce into apricot preserves. Add apricot mixture to wok and bring to a simmer over same heat. Add snow peas and cook for 30 seconds. Remove from heat and season with salt and pepper. Serve scallop mixture over noodles.

**Nutrients per serving (1½ cups scallop mixture and 2 cups noodles):** *Calories: 422, Total Fat: 5 g, Sat. Fat: 0.5 g, Omega-3s: 450 mg, Omega-6s: 70 mg, Carbs: 51 g, Fiber: 4 g, Sugars: 15 g, Protein: 42 g, Sodium: 477 mg, Cholesterol: 75 mg*

**Nutritional Bonus:**
Our Apricot-Glazed Scallops offer more than just sweet-savory flavor; they may help boost cardiovascular health, thanks to a trio of nutrients. Vitamin B12 may decrease the amount of homocysteine in your blood, an amino acid that has been linked to heart disease and stroke when found in elevated levels. Omega-3s may decrease triglycerides and slow the rate of arterial plaque, while magnesium helps maintain a normal heart rate and reduce the risk of high blood pressure in women.

Apricot-Glazed Scallops

Halibut &
Black Bean
Burrito
Casserole

# Halibut & Black Bean Burrito Casserole

*Serves 6. **Hands-on time:** 15 minutes. **Total time:** 40 minutes.*

A small portion of flaky halibut is all that's needed to impart flavor to this fresh-tasting casserole of beans and brown rice. For variety or to satisfy picky eaters, you can also opt for diced cooked chicken or shrimp for an equally delicious and savory alternative to the halibut.

### INGREDIENTS:

- Olive oil cooking spray
- 10 oz boneless, skinless Pacific halibut fillet, cut crosswise into ¼-inch pieces (about 18 pieces)
- 3 tsp fresh lime juice, divided
- ½ tsp ground cumin, divided
- 1 cup cooked or BPA-free canned black beans, drained and rinsed
- 1 cup cooked brown rice
- 2 green onions, thinly sliced (about ½ cup)
- ½ cup corn kernels (thawed, if frozen)
- ½ tsp finely grated lime zest
- ¼ cup finely diced roasted red pepper (TIP: If you're opting for store-bought roasted peppers, select a variety that's jarred in water, not oil.)
- 1 Tbsp chopped fresh cilantro
- 6 whole-wheat tortillas (7 inches each)
- 1½ oz low-fat Monterey Jack or cheddar cheese, finely grated (about ¾ cup)
- ½ cup low-fat sour cream or low-sodium salsa for garnish, optional

### INSTRUCTIONS:

**ONE:** Preheat oven to 400°F. Lightly mist an 11-cup casserole dish with cooking spray; set aside.

**TWO:** In a small bowl, toss halibut with 1 tsp lime juice and ¼ tsp cumin; set aside.

**THREE:** In a large bowl, combine remaining 2 tsp lime juice, remaining ¼ tsp cumin, beans and following 6 ingredients; stir to combine.

**FOUR:** Lay tortillas out on a flat work surface and mound ⅓ cup bean mixture onto center of each. Arrange 3 pieces of halibut in a single layer on top of bean mounds. Roll each tortilla to enclose filling but keep ends open. Arrange filled tortillas, seam sides down, in one layer in prepared casserole dish. Sprinkle with cheese and bake, covered with aluminum foil, for 10 minutes. Then remove foil and continue baking until burritos are crispy and cheese is golden brown, about 15 minutes more. Serve burritos with sour cream or salsa, if desired.

**Nutrients per burrito:** *Calories: 298, Total Fat: 6 g, Sat. Fat: 1 g, Omega-3s: 210 mg, Omega-6s: 180 mg, Carbs: 40 g, Fiber: 6 g, Sugars: 2 g, Protein: 19 g, Sodium: 414 mg, Cholesterol: 19 mg*

# Linguine ai Frutti di Mare

*Serves 4. **Hands-on time:** 35 minutes. **Total time:** 45 minutes.*

**The actual cooking of this dish happens very quickly – so it's best to have all your ingredients prepped and ready to go before you turn on the heat.**

### INGREDIENTS:

- 8 oz whole-wheat linguine
- 4 tsp extra-virgin olive oil
- ½ onion, diced into ¼-inch pieces
- 4 cloves garlic, minced
- ½ tsp dried crushed red pepper flakes
- ½ lb clams, scrubbed
- ½ lb mussels, scrubbed and debearded
- ¾ cup bottled clam juice, divided
- ½ lb cleaned calamari tubes and tentacles, tubes cut crosswise into ½-inch pieces
- ½ lb medium to large raw peeled and deveined shrimp, preferably tail on
- 1 cup chopped fresh tomatoes
- 1 tsp red wine vinegar
- 1 tsp arrowroot
- 2 Tbsp fresh flat-leaf parsley, chopped

### INSTRUCTIONS:

**ONE:** In a large pot of boiling water, cook pasta according to package directions.

**TWO:** Meanwhile, heat oil in a large skillet on medium-high. Add onion and cook, stirring occasionally and adjusting heat to avoid browning, until tender, about 3 minutes. Add garlic and pepper flakes and cook, stirring occasionally, for 30 seconds. Stir in clams, mussels and ½ cup clam juice and bring to a boil. Reduce to a simmer, cover and cook for 2 minutes. Stir in calamari and shrimp, increase heat to medium-high and return to boil. Reduce to a simmer, re-cover and cook for 2 minutes. Stir in tomatoes, re-cover and cook until mussels and clams are open and calamari and shrimp are cooked through, 2 to 4 minutes (discard any mussels or clams that don't open).

**THREE:** While seafood is cooking, in a small bowl, whisk together remaining ¼ cup clam juice, vinegar and arrowroot. Set aside.

**FOUR:** Drain pasta and transfer it to a serving bowl or to individual bowls. Use a slotted spoon to arrange seafood on top, reserving sauce in skillet. Return skillet to a boil on medium-high. Add arrowroot mixture to sauce, stirring until sauce thickens, 30 to 60 seconds.

**FIVE:** Spoon sauce over seafood and pasta, top with parsley and serve.

**Nutrients per serving (about 1¾ cups seafood mixture, ⅓ cup sauce, 1 cup pasta):** *Calories: 390, Total Fat: 8 g, Sat. Fat: 1 g, Monounsaturated Fat: 4 g, Polyunsaturated Fat: 1 g, Omega-3s: 660 mg, Omega-6s: 520 mg, Carbs: 52 g, Fiber: 1 g, Sugars: 3 g, Protein: 30 g, Sodium: 320 mg, Cholesterol: 169 mg*

# Baked Manicotti Bundles
## STUFFED WITH TILAPIA & MOZZARELLA

*Serves* 4. ***Hands-on time:*** *35 minutes.* ***Total time:*** *50 minutes.*

**There's often a misconception that comforting Italian classics have to be heavy in order to be delicious. Well, we've debunked that myth before, and we're doing it again! In this lightened-up manicotti, you'll find airy tilapia instead of red meat and low-fat dairy products in place of heavy creams and cheeses. And, by opting for whole-wheat noodles, you'll ensure that you won't be left with hunger pangs post-dinnertime.**

## INGREDIENTS:

- Olive oil cooking spray
- 3 to 4 green onions (enough to yield 10 layers)
- 10 whole-wheat lasagna noodles
- 1 carrot, peeled
- 1 tsp extra-virgin olive oil
- 12 oz fresh tilapia fillets (or other mild white fish)
- 4 oz light cream cheese
- ½ cup skim milk
- ½ tsp dried dill
- ½ tsp sea salt
- 2 oz reduced-fat mozzarella cheese, grated, divided
- Fresh dill for garnish, optional

## INSTRUCTIONS:

**ONE:** Preheat oven to 350°F. Lightly mist an 8 x 8-inch glass baking dish with cooking spray; set aside.

**TWO:** Rinse onions well, trim off white tops and discard. With the tip of a paring knife, score the upper end of the connected layers one by one so that each can be carefully removed and set aside.

**THREE:** Prepare lasagna noodles according to package directions. During the final 90 seconds of cooking, add reserved onion layers. Then lift out layers with heat-proof tongs and set aside before draining pasta. Rinse pasta well and set aside.

**FOUR:** Grate carrot into a small bowl. Set aside.

**FIVE:** Place a large nonstick pan on medium heat and add oil. Heat for 1 minute, then add tilapia, briefly shaking pan to prevent fish from sticking. Cover and cook for 3 minutes. Carefully flip fillets over and cook for 1 minute. Break fillets up with a heat-proof spatula. If pieces are not cooked through and opaque, cook for 1 more minute. Remove from heat and set aside.

**SIX:** Add cream cheese, milk, dried dill and salt to a medium saucepan. Use a knife or spatula to break cream cheese up into smaller pieces. Place pan on low heat and cook, whisking constantly, for about 1 minute or until cream cheese has melted. Add half of mozzarella and continue heating and whisking for 30 seconds or until mixture is smooth. Remove from heat and scoop out ½ cup cheese mixture; set aside and reserve.

**SEVEN:** Stir carrots and tilapia into pan with cheese mixture. Lay lasagna noodles out on a large cutting board with shorter edges parallel to bottom edge of cutting board. Place 2 Tbsp tilapia-cheese mixture on bottom edge of each noodle. Gently roll each noodle from the bottom edge to the top, pressing lightly and making a bundle that stays together without squeezing filling out. Tie each bundle with an onion layer and place in prepared glass dish.

**EIGHT:** Spoon reserved ½ cup cheese mixture over bundled manicotti and top with remaining mozzarella. Bake for 25 minutes or until mozzarella is melted and beginning to turn golden brown. Garnish with fresh dill, if desired, and serve.

*Nutrients per 2½ bundles: Calories: 447, Total Fat: 12 g, Sat. Fat: 5 g, Monounsaturated Fat: 3 g, Polyunsaturated Fat: 1 g, Omega-3s: 210 mg, Omega-6s: 420 mg, Carbs: 49 g, Fiber: 9 g, Sugars: 3 g, Protein: 35 g, Sodium: 507 mg, Cholesterol: 64 mg*

# How to Assemble Your Manicotti Bundles

**ONE:** Lay lasagna noodles out on a large cutting board with shorter edges parallel to bottom edge of cutting board. Place 2 Tbsp tilapia-cheese mixture on bottom edge of each noodle.

**TWO:** Gently roll each noodle from the bottom edge to the top, pressing lightly and making a bundle that stays together without squeezing filling out.

**THREE:** Tie each bundle with an onion layer and place in prepared glass pan.

Pita
Panini

# Pita Panini

WITH TUNA, SPROUTS, ZUCCHINI & AVOCADO CREAM

*Serves 4. **Hands-on time:** 20 minutes. **Total time:** 20 minutes.*

Panini, or "little breads" in Italian, are traditionally made in a panini press. But for those going without the countertop appliance, a toaster oven and a quick press with your hand works too. Alternatively, you can heat the pitas on a grill pan with another pan over top for pressure to get those signature grill marks.

## INGREDIENTS:

- 1 avocado, halved, pitted and peeled
- 1 clove garlic, minced
- Juice ½ lemon (about 4 tsp)
- 2 6.4-oz pouches cooked tuna in water
- 4 whole-wheat pitas (each 6 inches in diameter), halved and pockets opened
- 4 oz alfalfa sprouts
- 1 zucchini, thinly sliced into rounds
- 1 Roma tomato, thinly sliced into rounds

## INSTRUCTIONS:

**ONE:** Prepare Avocado Cream: In a medium bowl, add avocado, garlic and lemon juice. Mash with a fork and mix well. Set aside.

**TWO:** Divide tuna evenly among pita halves, then top with equal amounts sprouts, zucchini and tomato. Finish by spreading 1½ Tbsp Avocado Cream in each half

**THREE:** Toast pita halves in a toaster oven for 3 minutes, until cut edges are just beginning to brown. (Alternatively, you can place pita halves on a baking sheet and bake in a 350°F oven for 8 minutes or until edges are just beginning to brown.) Place a clean, dry washcloth on top of each hot pita half and press down gently with your hand, making sure to apply even, smooth pressure so panini are compressed instead of smashed. Serve immediately.

*Nutrients per 2 filled pita halves (3 Tbsp Avocado Cream, ¼ tomato, ¼ zucchini, 1 oz sprouts, 1 pita, 3 oz tuna): Calories: 378, Total Fat: 10 g, Sat. Fat: 1 g, Monounsaturated Fat: 5 g, Polyunsaturated Fat: 2 g, Omega-3s: 410 mg, Omega-6s: 1,620 mg, Carbs: 43 g, Fiber: 10 g, Sugars: 2 g, Protein: 27 g, Sodium: 410 mg, Cholesterol: 27 mg*

**NUTRITIONAL BONUS: Sprouted seeds, beans, nuts and grains are nutritional powerhouses. The sprouting process breaks down phytic acid, an anti-nutrient that normally binds with minerals such as iron and calcium, and prevents their absorption. Cooking, soaking and marinating foods can also reduce phytic acid to some degree.**

# Puttanesca Calzone

*Serves 4. **Hands-on time:** 15 minutes. **Total time:** 45 minutes.*

**Puttanesca is a traditional, spicy tomato pasta sauce that combines capers and olives, along with tuna in some versions. We decided to use that same flavor profile but added a twist by tucking the classic ingredients and fresh fish into whole-wheat pizza dough. The result? A rich calzone that'll make you forget about every pizza-shop version.**

## INGREDIENTS:

- 2 tsp olive oil
- 3 cloves garlic, chopped
- 6 medium tomatoes (about 2 lb), chopped
- 2 oz green beans (about 16), cut into thirds
- 4 oz asparagus spears (about 8), thinly sliced
- 8 oz whole-wheat pizza dough, defrosted according to package directions
- 4 bay scallops, quartered
- 4 oz wild-caught salmon, skin and bones removed, cut into 1-inch chunks
- 8 Kalamata olives, pitted and chopped
- 1 Tbsp capers, well rinsed and chopped
- 2 oz part-skim mozzarella cheese, grated

## INSTRUCTIONS:

**ONE:** Preheat oven to 400°F. In a large skillet, heat oil and garlic over medium heat for 2 to 3 minutes, until garlic begins to brown. Carefully add tomatoes and 1 cup water and cook for 10 to 15 minutes, stirring often, until tomatoes break down. Remove mixture from heat and stir in beans and asparagus. Set aside to cool slightly.

**TWO:** Cut pizza dough into 4 equal sections. Roll out each section into a circle, about 8 inches in diameter. Divide 4 dough circles among two baking sheets. Add scallops, salmon, olives and capers to skillet with tomato mixture, stirring to combine. Add tomato mixture and cheese to one side of each dough circle, dividing evenly. Fold each dough circle over and crimp edges with your fingers or a fork to seal.

**THREE:** Transfer baking sheets to oven and bake for 25 to 30 minutes, until crust is golden and firm. Let cool for 5 minutes before slicing and serving.

*Nutrients per calzone: Calories: 312, Total Fat: 10 g, Sat. Fat: 2 g, Monounsaturated Fat: 2 g, Polyunsaturated Fat: 1 g, Omega-3s: 570 mg, Omega-6s: 380 mg, Carbs: 67 g, Fiber: 6 g, Sugars: 5 g, Protein: 18 g, Sodium: 342 mg, Cholesterol: 30 mg*

# Homemade Dashi

*Makes 3 cups. **Hands-on time:** 3 minutes. **Total time:** 7 minutes.*

### INGREDIENTS:

- 3 cups cold water
- 1 3-inch piece kombu (dried kelp)
- ½ cup katsuobushi (dried bonito flakes)

### INSTRUCTIONS:

**ONE:** In a medium saucepan, combine water and kombu. Bring to a boil over medium heat, then remove from heat and discard kombu. Stir in katsuobushi, cover and let steep for 3 minutes.

**TWO:** Strain mixture through a very fine sieve. Cool, then store, covered, in refrigerator for up to a week.

**OPTION: We recognize that our dashi sauce is slightly high in sodium (but sourced from whole foods and packed with nutrients). If sodium is a concern, feel free to either increase the 3 cups cold water to 5 cups, reduce the serving size or skip the sauce altogether!**

*Nutrients per 3-Tbsp serving: Calories: 54, Total Fat: 0.5 g, Sat. Fat: 0 g, Carbs: 4 g, Fiber: 0 g, Sugars: 0 g, Protein: 83 g, Sodium: 446 mg, Cholesterol: 6 mg*

# Shrimp & Vegetable Tempura

*Serves: 4. **Hands-on time:** 30 minutes. **Total time:** 50 minutes.*

**Traditionally, tempura is served over steamed rice or soba (buckwheat) noodles. But feel free to enjoy your tempura any way your heart desires.**

### INGREDIENTS:

- Olive oil cooking spray
- 12 large raw shrimp, peeled and tail on
- 2 cups brown rice flour
- 4½ tsp low-sodium baking powder
- 4 tsp sesame oil
- 2½ cups ice water
- 1 small sweet potato or yam (about 6 oz), peeled and cut into ¼-inch slices
- 2 cups large broccoli florets
- 8 large shiitake mushrooms, stemmed
- ½ cup dashi (see recipe, left) or 3 Tbsp vegetable broth mixed with 5 Tbsp water
- 2 Tbsp low-sodium soy sauce
- 3 Tbsp finely grated daikon radish (from about 2-inch piece)
- 1½ tsp finely grated fresh ginger (from about ¾-inch piece)

### INSTRUCTIONS:

**ONE:** Preheat oven to 500°F. Arrange racks in the top third and bottom third of oven. Thoroughly coat two large rimmed baking sheets with cooking spray.

**TWO:** Make several shallow cuts across inside curve of each shrimp. Gently press shrimp flat on work surface (to help prevent curling during cooking).

**THREE:** In a large mixing bowl, whisk together flour, baking powder and oil. Gradually and gently whisk in ice water, mixing until dry ingredients are just moistened.

**FOUR:** One piece at a time, dip shrimp, sweet potato slices, broccoli florets and mushrooms into batter, shake off excess and arrange on prepared baking sheets. Bake until lightly browned, 15 to 20 minutes.

**FIVE:** Meanwhile, in small saucepan, combine dashi, soy sauce, radish and ginger. Bring to a simmer over medium heat. Remove from heat and cover to keep warm.

**SIX:** Serve tempura immediately with dipping sauce on the side.

*Nutrients per serving (3 shrimp, 3 Tbsp sauce, 2 to 3 pieces each sweet potato, broccoli and mushrooms): Calories: 421, Total Fat: 7.5 g, Sat. Fat: 1 g, Monounsaturated Fat: 3 g, Polyunsaturated Fat: 3 g, Omega-3s: 190 mg, Omega-6s: 810 mg, Carbs: 75 g, Fiber: 6 g, Sugars: 3 g, Protein: 13 g, Sodium: 382 mg, Cholesterol: 32 mg*

Shrimp & Vegetable Tempura with Homemade Dashi

Baked Pecan-Crusted Flounder

# Baked Pecan-Crusted Flounder
## WITH SQUASH SAUTÉ

**Serves** 4. **Hands-on time:** 13 minutes. **Total time:** 25 minutes.

**Take a break from your beige rice and potato sides! Instead, add a splash of color and comfort to this delicately spiced, nutty fish with a pile of sautéed yellow squash and richly browned onions.**

## INGREDIENTS:

### FISH

- Olive oil cooking spray
- 4 4-oz boneless, skinless Pacific flounder fillets, rinsed and patted dry
- 1½ tsp raw honey
- 1½ tsp prepared mustard
- 1 packet stevia
- ¼ tsp sea salt
- ⅛ tsp ground cayenne pepper
- ¼ cup unsalted pecan pieces, toasted and finely chopped

### SQUASH

- 2 tsp safflower oil
- 1 cup diced onion
- 2 medium yellow squash, sliced
- ¼ tsp sea salt
- ¼ tsp fresh ground black pepper

## INSTRUCTIONS:

**ONE:** Preheat oven to 425°F. Line a large baking sheet with aluminum foil and coat foil with cooking spray. Place fillets on foil.

**TWO:** In a small bowl, combine honey, mustard, stevia, salt and cayenne. Brush tops of fillets with mustard mixture, dividing evenly. Sprinkle pecans over top, dividing evenly, and coat tops of fillets with cooking spray. Bake for 12 minutes or until fish flakes easily with a fork.

**THREE:** Meanwhile, prepare squash: Heat oil in a large nonstick skillet on medium-high. Add onion and cook for 5 minutes or until it begins to richly brown, stirring frequently. Add squash and cook for 4 minutes or until edges begin to brown. Add salt and pepper, and stir gently.

**FOUR:** To serve, place equal amounts of squash mixture on each of four dinner plates, then top with a fillet. Or, serve family-style on a platter.

**Nutrients per serving (3 oz fish and ½ cup squash mixture):** *Calories: 220, Total Fat: 9 g, Sat. Fat: 1 g, Monounsaturated Fat: 2 g, Polyunsaturated Fat: 1 g, Omega-3s: 290 mg, Omega-6s: 100 mg, Carbs: 11 g, Fiber: 2 g, Sugars: 5 g, Protein: 24 g, Sodium: 365 mg, Cholesterol: 54 mg*

# Sweet & Hot Shrimp Tacos
## WITH CHERRY GINGER GLAZE

**Serves** 4. **Hands-on time:** 15 minutes. **Total time:** 25 minutes.

**Cherries and chiles mingle in this Mexican-inspired taco sauce with sophisticated flavor that is simple to create. And, by using shrimp instead of the traditional ground-beef taco filling, this dinner is ideal for lighter al-fresco dining and summer entertaining.**

## INGREDIENTS:

- 1 cup fresh or frozen pitted red cherries (if frozen, no need to thaw)
- 1 to 2 jalapeño peppers, cut in half and seeded (TIP: Use 1 for mild, 2 for medium to hot.)
- 1 2-inch piece ginger, peeled and quartered
- 4 tsp raw honey
- 24 large raw shrimp (just over 1 lb), shells and tails removed
- ¼ tsp sea salt
- 1 Tbsp olive oil
- 8 whole-grain corn soft taco shells
- 1 small head radicchio, thinly sliced (8 oz)
- 4 large carrots, peeled and grated (8 oz)
- Cilantro leaves for garnish, optional

## INSTRUCTIONS:

**ONE:** Place cherries, jalapeño, ginger and honey in a mini chopper or blender along with ¼ cup water. Blend until smooth (there may be very small bits of cherry).

**TWO:** Season shrimp with salt. Heat a large skillet over high. Add oil and shrimp and cook for 2 to 3 minutes, turning occasionally, until shrimp are pink on the outside but not cooked through. Reduce heat to medium and carefully add cherry mixture. Simmer for about 2 minutes, until sauce reduces slightly and shrimp are cooked through.

**THREE:** Preheat an oven or toaster oven to 400°F and warm taco shells for 2 minutes. Spoon 3 shrimp and 1 Tbsp cherry sauce into each taco and top with 2 Tbsp each radicchio and carrots. Garnish with cilantro, if desired. Serve immediately.

**Nutrients per 2 tacos:** *Calories: 348, Total Fat: 11 g, Sat. Fat: 2 g, Monounsaturated Fat: 5 g, Polyunsaturated Fat: 2 g, Carbs: 39 g, Fiber: 5 g, Sugars: 14 g, Protein: 26 g, Sodium: 528 mg, Cholesterol: 172 mg*

**NUTRITIONAL BONUS: Hot chiles such as jalapeños contain capsaicin, the compound responsible for bringing on the burn and tingling taste buds. Capsaicin is also being studied for its powerful anti-inflammatory properties and ability to help combat arthritis pain.**

# Homemade Ketchup

**Makes** 1⅓ cups. **Hands-on time:** 5 minutes. **Total time:** 30 minutes (plus 1 hour to chill).

## INGREDIENTS:

- 1½ cups boxed diced tomatoes, no salt added (TRY: Pomi Chopped Tomatoes)
- ½ medium yellow onion, diced
- 1 Tbsp tomato paste
- 3 Tbsp apple cider vinegar
- 3 Tbsp raw honey
- ¼ tsp sea salt
- Pinch each ground allspice and cloves

## INSTRUCTIONS:

In a small saucepan, combine all ingredients and bring to a boil on high heat. Reduce heat to medium-low and simmer for 20 to 25 minutes, stirring frequently, until reduced by about half and thickened. Remove from heat and cool for 5 minutes. Purée mixture in a food processor or blender until smooth. Transfer to sealable container and refrigerate until cooled. (**NOTE:** Only ½ cup Homemade Ketchup is needed for Ultimate Shrimp Cocktail recipe. Reserve leftovers for future use.) Homemade Ketchup can be stored, covered and refrigerated, for up to 1 week.

# Mackerel
## WITH PECAN COATING

**Serves 4. Hands-on time:** 10 minutes. **Total time:** 25 minutes.

**Holy mackerel! This delectable dish is loaded with more than 100% of your daily vitamin D quota.**

## INGREDIENTS:

- 4 4-oz Atlantic mackerel fillets, skin left intact and bones removed
- ⅛ tsp each sea salt and fresh ground black pepper
- Olive oil cooking spray
- 2 Tbsp Dijon mustard
- 1 to 2 Tbsp raw honey
- ¼ cup whole-wheat panko bread crumbs
- 4 tsp unsalted pecans, chopped
- ¼ cup fresh Italian parsley, chopped

## INSTRUCTIONS:

**ONE:** Preheat oven to 450°F. Sprinkle fillets with salt and pepper and place skin side down in a 13 x 9-inch baking dish. Mist tops of fillets with cooking spray.

**TWO:** In a small bowl, combine Dijon and honey. Brush tops of fillets with Dijon mixture, dividing evenly. In a separate medium bowl, combine panko, pecans and parsley. Sprinkle panko mixture over top of fillets, dividing evenly.

**THREE:** Bake at 450°F for 13 to 15 minutes or until fish flakes easily with a fork.

**Nutrients per 4-oz serving:** *Calories: 310, Total Fat: 19 g, Sat. Fat: 3.5 g, Monounsaturated Fat: 7 g, Polyunsaturated Fat: 4 g, Omega-3s: 2,810 mg, Omega-6s: 970 mg, Carbs: 14 g, Fiber: 1 g, Sugars: 10 g, Protein: 22 g, Sodium: 350 mg, Cholesterol: 79 mg*

# Ultimate Shrimp Cocktail

**Serves 6. Hands-on time:** 20 minutes. **Total time:** 30 minutes (plus 30 minutes for chilling).

**The venerable shrimp cocktail is a crowd-pleaser at any time of year, and homemade ketchup for the cocktail sauce dressing provides the perfect tangy base. Ditch the shrimp ring and impress your guests with this tangy ceviche-style revamp.**

## INGREDIENTS:

- 1 lemon, halved
- 2 medium white onions, quartered
- 1 tsp sea salt, optional, plus additional to taste
- 1½ lb raw shrimp (16 to 20 per lb), peeled and deveined, tails off
- 1 large ripe avocado, pitted, peeled and diced into chunks
- 2 plum tomatoes, seeded and diced
- 1 serrano pepper, seeded and minced
- 1 cup diced English cucumber, unpeeled
- ½ cup diced jicama
- ½ cup Homemade Ketchup (see recipe, left)
- ⅓ cup fresh lemon juice
- 3 Tbsp each chopped fresh cilantro and dill, plus additional sprigs for garnish
- 3 Tbsp fresh grated horseradish
- 2 Tbsp olive oil
- Fresh ground black pepper, to taste
- 3 cups shredded iceberg lettuce

## INSTRUCTIONS:

**ONE:** In a medium saucepan, bring 8 cups water to a boil. Squeeze lemon halves into pan and gently drop in lemon halves, onions and salt, if desired. Reduce heat to medium and simmer for 10 minutes for flavors to meld.

**TWO:** Remove from heat, strain liquid through a fine mesh strainer and return seasoned water to pan, discarding solids. Bring to a boil again and gently immerse shrimp. Cook shrimp for about 2 minutes or until just pink and opaque, and starting to curl (do not overcook). Strain through a fine mesh strainer or colander, and transfer shrimp to a paper towel-lined baking sheet. Cool to room temperature, then transfer shrimp to a large mixing bowl.

**THREE:** Add to bowl with shrimp: avocado, tomatoes, serrano pepper, cucumber, jicama, ketchup, lemon juice, cilantro, dill, horseradish and oil. Stir gently to combine and season with salt and pepper. Cover and refrigerate for 30 minutes or up to 2 hours.

**FOUR:** Divide lettuce evenly among six martini or rocks glasses. Top each with sixth of shrimp cocktail mixture and garnish with additional cilantro or dill sprigs.

**Nutrients per serving (1 cup shrimp cocktail and ½ cup lettuce):** *Calories: 261, Total Fat: 11.5 g, Sat. Fat: 2 g, Monounsaturated Fat: 7 g, Polyunsaturated Fat: 2 g, Carbs: 15.5 g, Fiber: 4.5 g, Sugars: 6 g, Protein: 25 g, Sodium: 520 mg, Cholesterol: 172 mg*

## Nutritional Bonus:
Shrimp have a bad reputation for high cholesterol content, but there is a silver lining: Not only does a 4-oz serving of shrimp contain almost 50% of your recommended daily protein intake, but a recent study showed that participants who ate shrimp daily had a 13% decrease in triglyceride levels, a form of fat that circulates in the blood.

# Meatless

If you're an omnivore who thinks most meatless meals consist of a lifeless lump of tofu sitting on a plate, think again! The 18 supremely satisfying recipes in this chapter will make your taste buds tingle as your waistline shrinks. In fact, we've got something for everyone: Your kids will love the Butternut Squash Lasagna and Pizza per Uno, and even the most ardent meat fan will fall in love with our Meatless "Sausage" & Pepper Penne or Fiery Chipotle Veggie Sausages. You'll also be pleased to discover just how nutritious and economical plant-based meals can be.

## Sesame Noodles
### WITH ASPARAGUS & CARROTS

*Serves 4. **Hands-on time:** 15 minutes. **Total time:** 25 minutes.*

**Elegant, indulgent and satisfying: This easy meatless dish may be low-cal, but it definitely doesn't skimp on taste.**

INGREDIENTS:

- 2 Tbsp tahini
- 1 Tbsp sesame oil
- 2 Tbsp apple cider vinegar
- 2 tsp raw honey
- Pinch crushed red pepper
- ¼ tsp sea salt
- 8 oz whole-wheat spaghetti
- 16 medium asparagus spears, cut into 2-inch pieces
- 2 medium carrots, peeled and cut into matchsticks
- ½ cup thinly sliced scallions
- 1 Tbsp sesame seeds

INSTRUCTIONS:

ONE: Bring a large pot of water to a boil. Meanwhile, prepare sesame dressing: In a small bowl, whisk together tahini, oil, vinegar, 2 Tbsp water, honey, crushed red pepper and salt; set aside.

TWO: Add spaghetti to boiling water and cook until al dente, according to package directions; drain.

THREE: While pasta is cooking, add about 2 inches of water to another saucepan, then fit with a steamer basket. Bring water to a boil. Add asparagus to basket and steam just until tender, about 2 minutes.

FOUR: In a large bowl, add asparagus, carrots and scallions. Add spaghetti and sesame dressing; toss to combine. Sprinkle mixture with sesame seeds. Serve warm or chilled.

**Nutrients per 1½-cup serving:** *Calories: 328, Total Fat: 10 g, Sat. Fat: 1 g, Monounsaturated Fat: 3 g, Polyunsaturated Fat: 4 g, Carbs: 53 mg, Fiber: 9 g, Protein: 11 g, Sugars: 8 g, Sodium: 179 mg, Cholesterol: 0 mg*

**Nutritional Bonus:**
Tahini, a paste made from ground sesame seeds, is rich in beneficial minerals such as copper (in fact, a single serving of this recipe offers almost 30% of your daily requirement). Copper plays a key role in the production of collagen – a component of bones, connective tissue and hemoglobin, the main iron in red blood cells.

Fiery Chipotle Veggie Sausages

Baked Parmesan Fries

## Nutritional Bonus:
One small spud offers 15% of your day's recommended intake of vitamin B6. The water-soluble B vitamin is vital in the production of serotonin and melatonin, neurotransmitters that help regulate your sleep and mood.

# Fiery Chipotle Veggie Sausages
## WITH CUCUMBER-AVOCADO SALSA

*Serves 4.* **Hands-on time:** *11 minutes.* **Total time:** *20 minutes.*

The level of spiciness varies from brand to brand of sausages, but our topping of creamy avocado and crisp cucumbers will cool even the fieriest heat. Pair these sausages with the Baked Parmesan Fries (right) and you'll have a classic summertime meal – yes, it's clean eating!

## INGREDIENTS:

- Olive oil cooking spray
- 4 3.5-oz natural vegetarian sausages, preferably chipotle flavored
- 4 whole-wheat hot dog buns
- ⅓ medium cucumber, peeled, seeded and diced
- ⅓ cup diced yellow bell pepper
- ¼ cup finely chopped red onion
- ½ ripe medium avocado, pitted, peeled and diced
- 2 Tbsp chopped fresh cilantro
- 2 tsp fresh lime juice
- ½ oz reduced-fat blue cheese, crumbled (2 Tbsp)
- 1 medium lime, cut into wedges, optional

## INSTRUCTIONS:

ONE: Preheat grill to medium-high and lightly coat grill basket with cooking spray. Place sausages in grill basket. (**TIP:** It's best to cook these dogs in your grill basket as the veggie varieties can be a bit more fragile.) Cook according to package directions. Gently open buns, but do not split in half. Grill buns briefly on each side while sausages cook for final 2 minutes.

TWO: Meanwhile, in a medium bowl, combine cucumber, pepper and onion. Gently fold in all remaining ingredients, except lime wedges.

THREE: To serve, place 1 sausage in center of each bun and spoon equal amounts of vegetable mixture over top of each. Serve with lime wedges, if desired.

Nutrients per dog (1 sausage, 1 bun, ½ cup salsa): *Calories: 338, Total Fat: 9 g, Sat. Fat: 1 g, Monounsaturated Fat: 3 g, Polyunsaturated Fat: 1 g, Carbs: 48 g, Fiber: 8 g, Sugars: 6 g, Protein: 29 g, Sodium: 517 mg, Cholesterol: 2 mg*

# Baked Parmesan Fries

*Serves 4.* **Hands-on time:** *8 minutes.* **Total time:** *23 minutes.*

Whether you like your fries piping hot or cooled to room temperature, the taste and texture of our Parm variety won't disappoint. But be sure to use Yukon gold or red potatoes for a moist end result. Avoid using the russet spuds you may have on hand, as they have a drier, starchier texture.

**FOR A TWIST: Try grated Asiago cheese in place of the Parmesan and dried red pepper flakes in lieu of the ground black pepper.**

## INGREDIENTS:

- 1 lb Yukon gold or red potatoes, scrubbed and cut into ½-inch-thick strips
- 1 Tbsp extra-virgin olive oil
- 2 tsp dried Italian seasoning
- ½ tsp garlic powder
- ¼ to ½ tsp coarsely ground black pepper, to taste
- Sea salt, to taste
- ¼ cup grated Parmesan cheese

## INSTRUCTIONS:

ONE: Preheat oven to 425°F. Line a large baking sheet with foil. Place potatoes on baking sheet, drizzle evenly with oil and sprinkle with Italian seasoning, garlic powder and pepper. Toss to coat, then arrange potatoes in a single layer. Bake in center of oven for 10 minutes, then flip and stir, and bake for 5 minutes more or until lightly golden.

TWO: Remove from oven. Sprinkle with salt and Parmesan. Serve immediately or at room temperature.

Nutrients per ⅔-cup serving: *Calories: 150, Total Fat: 5.5 g, Sat. Fat: 1.5 g, Carbs: 20 g, Fiber: 1 g, Sugars: 0 g, Protein: 6 g, Sodium: 162 mg, Cholesterol: 5 mg*

# Black-Eyed Pea & Onion Fritters
## WITH HORSERADISH SOUR CREAM & SPINACH-RICE

*Serves 4. **Hands-on time:** 18 minutes. **Total time:** 30 minutes.*

Black-eyed peas are a staple in the South and, when coupled with whole grains (think brown rice or cornbread), they become a complete meatless protein. However, the bacon grease and other fatty pork products that peas are routinely cooked with often overshadow the health benefits of this favorite legume. We've chosen to cut the pork fat, opting to cook our fritters in a minimal amount of oil. Plus, we call upon low-cal, zero-fat and cholesterol-free egg whites to act as the binder, or "glue," that holds it all together.

## INGREDIENTS:

**FRITTERS**

- 15.5 oz no-salt-added cooked or canned black-eyed peas, rinsed and drained (TRY: Eden Organic Black Eyed Peas)
- 1 1-oz slice whole-wheat bread, torn into small pieces
- 2 scallions, finely chopped
- ½ red bell pepper, diced
- 1 clove garlic, minced
- 3 egg whites
- ½ tsp dried thyme
- 2 jalapeño peppers, finely chopped, seeded if desired
- ¼ tsp sea salt
- ¼ tsp fresh ground black pepper
- 1 Tbsp extra-virgin olive oil, divided

**SAUCE**

- ½ cup light sour cream
- 1½ to 2 tsp prepared horseradish

**RICE**

- 2 cups cooked brown rice
- 1 oz baby spinach, coarsely chopped (1 cup)
- 1 Tbsp extra-virgin olive oil
- 1 clove garlic, minced
- ¼ tsp sea salt

## INSTRUCTIONS:

**ONE:** Prepare fritters: In a medium bowl, add peas and partially mash with a fork or potato masher. Place bread in a blender and grind into coarse bread crumbs. Add bread crumbs to peas with scallions, bell pepper, garlic, egg whites, thyme, jalapeños, salt and pepper.

**TWO:** Heat 1½ tsp oil in a large nonstick skillet on medium. Working in two batches, spoon fritter batter into skillet in ¼-cup mounds, flattening slightly so they measure 2½ inches in diameter. Cook for 3 minutes per side or until lightly golden. Once cooked, set aside on a separate plate. Repeat with remaining batter and 1½ tsp oil.

**THREE:** Meanwhile, prepare sauce: In a small bowl, stir together sour cream and horseradish.

**FOUR:** Prepare rice: In a medium bowl, combine rice ingredients and toss gently.

**FIVE:** To serve, divide rice mixture, fritters and sauce evenly among 4 plates.

*Nutrients per serving (2 fritters, ½ cup rice mixture, 2 Tbsp sauce): Calories: 331, Total Fat: 12 g, Sat. Fat: 3 g, Monounsaturated Fat: 6 g, Polyunsaturated Fat: 1 g, Carbs: 45 g, Fiber: 7 g, Sugars: 3 g, Protein: 13 g, Sodium: 382 mg, Cholesterol: 10 mg*

---

**NEW!**

# Baked Falafel
## WITH YOGURT TAHINI SAUCE

*Serves 6. **Hands-on time:** 25 minutes.*
*Total time: 40 minutes (plus 2 hours for chilling).*

Forget deep-fried falafel! Our baked version has a fantastic texture and is loaded with flavor. Falafel is a Middle Eastern street food that is, typically, a deep-fried patty made of chickpeas or fava beans (or sometimes both), garlic, parsley, cilantro and cumin. Dried chickpeas are the key to this recipe, giving it a chewy texture. Serve these little bites as an appetizer or on a whole-grain pita with lettuce, cucumber, tomatoes and a little low-fat feta cheese.

## INGREDIENTS:

- 1 cup dried chickpeas (aka garbanzo beans), soaked overnight in fridge in cold water, covered by 3 inches
- ½ medium white onion, chopped (about ¾ cup)
- 3 cloves garlic, minced
- 5 Tbsp chopped fresh flat-leaf parsley, divided
- 3 Tbsp chopped fresh cilantro
- 1 Tbsp fresh lemon juice
- 1½ tsp ground cumin
- ¾ tsp sea salt
- ⅛ tsp ground cayenne pepper
- 1 tsp baking powder
- 6 Tbsp white whole-wheat flour or whole-wheat flour, divided
- Olive oil cooking spray

**YOGURT TAHINI SAUCE**

- 1 cup nonfat plain Greek yogurt
- 3 Tbsp tahini paste
- 2 tsp fresh lemon juice
- ½ tsp ground cumin
- ¼ tsp each sea salt and fresh ground black pepper

## INSTRUCTIONS:

**ONE:** Drain chickpeas in a colander and rinse under cold water. Transfer chickpeas to a paper-towel-lined tray, in a single layer, and pat dry with paper towel.

**TWO:** Place chickpeas, onion, garlic, 3 Tbsp parsley, cilantro, lemon juice, cumin, salt and cayenne into the bowl of a food processor and pulse until onion is finely chopped and mixture resembles small crumbs. Add baking powder and 4 Tbsp flour and pulse until just combined. Scrape mixture out of food processor and transfer to a mixing bowl. Cover and refrigerate for about 2 hours.

**THREE:** While falafel is resting, prepare Yogurt Tahini Sauce: In a medium bowl, whisk together yogurt, tahini, lemon juice, cumin, salt and pepper until smooth. Cover and refrigerate until needed.

**FOUR:** Preheat oven to 350°F.

**FIVE:** Scoop out 1 heaping Tbsp chickpea mixture and form into a ball. Mixture should be dough-like and should not stick to your hands. Fold in up to 2 Tbsp more flour, as needed. Form remaining chickpea mixture into 1½-Tbsp balls and arrange in a single layer on a parchment-lined baking sheet. Mist falafel with cooking spray. Bake in oven for 15 to 18 minutes, turning once and re-misting with cooking spray, until golden brown, crisp, and hot and fluffy in center.

**SIX:** Arrange falafel on a platter with a bowl of Yogurt Tahini Sauce for dipping. Sprinkle with remaining 2 Tbsp parsley.

*Nutrients per serving (3 falafel and 3 Tbsp Yogurt Tahini Sauce): Calories: 214, Total Fat: 6 g, Sat. Fat: 0.5 g, Monounsaturated Fat: 1.5 g, Polyunsaturated Fat: 2 g, Carbs: 30 g, Fiber: 7 g, Sugars: 5 g, Protein: 12 g, Sodium: 348 mg, Cholesterol: 0 mg*

Baked
Falafel

## Nutritional Bonus:
Chickpeas are well known as a great source of fiber, boasting a whopping 35 g per cup of dried beans. Even better news is that recent studies show that fiber from chickpeas helps regulate blood fat, lower LDL cholesterol, lower total cholesterol and lower triglycerides better than other fiber sources.

THE BEST OF CLEAN EATING 2

Quinoa-
Stuffed
Collard
Green Rolls

# Quinoa-Stuffed Collard Green Rolls

*Serves 6. **Hands-on time:** 45 minutes. **Total time:** 1 hour, 20 minutes.*

**Collard greens are a versatile staple in any kitchen, and their sturdy texture makes them a perfect substitute for cabbage in our hearty version of cabbage rolls. The tomato sauce, filling and leaves may all be prepared in advance if desired. Rolls may also be prepared in advance, frozen in a single layer on a parchment-lined baking sheet and transferred into sealable freezer-safe containers. Simply thaw overnight in the fridge, transfer to casserole dish with tomato sauce and bake as directed for a quick meal any time.**

## INGREDIENTS:

- 4 tsp olive oil, divided
- 3 medium yellow onions, diced, divided
- 4 cloves garlic, minced, divided
- 1 tsp dried Italian seasoning blend, divided
- 2 cups boxed diced tomatoes, no salt added (TRY: Pomi Chopped Tomatoes)
- 1 Tbsp raw honey
- 2¼ cups low-sodium vegetable broth or water, divided
- Sea salt and fresh ground black pepper, to taste

- 18 large collard green leaves, stems removed and discarded
- 1 cup quinoa
- 2 cups cremini mushrooms, thinly sliced
- 1 each red and green bell pepper, diced
- 1 cup cooked white navy beans (or BPA-free no-salt-added canned white navy beans, drained and rinsed)
- 2 Tbsp chopped fresh dill
- Pinch ground cayenne pepper

## INSTRUCTIONS:

**ONE:** In a medium saucepan, heat 2 tsp oil on medium-high. Stir in third of onions and half of garlic. Cook for 3 to 4 minutes, until onions are softened. Stir in ½ tsp Italian seasoning and tomatoes. Bring to a boil, reduce heat to medium and simmer for 20 minutes, until thickened. Remove from heat, add honey and ¼ cup broth, and season with salt and pepper. Set aside.

**TWO:** Meanwhile, bring a large pot of salted water to a boil and prepare a large bowl filled with ice and water. Add 3 to 4 collard leaves to pot, immerse and blanch for about 1 minute, until tender. Transfer to ice water to cool, then place onto a paper towel-lined tray and pat leaves dry with paper towel. Repeat with remaining collard leaves. Place 1 leaf onto a cutting board, thick protruding stem side of leaf facing up. Holding a small knife parallel to cutting board, trim off thick part of stem (this will make leaves easier to roll). Repeat with remaining collard leaves. Set aside.

**THREE:** In a separate medium saucepan, bring remaining 2 cups broth and quinoa to a boil on high heat. Reduce heat to low, cover with a tight-fitting lid and cook for 12 to 15 minutes. Remove from heat, uncover and let rest for 5 minutes. Fluff quinoa with a fork and transfer to a large bowl. Set aside.

**FOUR:** While quinoa cooks, heat remaining 2 tsp oil in a large sauté pan on medium-high. Add remaining onions and garlic. Stirring frequently, cook for 2 to 3 minutes, until onions are softened. Add remaining ½ tsp Italian seasoning, mushrooms and bell peppers and cook for an additional 4 to 6 minutes, stirring frequently. Transfer mixture to bowl with quinoa. Stir in beans, dill and cayenne until combined, and season with salt and pepper.

**FIVE:** Assemble rolls: Spread half of tomato sauce evenly into the bottom of a 9 x 13-inch casserole dish; set aside. Place 1 collard leaf onto cutting board, trimmed side up and stem to you. Scoop about ¼ to ⅓ cup quinoa filling onto leaf (depending on size), about a third of the way from the stem end. Fold sides of leaf over filling, then roll stem end over filling, tucking it in behind the filling, and continue to roll into a cylinder shape. Place into casserole dish, seam side down, and repeat assembly with remaining leaves and filling, placing rolls snugly into casserole dish. Top with remaining tomato sauce. Cover pan tightly with aluminum foil and bake in oven for 30 to 35 minutes, until hot throughout and sauce is bubbling.

**NOTE: To save a bit of time and skip Step One, substitute 1½ cups store-bought jarred tomato sauce for our homemade version.**

*Nutrients per serving (3 rolls and ¼ cup sauce): Calories: 261, Total Fat: 5 g, Sat. Fat: 1 g, Monounsaturated Fat: 3 g, Polyunsaturated Fat: 1 g, Carbs: 43 g, Fiber: 9 g, Sugars: 10 g, Protein: 10 g, Sodium: 124 mg, Cholesterol: 0 mg*

## Nutritional Bonus:
**Although collard greens do not get much attention, they are one of the healthiest leafy greens! Collards are a cruciferous green vegetable, containing sulphur, antioxidant vitamins A, C and K and loads of fiber. This combination makes them an ideal choice to aid in detoxification.**

# Rustic Genovese Basil Pesto Pasta

*Serves 6.*

This pasta recipe from Chef Christina Machamer is creamy and comforting enough for the chilly days of winter and clean enough to be in this book.

## INGREDIENTS:

### BASIL PESTO

- 4 cups loosely packed fresh basil leaves
- 3 to 4 Tbsp extra-virgin olive oil (or as needed)
- 2 to 3 cloves garlic, peeled and sliced thin
- 2 Tbsp pine nuts, lightly toasted
- 2 Tbsp (heaping full) Fontinella cheese or low-fat Parmesan cheese, grated
- Kosher salt, to taste

### PASTA

- 1 cup cherry tomatoes, halved
- 10 sprigs thyme
- Kosher salt and finely ground black pepper, to taste
- 1½ Tbsp extra-virgin olive oil
- 1 small russet potato, peeled
- 1 cup green beans, sliced ¼-inch on the bias
- 12 oz whole-wheat pasta (Machamer recommends tagliatelle or fettuccine)

## INSTRUCTIONS:

**ONE:** Prepare pesto: Bring 1 gallon salinated water to a rapid boil. Blanch and shock basil leaves by adding them to boiling water for about 5 seconds, then quickly submerging them in an ice bath. (This will set the chlorophyl in the basil so the pesto remains bright green.) Squeeze excess water out of basil and roughly chop.

**TWO:** In a blender or food processor, process basil with enough oil to emulsify, about 3 to 4 Tbsp. Add garlic, nuts and cheese and season with salt. Continue blending just enough to emulsify. (Pesto should have a slightly course texture.) Chill until needed. Pesto will keep up to 2 days but is best served the day it is made.

**THREE:** Prepare pasta: Preheat oven to 350°F. In an oven-safe baking dish, arrange tomatoes cut side up. Arrange thyme sprigs over top, season with salt and pepper, and drizzle with oil. Bake tomatoes until they just begin to brown and caramelize, approximately 15 minutes.

**FOUR:** Bring 1 gallon salinated water to a rapid boil. Meanwhile, mince potato either by hand or in a food processor. Blanch beans in boiling water for about 4 minutes, then quickly submerge in an ice bath. Set aside. In the same water, add pasta and potato and cook until pasta is tender. (Cooking time will vary by pasta type used, but standard time is 7 to 9 minutes.) Strain pasta along with potato.

**FIVE:** In a large mixing bowl, combine tomatoes, pesto, beans and pasta-potato mixture. Toss until well combined.

**NOTE:** Pasta may only be reheated under low heat. High heat will cause the oil in the pesto to separate.

Nutrients per serving (4 oz pasta and 1 oz pesto): *Calories: 460, Total Fat: 14 g, Sat. Fat: 2.5 g, Carbs: 69 g, Fiber: 14 g, Sugars: 5 g, Protein: 19 g, Sodium: 120 mg, Cholesterol: 0 mg*

# Meatless "Sausage" & Pepper Penne

*Serves 4. Hands-on time: 15 minutes. Total time: 35 minutes.*

Traditional sausage and pepper penne often contains a heaping amount of fat, salt and preservatives. To keep things clean, we've replaced the meat with crumbled tempeh and added a variety of herbs to mimic the smoky sausage flavor.

## INGREDIENTS:

- 3 oz uncooked whole-wheat penne pasta (about 1 cup)
- 3 tsp olive oil, divided
- 8 oz tempeh, crumbled (about 2 cups)
- 2 cloves garlic, minced
- 2 tsp fennel seeds
- ½ tsp paprika
- ⅛ tsp red chile flakes
- ½ medium white onion, thinly sliced
- ½ medium red bell pepper, thinly sliced
- ½ medium green bell pepper, thinly sliced
- 2 cups Everyday Marinara Sauce (see recipe, p. 133)
- 2 Tbsp chopped fresh oregano leaves
- Sea salt and fresh ground black pepper, to taste

## INSTRUCTIONS:

**ONE:** Cook penne according to package directions. Drain, set aside and keep warm.

**TWO:** Heat 2 tsp oil in a large nonstick sauté pan over medium. Add tempeh and garlic and sauté for 3 to 4 minutes or until browned. Reduce heat to medium-low and add fennel seeds, paprika and chile flakes. Continue to cook for 3 to 4 minutes, until fragrant. (**CAUTION:** Pan will be dry at this point. While it won't burn, do not leave unattended.) Transfer tempeh mixture to a mixing bowl and return pan to heat.

**THREE:** Increase heat to medium-high, add remaining 1 tsp oil and sauté onion for 2 to 3 minutes. Add bell peppers and continue to sauté for an additional 2 to 3 minutes, until softened. Put tempeh mixture back in pan, stir to combine and add Everyday Marinara Sauce. Reduce heat to medium-low and simmer for about 3 minutes, until bubbling and fragrant. Add oregano and season with salt and pepper.

**FOUR:** To serve, toss penne with tempeh mixture, then divide evenly among 4 pasta bowls. Serve immediately.

**MEAT FREE: If you're trying to incorporate more vegetarian meals into your diet, marinate tempeh and use it in place of meat in recipes. The soybean product easily absorbs flavors and has a pleasant texture, making it a vegetarian favorite.**

Nutrients per 1½-cup serving: *Calories: 301, Total Fat: 13 g, Sat. Fat: 2 g, Monounsaturated Fat: 5 g, Polyunsaturated Fat: 3 g, Carbs: 35 g, Fiber: 7 g, Sugars: 7 g, Protein: 17 g, Sodium: 71 mg, Cholesterol: 0 mg*

Meatless "Sausage" & Pepper Penne

Pea
Ravioli

# Pea Ravioli

*Serves 4. **Hands-on time:** 40 minutes. **Total time:** 40 minutes.*

One of the world's oldest known vegetables, peas are actually a member of the legume family and an impressive source of vegetarian protein (this meat-free pasta offers 21 grams per serving!).

## INGREDIENTS:

- 1 Tbsp extra-virgin olive oil
- 1 medium shallot, finely chopped (about ¼ cup)
- 1 clove garlic, finely chopped
- ½ cup low-sodium vegetable or chicken broth
- 1¼ cups fresh or frozen peas, divided
- Sea salt and fresh ground black pepper, to taste
- ⅓ cup low-fat ricotta cheese
- 5 Tbsp grated Pecorino Romano cheese, divided
- 2 Tbsp chopped fresh chives, plus additional for garnish
- ½ tsp lemon zest
- 32 whole-wheat wonton wrappers

**TIP:** Look for whole-wheat wonton wrappers in the organic section of your supermarket and at natural food stores. Or, try our Make-Your-Own Whole-Wheat Wonton Wrappers at cleaneating.com/june-2011. Triple our online recipe to make enough wrappers for this Pea Ravioli. You can also use egg roll wrappers that have been cut into quarters.

## INSTRUCTIONS:

**ONE:** In a medium saucepan, heat oil on medium. Add shallot and cook until soft and translucent, about 3 minutes. Add garlic and cook, stirring constantly, for 1 minute. Add broth and bring to a simmer. Add 1 cup peas and simmer until just tender, 2 to 3 minutes. Season with salt and pepper. With a slotted spoon, transfer pea-shallot mixture to a food processor. Cover saucepan and set broth aside. To a food processor, add ricotta, 3 Tbsp Pecorino Romano, chives and lemon zest; purée. Taste and adjust seasoning, if desired.

**TWO:** Bring a large pot of water to a boil while you make ravioli. Arrange a small bowl of water and a baking sheet near your work surface. Place 2 wonton wrappers in front of you; keep remaining wrappers covered with a kitchen towel to prevent them from drying out. Place 1 Tbsp pea purée on 1 wrapper. Dip your finger into water and moisten edges of wrapper. Place second wrapper over top and press edges together firmly to seal. Transfer to baking sheet. Repeat with remaining pea purée and wrappers.

**THREE:** Just before cooking ravioli, return reserved broth to a simmer. Add remaining ¼ cup peas to broth and cook, uncovered, until tender, 2 minutes.

**FOUR:** Meanwhile, add ravioli to pot with boiling water and cook for 2 minutes, until dough is al dente and ravioli rise to the surface. With a slotted spoon or skimmer, transfer directly to four shallow serving bowls. Divide pea-broth mixture evenly among bowls and sprinkle with remaining 2 Tbsp Pecorino Romano (½ Tbsp per bowl). Garnish with additional chives and serve.

**Nutrients per serving (4 ravioli, 1 Tbsp peas plus broth, ½ Tbsp Pecorino Romano):** *Calories: 414, Total Fat: 9 g, Sat. Fat: 3 g, Monounsaturated Fat: 3 g, Polyunsaturated Fat: 1 g, Carbs: 68 g, Fiber: 12 g, Sugars: 1.5 g, Protein: 21 g, Sodium: 445 mg, Cholesterol: 16 mg*

# Butternut Squash Risotto

*Serves 4. **Hands-on time:** 45 minutes. **Total time:** 1 hour.*

Yes, butternut squash does add a warm, rich color to this risotto, but our deep orange friend is not just here for its looks. The squash also lends this dish a creamy texture and sweet and nutty flavor (and it's loaded with nutrients). For more on how to pick, prepare and cook squash, see p. 206.

## INGREDIENTS:

- 3 cups peeled, diced fresh butternut squash
- Extra-virgin olive oil or olive oil cooking spray
- Sea salt and fresh ground black pepper, to taste
- 4 cups low-sodium organic chicken broth
- ½ cup onion, diced
- 1 Tbsp extra-virgin olive oil
- 8 oz mushrooms, sliced (2 cups)
- 1 Tbsp garlic, minced
- 1 cup arborio rice
- 1 Tbsp fresh thyme leaves
- 1 Tbsp fresh sage, minced
- ½ cup fresh or frozen peas (thawed if frozen)
- ¼ cup shredded fontina or Parmesan cheese
- 2 Tbsp chopped walnuts, toasted

## INSTRUCTIONS:

**ONE:** Preheat oven to 425°F. Toss squash with a little oil or mist with cooking spray; season with salt and pepper. Spread squash in an even layer on a rimmed baking sheet. Bake until tender, about 25 minutes, stirring every 10 minutes. Set squash aside.

**TWO:** Meanwhile, bring broth to a simmer in a saucepan over medium heat; keep warm.

**THREE:** While broth is heating, sauté onion in 1 Tbsp oil in a large sauté pan over medium-high heat for 3 minutes. Add mushrooms and sauté until they start to soften, 5 minutes. Add garlic and sauté for 1 minute more. Add rice and stir to coat with oil and vegetables.

**FOUR:** Add ½ cup warm broth; simmer and stir with a wooden spoon until liquid evaporates, about 2 minutes. Stir in another ½ cup warm broth; simmer, stirring occasionally, until liquid is almost all evaporated. Continue adding broth in ½-cup increments, adding more only after previous addition has been absorbed. Taste rice after three-quarters of the broth has been added. Rice is done when it's tender but still slightly firm and white in the very center (not chalky). Continue adding broth until only ½ cup remains.

**FIVE:** Add thyme, sage, peas and cheese to pan with last ½ cup broth; stir until cheese melts, 1 to 2 minutes. Remove pan from heat before all liquid is absorbed. Gently fold in cooked squash and walnuts. Season risotto with salt and pepper. Garnish with additional thyme, if desired, and serve warm.

**Nutrients per 1½-cup serving:** *Calories: 359, Total Fat: 9 g, Sat. Fat: 2.5 g, Monounsaturated Fat: 4 g, Polyunsaturated Fat: 2.5 g, Carbs: 60 g, Fiber: 6 g, Sugars: 4 g, Protein: 14 g, Sodium: 163 mg, Cholesterol: 8 mg*

# CE's Whole-Wheat Pizza Dough

*Makes* 2 dough balls (about 1 lb each). *Hands-on time:* 30 minutes. *Total time:* 2 hours.

## INGREDIENTS:

- 1 Tbsp raw honey
- 1 cup less 1½ Tbsp lukewarm water (105°F to 110°F), divided
- 1 pkg active dry yeast (¼ oz or 2½ tsp)
- 2½ cups whole-wheat flour, divided
- 4 tsp vital wheat gluten (TRY: Bob's Red Mill)
- 1 tsp sea salt
- 3 Tbsp olive oil, divided

## INSTRUCTIONS:

**ONE:** In a large bowl, mix together honey and ⅓ cup water. Sprinkle in yeast and allow to proof, undisturbed (do not stir or move bowl), for 10 minutes or until yeast is foamy. (**NOTE:** If yeast does not foam, it is dead and your dough will not rise. Discard and start again with fresh ingredients.)

**TWO:** While yeast is proofing, mix together 2 cups flour, wheat gluten and salt in another large bowl.

**THREE:** Once yeast is foamy, add remaining water and 2 Tbsp oil to yeast mixture. Pour in flour mixture and gently fold in until just combined. Mixture will form a very wet ball. Coat the bottom of another large bowl with remaining oil. Transfer dough to bowl, rolling ball just to coat with oil. Cover bowl tightly with plastic wrap and set aside at room temperature to rise for 1 hour. Dough will be very soft and sticky.

**FOUR:** Lightly dust counter with about ¼ cup flour. Transfer dough to floured surface and roll lightly in flour, dusting your hands with additional remaining flour as needed. Gently knead dough, using remaining flour as needed, for about one minute. Form dough into a ball and place back into bowl. Cover again tightly with plastic wrap and set aside at room temperature to rise for 30 minutes.

**FIVE:** Transfer dough back to floured surface, adding more flour if needed, and cut dough in half to form 2 balls. Lightly knead each for about 30 seconds and reform into balls. Dough is now ready to use or freeze. To store, wrap each dough ball individually in plastic wrap. Dough can be kept refrigerated for 24 hours or frozen for up to 1 month.

**Nutrients per serving (⅛ of each dough ball):** *Calories: 96, Total Fat: 3 g, Sat. Fat: 0.5 g, Carbs: 15 g, Fiber: 2 g, Sugars: 1 g, Protein: 3 g, Sodium: 121 mg, Cholesterol: 0 mg*

Mushroom & Radicchio Thin-Crust Pizzetta

## To Make CE's Whole-Wheat Pizza Dough Gluten Free:

- Swap whole-wheat flour for an all-purpose gluten-free baking flour mix. (TRY: Bob's Red Mill)

- Remove vital wheat gluten from recipe.

- Increase yeast to 2 packages.

- Add 1 tsp baking powder to flour mixture.

- Reduce water to ⅓ cup.

- Add ⅓ cup egg whites in Step Three when adding flour to proofed yeast.

- Have a bit of extra water on hand in case mixture is dry.

- Add 4 tsp xanthan gum (available at health food stores) to dry ingredients.

- Add 2 tsp apple cider vinegar after combining yeast and dry ingredients.

# Mushroom & Radicchio Thin-Crust Pizzetta

*Serves 6. **Makes** 1 pizza. **Hands-on time:** 30 minutes. **Total time:** 45 minutes.*

Meaning "little pizza" in Italian, a *pizzetta* is light in size but big on taste. In our far-from-ordinary recipe, the crisp radicchio complements the creaminess of the mushrooms and goat cheese.

## INGREDIENTS:

- Olive oil cooking spray
- 2 cloves garlic, minced
- 2 cups cremini mushrooms, thinly sliced
- 2 tsp rosemary sprigs, finely chopped, divided
- Sea salt and fresh ground black pepper, to taste
- 2 tsp cornmeal (if pkg specifies a grind, opt for fine, not coarse)
- 1 1-lb ball CE's Whole-Wheat Pizza Dough (see recipe, left) or 1 1-lb pkg store-bought whole-wheat pizza dough
- 1 tsp plus 1 Tbsp olive oil, divided
- 2 medium plum tomatoes, diced
- 2 oz goat cheese, crumbled
- 3 Tbsp white balsamic vinegar
- ¼ medium radicchio, thinly sliced and soaked in cold water for 30 minutes
- 2 cups baby arugula

## INSTRUCTIONS:

**ONE:** Preheat oven to 475°F.

**TWO:** Coat a large sauté pan with cooking spray and set over medium-high. Add garlic and mushrooms and sauté for 4 to 6 minutes or until tender, light golden brown in color and no liquid remains in pan. Transfer garlic-mushroom mixture to a bowl, season with ½ tsp rosemary, salt and pepper and mix well. Set aside at room temperature.

**THREE:** Line a large baking sheet with parchment paper and sprinkle with cornmeal.

**FOUR:** Roll out pizza dough into a rectangular shape, as thin as possible, about 12 x 16 inches in size. Transfer dough onto baking sheet and brush with 1 tsp oil. Top pizza with remaining rosemary, tomatoes and cheese and season with salt and pepper. Place pan in oven and bake for 8 to 10 minutes, until crust is golden brown and crisp. Remove from oven and slice crust in half lengthwise, then cut each half into 6 pieces.

**FIVE:** While pizzetta is baking, prepare dressing: In a small bowl, whisk remaining 1 Tbsp oil into vinegar. Drain radicchio well and place into a large bowl. Add arugula and dressing to radicchio and toss well, seasoning with salt and pepper.

**SIX:** Top each pizzetta slice with radicchio salad and garlic-mushroom mixture, dividing evenly. Serve immediately.

*Nutrients per 2-slice serving: Calories: 221, Total Fat: 11 g, Sat. Fat: 3 g, Carbs: 24 g, Fiber: 4 g, Sugars: 4 g, Protein: 8 g, Sodium: 240 mg, Cholesterol: 10 mg*

# Pizza per Uno
## WITH GARLIC, SPINACH & FRESH MOZZARELLA

*Makes 2 pizzas. **Hands-on time:** 10 minutes. **Total time:** 18 to 20 minutes.*

These quick and easy pizzas use pita bread for a traditionally thin and crispy crust. Vary the toppings to your taste preferences: Add diced Roma or sun-dried tomatoes, chopped olives or even leftover cooked broccoli.

**TIP:** Pitas are a fast, easy and convenient alternative to a full-size pizza crust. Plus, you won't feel guilty about indulging in the whole pie!

## INGREDIENTS:

- ½ cup natural salt-free tomato sauce
- ¼ to ½ tsp red pepper flakes, or to taste
- 2 to 3 medium cloves garlic, passed through a garlic press or very finely minced
- 2 whole-wheat, sprouted-wheat or gluten-free pitas
- 1 cup loosely packed spinach or other winter greens, finely chopped
- 2 oz fresh mozzarella, thinly sliced into rounds
- 2 Tbsp minced fresh basil leaves

## INSTRUCTIONS:

**ONE:** Preheat oven to 400°F.

**TWO:** In a small bowl, combine tomato sauce, red pepper flakes and garlic; stir to mix well.

**THREE:** Place both pitas on a baking sheet. Using a pastry brush or spoon, evenly divide sauce mixture between pitas, leaving a ¼-inch border around edges. Sprinkle with spinach, then arrange mozzarella rounds over top of greens, dividing both evenly.

**FOUR:** Bake for 8 to 10 minutes, until greens are wilted and mozzarella is melted. Remove from oven, sprinkle with basil, dividing evenly, and serve immediately. If you're enjoying 1 pizza, loosely wrap remaining pizza in aluminum foil or store in a sealable container for up to 2 days in refrigerator. Reheat in a warm oven or serve at room temperature.

*Nutrients per pizza: Calories: 183, Total Fat: 5 g, Sat. Fat: 3 g, Carbs: 24 g, Fiber: 4 g, Sugars: 3 g, Protein: 11 g, Sodium: 351 mg, Cholesterol: 18 mg*

**NUTRITIONAL BONUS: Popeye had it right — spinach does make you stronger. Just ½ cup contains almost all of your recommended daily intake of vitamin K, which activates osteocalcin – a protein found in bones – to help you maintain strong and healthy bones.**

Mediterranean
Vegetable,
White Bean &
Feta Penne

# Mediterranean Vegetable, White Bean & Feta Penne

Serves 4. **Hands-on time:** 7 minutes. **Total time:** 17 minutes.

Our Mediterranean-inspired pasta offers multiple layers of flavor in every bite, but that doesn't mean that the recipe is accompanied by a kitchen-intensive list of instructions.

## INGREDIENTS:

- 6 oz whole-grain penne pasta
- 1 cup cooked or BPA-free canned white beans (such as navy or cannellini), drained and rinsed well
- 2 medium tomatoes, chopped
- 4 cloves garlic, minced, divided
- 1 Tbsp balsamic vinegar
- 1 tsp dried basil
- ¼ tsp red pepper flakes
- ¼ tsp sea salt
- 1 Tbsp plus 1 tsp extra-virgin olive oil, divided
- 1 medium zucchini, cut into eighths lengthwise, then cut into 2-inch pieces
- 1 medium green bell pepper, cut into thin strips, then cut into 2-inch pieces
- ½ tsp dried rosemary
- 1 cup crumbled reduced-fat feta

## INSTRUCTIONS:

ONE: Cook penne according to package directions, adding beans during the last minute of cooking.

TWO: Meanwhile, in a medium bowl, combine tomatoes, 2 cloves garlic, vinegar, basil, pepper flakes and salt; set aside.

THREE: Heat 1 tsp oil in a large nonstick skillet on medium-high, tilting skillet to coat bottom lightly. Add zucchini and bell pepper and cook for 4 minutes or until edges begin to brown, stirring frequently. Add remaining 2 cloves garlic and cook for 15 seconds, stirring constantly. Remove from heat, stir in tomato mixture and drizzle with remaining 1 Tbsp oil. Cover to keep warm.

FOUR: Drain penne-bean mixture, place in a serving bowl, sprinkle evenly with rosemary and all but ¼ cup feta. Spoon zucchini mixture over top and finish with remaining feta.

Nutrients per 1½-cup serving: Calories: 353, Total Fat: 12 g, Sat. Fat: 4 g, Monounsaturated Fat: 3.5 g, Polyunsaturated Fat: 0.5 g, Carbs: 44 g, Fiber: 11 g, Sugars: 6 g, Protein: 18 g, Sodium: 631 mg, Cholesterol: 10 mg

# The Loaded Bowl

Serves 12. **Hands-on time:** 25 minutes. **Total time:** 25 minutes.

*Clean Eating* Editor in Chief Alicia Rewega enjoys this dish as a complete dinner, but you can also try it as a side salad. Says Alicia, "I love its versatility: At times, I swap the quinoa for brown rice or sprinkle in a little cayenne pepper and chile powder for extra heat. I will also add chunks of grilled chicken breast for a little more protein after an intense workout. The options are endless!"

## INGREDIENTS:

- 3 cups quinoa, rinsed and drained
- 1 15-oz can Eden Organic Black Beans, rinsed well and drained (or 2 cups cooked black beans)
- 1 pint cherry or grape tomatoes, halved
- 1 cup fresh cilantro, chopped (TIP: Feel free to add more or less depending on your preference.)
- 2 avocados, pitted and peeled
- Fresh lemon juice, to prevent avocado from browning
- Sea salt and fresh ground black pepper, to taste
- Juice 4 limes
- Zest 1 lime

### DRESSING

- ¼ cup extra-virgin olive oil
- ¼ cup white vinegar
- 2 or 3 cloves garlic, minced
- Sea salt and fresh ground black pepper, to taste

## INSTRUCTIONS:

ONE: Prepare quinoa according to package directions, cover and set aside.

TWO: In a large mixing bowl, add beans, tomatoes and cilantro, tossing to combine.

THREE: Dice avocados, drizzle with lemon juice and set aside in fridge.

FOUR: Add all dressing ingredients to a food processor or mini chopper. Pulse until garlic is blended and dressing appears creamy. Set aside in fridge.

FIVE: Fluff quinoa with a fork and add bean mixture. Season with salt and pepper and add lime juice and zest; toss to combine. Serve in bowls, topped with avocado and drizzled with dressing, dividing evenly. If desired, garnish with a few more sprigs of cilantro.

STORAGE: **This grain salad keeps well, covered, in the refrigerator for 3 to 4 days. But you can make your leftovers last even longer (stretching your dollar!) by slicing the avocado fresh and adding it to the mix just before serving. Without the avocado, the dish will last up to 5 or 6 days in the fridge. And, you can freeze it too!**

Nutrients per 1-cup serving: Calories: 293, Total Fat: 12 g, Sat. Fat: 1 g, Monounsaturated Fat: 6.5 g, Polyunsaturated Fat: 1 g, Carbs: 39 g, Fiber: 6 g, Sugars: 1 g, Protein: 9 g, Sodium: 59 mg, Cholesterol: 0 mg

NUTRITIONAL BONUS: **Mother Nature offers a complete health-boosting package in avocados. Rich in oleic acid, a monounsaturated fat, the creamy fruit may help improve cholesterol levels. Avocados also contain concentrated amounts of lutein and other carotenoids.**

# Wild Mushroom Tamale Pie

*Serves 4.*

Chef Jason Gaskins' relationship with San Francisco's thriving local organic farming movement results in stunning healthy fare at his Roots restaurant. Don't fret if you can't make it to San Fran, though – here's one of Jason's fresh and fuss-free creations for you to try at home.

## INGREDIENTS:

- 2 cups yellow onion, finely diced
- 2 Tbsp olive oil
- 1 Tbsp garlic, finely diced
- 3 cups vine-ripened tomatoes, diced, divided
- 2 cups vegetable stock
- 2 ears fresh corn kernels
- 1 cup black trumpet mushrooms or any seasonal exotic mushroom

## SEASON TO TASTE WITH:

- Ground cayenne pepper
- Kosher salt
- Fresh ground black pepper
- Fresh ground cumin

## TO GARNISH:

- 1 cup prepared corn bread batter (TRY: Bob's Red Mill Cornbread Mix)
- 2 oz goat cheese, crumbled
- 2 Tbsp cilantro, chopped

## INSTRUCTIONS:

ONE: Preheat oven to 350°F.

TWO: In a saucepot, sauté onion with olive oil until translucent. Add garlic, without caramelizing. Then add half of the tomatoes and reduce heat to simmer for about 20 to 30 minutes.

THREE: In a sauté pan, bring vegetable stock to a boil. Add corn and a pinch of cayenne pepper. Cook for about 3 minutes and then add remaining tomatoes and all of the mushrooms. Continue cooking for another few minutes and then add this mixture to the saucepot.

FOUR: Season mixture to taste with cayenne, salt, pepper and cumin.

FIVE: Spoon the mixture into casserole dishes. Using a soup spoon, dollop each surface with corn bread batter, making a pattern of uniform dots.

SIX: Bake for 10 to 15 minutes, until golden brown.

SEVEN: Garnish with dime-sized pieces of goat cheese and a sprinkle of cilantro.

*Nutrients per serving: Calories: 320, Total Fat: 7 g, Sat. Fat: 3.5 g, Omega-3: 20 mg, Omega-6: 540 mg, Carbs: 53 g, Fiber: 7 g, Sugars: 12 g, Protein: 13 g, Sodium: 500 mg, Cholesterol: 15 mg*

# Maitake Mushroom Pesto over Pasta

*Serves 6. **Hands-on time:** 10 minutes. **Total time:** 30 minutes.*

This tasty spin works with pasta, wild rice, risotto and even spread on sandwiches.

## INGREDIENTS:

- 12 oz whole-wheat penne or rotini pasta
- 3 Tbsp safflower oil, divided
- 2 cloves garlic, coarsely chopped
- ½ cup coarsely chopped white onion
- 7 oz maitake mushrooms, coarsely chopped
- Pinch sea salt
- ¼ cup unsalted walnuts
- ¼ cup fresh grated Parmesan cheese
- ¾ cup packed fresh basil leaves, washed and dried
- ¾ cup fresh Italian parsley leaves, washed and dried
- 2 Tbsp chopped fresh basil leaves

## INSTRUCTIONS:

ONE: Cook pasta according to package directions until al dente, stirring occasionally, about 12 to 15 minutes.

TWO: Heat 1 Tbsp oil in a large nonstick skillet over medium-high. Add garlic and onion and sauté for about 2 minutes. Add mushrooms and salt and sauté until liquid has evaporated and mushrooms are soft, about 6 to 8 minutes.

THREE: Transfer mushroom mixture to a food processor fitted with a standard blade. Add walnuts, Parmesan, basil, parsley and remaining 2 Tbsp oil. Pulse until finely minced.

FOUR: Drain pasta and toss with pesto. Garnish with chopped basil and serve.

*Nutrients per 1½-cup serving: Calories: 336, Total Fat: 13 g, Sat. Fat: 1 g, Monounsaturated Fat: 6 g, Polyunsaturated Fat: 3 g, Carbs: 48 g, Fiber: 7 g, Sugars: 3 g, Protein: 10 g, Sodium: 86 mg, Cholesterol: 3 mg*

Maitake Mushroom Pesto over Pasta

Butternut
Squash
Lasagna

# Butternut Squash Lasagna
## WITH CARAMELIZED ONIONS & WALNUTS

*Serves 12. **Hands-on time:** 30 minutes. **Total time:** 2 hours. \**

**Butternut squash layered with our Everyday Marinara Sauce provides a creamy, sweet base for this protein-packed vegetarian lasagna. For more on how to pick, prepare and cook squash, see p. 206.**

**\*TIME SAVERS: Try roasting the squash the evening before you put this lasagna together. You can even roast two – enjoy one for dinner tonight and slide the other into the fridge for tomorrow's lasagna. The caramelized onions may also be prepared ahead of time. Prepare both in large batches and refrigerate in 1-cup servings. To use, simply drain any excess water and use as desired. By using these time-saving tips, you can whip up our veggie lasagna in about 1 hour!**

### INGREDIENTS:

- 1 medium butternut squash (about 2 lbs)
- 2 tsp olive oil, divided
- 3 medium Spanish onions, thinly sliced
- 1 cup low-fat ricotta cheese
- ⅛ tsp ground nutmeg
- 4 large egg whites
- ¼ cup grated Parmesan cheese
- 10 sage leaves, finely chopped
- ⅛ tsp sea salt
- Fresh ground black pepper, to taste
- 2 cups shredded part-skim mozzarella cheese
- 2½ cups Everyday Marinara Sauce (see recipe, p. 133)
- ½ lb oven-ready whole-wheat lasagna noodles (about 12 noodles; TRY: DeLallo Organic Whole Wheat No-Boil Lasagna)
- ⅓ cup coarsely chopped walnuts, toasted

### INSTRUCTIONS:

**ONE:** Preheat oven to 375°F.

**TWO:** Cut squash in half lengthwise and scoop out seeds. Lightly brush cut sides with 1 tsp oil and place, cut sides down, onto a parchment-lined baking tray. Bake in oven for 25 minutes, until squash is tender when pierced with a fork. Remove from oven and let cool to room temperature.

**THREE:** Meanwhile, heat remaining 1 tsp oil in a large sauté pan over medium-high. Add onions, stir and sauté for 2 to 3 minutes, until onions begin to soften. Reduce heat to medium-low and continue to cook for about 40 minutes, stirring frequently, until onions are very soft and golden brown. Remove from heat and set aside until cooled to room temperature.

**FOUR:** Scoop out flesh of squash into the bowl of a food processor. Add ricotta, nutmeg, egg whites and Parmesan and process until smooth. Add sage and season with salt and pepper. Transfer mixture to a large mixing bowl and gently fold in caramelized onions.

**FIVE:** Reserve ½ cup mozzarella, cover and refrigerate until needed. Assemble lasagna: Cover bottom of 9 x 13-inch casserole dish with about ½ cup Everyday Marinara Sauce. Top with a single layer of lasagna noodles, overlapping slightly, then 1 cup butternut squash mixture and ½ cup mozzarella. Repeat layers once, starting with ½ cup Everyday Marinara Sauce. Sprinkle walnuts evenly over mozzarella. Repeat layers once again. Finish with ½ cup Everyday Marinara Sauce, a layer of noodles, remaining butternut squash (about ⅓ cup, depending on size of squash) and remaining ½ cup Everyday Marinara Sauce. Cover dish with foil, place onto a baking tray and bake in oven for 45 minutes at 375°F. Remove foil, top lasagna with reserved ½ cup mozzarella and bake for an additional 15 minutes.

**SIX:** Remove lasagna from oven and allow to rest and set for 15 to 20 minutes before cutting into 12 servings. Enjoy! Lasagna can be kept frozen for up to 3 months, refrigerated for 2 to 3 days.

**OPTION: Set a small bowl with additional heated Everyday Marinara Sauce at your table so your family members can drizzle even more over top of their lasagna, if they'd like.**

*Nutrients per 1½-cup serving: Calories: 260, Total Fat: 9 g, Sat. Fat: 3 g, Monounsaturated Fat: 2 g, Polyunsaturated Fat: 2 g, Carbs: 34 g, Fiber: 7 g, Sugars: 8 g, Protein: 14 g, Sodium: 250 mg, Cholesterol: 20 mg*

# Holiday Meals

Above: Roast Tenderloin of Beef with Orange & Garlic Gremolata, p. 204
Top Right: Farro Pilaf with Toasted Pine Nuts, Dried Apricots & Cranberries, p. 209
Lower Right: Steamed Broccolini with Caramelized Pearl-Onion Garnish, p. 209

# Your Holiday Menu

It's time to get excited about the holidays because *Clean Eating* magazine is here with a stress-free menu that keeps on giving. Our collection of holiday recipes contains classic, guiltless and fuss-free favorites, meaning less time in the kitchen and more time visiting with family and friends – not to mention, no concern of working off excess fat and calories in the New Year. Win, win, win!

# Roast Tenderloin of Beef
## WITH ORANGE & GARLIC GREMOLATA

*Serves 10. **Hands-on time:** 20 minutes. **Total time:** 55 minutes.*

"Elegance" is the perfect word for this main course, especially when accented with gremolata (a classic, savory mixture of minced parsley, garlic and citrus peel). When armed with an instant-read meat thermometer, any cook can succeed with this recipe – even a novice.

### INGREDIENTS:

**BEEF TENDERLOIN**

- 1 2¾-lb beef tenderloin
- 1½ Tbsp extra-virgin olive oil
- 1 Tbsp fresh thyme leaves, minced
- 1 large clove garlic, minced
- ½ tsp sea salt
- ¾ tsp fresh ground black pepper

**GREMOLATA**

- 4 large cloves garlic, minced
- Zest 2 large oranges
- 1 cup minced flat-leaf parsley

**NOTE: Ask your butcher to provide you with a peeled, tied and roast-ready tenderloin of beef. If the butcher is willing, have the tapered end tucked under and tied so it is about the same thickness as the other end. This way the roast will cook evenly.**

### INSTRUCTIONS:

**ONE:** Prepare gremolata: In a small bowl, thoroughly combine garlic, orange zest and parsley. Cover and set aside until ready to serve.

**TWO:** Prepare beef tenderloin: Remove tenderloin from refrigerator 1½ hours before cooking. Position rack in center of oven. Preheat oven to 400°F. Line a large rimmed baking sheet or pan with aluminum foil and place roasting rack on baking sheet (with 1-inch sides).

**THREE:** Rub oil all over tenderloin. In a small bowl, combine thyme, garlic, salt and pepper. Rub garlic mixture all over tenderloin. Place tenderloin on roasting rack in baking sheet or pan.

**FOUR:** Roast tenderloin for 25 minutes, then check internal temperature using an instant-read meat thermometer. Remove tenderloin when internal temperature is 125°F to 130°F for medium-rare or 130° to 140°F for medium doneness. The tenderloin may take anywhere from 25 to 35 minutes to roast, depending on your oven, exact weight of meat and desired level of doneness.

**FIVE:** Transfer meat to carving board and tent with foil. Let meat rest for 10 minutes to allow juices to set. Temperature of meat will increase another 5°F to 10°F as meat rests. Carve across the grain into ½-inch-thick slices. Serve, sprinkled generously with Orange & Garlic Gremolata.

**Nutrients per serving (4 oz beef and 1 Tbsp gremolata):** *Calories: 156, Total Fat: 6.5 g, Sat. Fat: 2 g, Monounsaturated Fat: 3 g, Polyunsaturated Fat: 0.25 g, Carbs: 6 g, Fiber: 0.5 g, Sugars: 0 g, Protein: 25 g, Sodium: 160 mg, Cholesterol: 66 mg*

**NUTRITIONAL BONUS: While slightly higher in saturated fat than other lean proteins, beef is a rich source of niacin, vitamins B6 and B12, iron, zinc and selenium. More than 60 different bodily enzymes require vitamin B6 to perform properly, while vitamin B12 relies upon its B cousin for assistance in adequate absorption of nutrients into your body.**

For a photo of this recipe, see page 202.

# Delicata Squash Soup

WITH POPCORN-SAGE GARNISH

*Serves* 10. ***Hands-on time:*** *25 minutes.* ***Total time:*** *1 hour, 10 minutes.*

**Delicata squash is a naturally sweet winter squash with smooth, nearly fiber-less flesh. Its beautiful yellow flesh and subtle flavor make it perfect for this seasonal puréed soup. To counterbalance the creamy texture, we've added popped popcorn as a fun, whimsical garnish that delivers an herbaceous flavor and crunch.**

**BUY IT: When buying delicata squash, look for firm cylindrical-shaped squash that have elongated ridges and yellow to pale-orange skin with green striations.**

## INGREDIENTS:

- 2 lb delicata squash, halved lengthwise and seeded
- 2 large Granny Smith apples (about 1 lb), unpeeled, halved lengthwise and cored
- 1 large clove garlic, halved lengthwise
- 2 Tbsp olive oil
- 4 cups low-sodium chicken broth, divided
- ½ cup low-fat sour cream
- ¼ tsp ground nutmeg
- 1 tsp sea salt
- Fresh ground white and/or black pepper, to taste

## GARNISH

- 1¼ cups air-popped popcorn
- 1¼ tsp finely minced fresh sage

## INSTRUCTIONS:

**ONE:** Preheat oven to 350°F.

**TWO:** Brush cut sides of squash, apples and garlic with oil. Arrange them, cut side down, on a large rimmed baking sheet. Tuck garlic under squash, placing halves in hollowed-out cavity. Roast in oven until squash and apples are tender when pierced with a fork, about 30 minutes. Set aside to cool slightly, about 20 minutes.

**THREE:** Using a spoon, scoop flesh from squash and apples; discard skins. Place roasted squash, apples and garlic in the bowl of a food processor fitted with a metal blade. Process to a smooth purée. Add 2 cups broth and continue processing until smooth. Transfer squash mixture to a medium saucepan over medium heat and add remaining 2 cups broth, sour cream, nutmeg and salt. Bring mixture to a simmer but do not boil. Cook for 10 minutes. Season with pepper, set aside and keep warm.

**FOUR:** Transfer popcorn to a bowl and toss with sage. To serve, ladle soup into warmed bowls and garnish with sage popcorn.

**Nutrients per ¾-cup serving:** *Calories: 100, Total Fat: 2 g, Sat. Fat: 1 g, Carbs: 19 g, Fiber: 3 g, Sugars: 8 g, Protein: 4 g, Sodium: 232 mg, Cholesterol: 65 mg*

# Squash

## Don't let its tough exterior fool you. Deep down, winter squash yields sweet and delicious flesh just waiting to be discovered.

If you're more inclined to make an autumn centerpiece out of hard squash than eat it, you're not alone. Cutting into the rough and bumpy outer shell can be intimidating, but that protective layer is actually a good thing. Thick-walled "winter" squash are harvested in the fall and can last up to six months without much special storage.

Irregular shapes and a subtly colored palette of stripes, dots and blemishes are some of the distinguishing traits of the squash family, which is made up of more than 100 unique members – no two are exactly alike. However, only a few types are well known and readily available: acorn, buttercup, butternut, hubbard and spaghetti squash.

Just like pumpkins, squash are native to Central America and part of the gourd family. They're the fruit of ground-covering vine plants that develop to maturity before they're picked, forming a hard rind surrounding dozens of tough seeds. But, unlike most common pumpkins, squash contain a smaller seed cavity and far more edible flesh. Zucchini, yellow squash and patty pans are also part of the squash family. They are harvested in the summer while still young and don't develop a thick rind. For this reason, summer squash don't last as long as winter squash, and they require just a short cooking time.

Undoubtedly a super-nutritious food choice, squash is an especially good source of fiber and beta-carotene, which may help protect you from the development of inflammation, heart disease and some cancers. The flesh of most squash is slightly sweet and can easily be incorporated into dishes ranging from soups and pasta to custards and pies. Getting past the rough exterior is truly worth a little extra effort, and you'll find the tasty and healthy rewards to be far more than skin deep.

### What You'll Need:

- Heavy-duty vegetable peeler
- Sharp chef's or Santoku knife
- Large spoon
- Rimmed baking sheet
- Heavy-duty foil
- Fork or skewer
- Olive oil & salt

## Squash the confusion

Part of the uncertainty with squash may be the fact that there are so many ways to prepare it. Squash can be cooked whole, in halves, in pieces or grated. It can be roasted, steamed, boiled, microwaved or stuffed. Let your recipe determine the best way to prepare the squash.

**COOKED WHOLE:** Easiest method for most small squash. Cut off top 1 inch of stem end before cooking (baking is usually the best method).

**COOKED IN HALVES OR LARGE PIECES:** Easiest method for most larger squash, because cutting into pieces reduces cooking time. Best for recipes where squash will be served as halves or pieces, mashed, scooped out of shells or puréed.

**PEELED AND DICED BEFORE COOKING:** Best for recipes where shape and size of diced squash needs be retained (not mashed or puréed), such as adding to stews, casseroles, pastas, salads or the Butternut Squash Risotto recipe on p. 193.

# How to Prep and Cook: Butternut Squash

ONE: Butternut is the easiest type of squash to peel before cooking because of its thin, smooth skin. Using a heavy-duty vegetable peeler, peel strips of skin from squash away from your body.

TWO: Cut ½ inch off the top and bottom of squash, then slice squash in half lengthwise. Scoop out the seeds with a spoon.

THREE: Dice squash into uniform-sized pieces.

FOUR: Toss squash pieces with a little olive oil and sprinkle with sea salt. Spread pieces in a single layer on a rimmed baking sheet. Bake in a 425°F oven until pieces are tender (easily pierced with a fork), 25 to 35 minutes, stirring every 10 minutes.

# How to Prep and Cook: Acorn Squash

ONE: Cut about ½ inch off the bottom end of the squash. This will make it easier to peel after baking and provides a flat edge for safer and easier cutting. (If stem is still attached to other end of squash, break it off.)

TWO: Position squash so it sits on flat end. Slice straight down through stem end to cut squash in half.

THREE: Scoop out seeds, rub a little olive oil over cut sides of squash and sprinkle with sea salt. Place halves cut side down on a foil-lined baking sheet. Bake in a 400°F oven until flesh is tender, 30 to 40 minutes. To test squash for doneness, stick a fork in the squash. If the fork meets just a little resistance, squash is good consistency for peeling and dicing. If fork slides easily in and out with no resistance, squash is good consistency for eating from shell, mashing or puréeing.

FOUR: To peel, set squash aside on baking sheet until cool enough to handle, about 5 minutes. Pull off strips of skin starting at the cut end.

# How to Prep and Cook: Spaghetti Squash

ONE: Hold squash firmly with one hand. Use a metal skewer or fork to poke holes over entire surface of squash to prevent it from bursting during baking. Place squash on a rimmed baking sheet and bake in oven at 400°F for 30 to 45 minutes, until soft.

TWO: When squash is cool enough to handle, cut it in half lengthwise.

THREE: Scoop out the seeds with a spoon.

FOUR: Scrape the flesh of the squash with a fork in a grating and twirling motion to shred the flesh and pull it away from the skin. Scoop shredded flesh onto a serving dish and finish as desired: Toss with extra-virgin olive oil, salt and pepper or serve with a clean sauce of choice.

**Farro Pilaf**

**Steamed Broccolini**

# Farro Pilaf

## WITH TOASTED PINE NUTS, DRIED APRICOTS & CRANBERRIES

*Serves 12. **Hands-on time:** 35 minutes. **Total time:** 40 minutes.*

Farro is one of the oldest un-hybridized forms of wheat – a whole grain with a sweet, nutty flavor and a firm, chewy texture, which it retains when cooked and reheated.

### INGREDIENTS:

- 4 cups low-sodium chicken broth
- 2 cups whole-grain farro
- ¾ cup unsalted pine nuts
- 2 Tbsp olive oil
- 1 large clove garlic, minced
- 1 yellow onion, diced
- 1 large carrot, trimmed and diced
- 1 large stalk celery, trimmed and diced
- 1 Tbsp finely chopped fresh thyme leaves
- ½ cup unsweetened dried cranberries
- ½ cup unsweetened dried apricots, diced
- ½ tsp each sea salt and fresh ground black pepper

**COOKING TIP:** While farro packages call for soaking the grains, this prep step has been removed from our Farro Pilaf recipe. When soaked in water, farro grains swell but do not gain flavor. That's why we've boosted taste by permeating the grains with the flavor of low-sodium chicken broth.

### INSTRUCTIONS:

**ONE:** Bring broth and 2 cups water to a boil in a 6-qt saucepan. Add farro, reduce heat so liquid just simmers and cook farro for about 20 to 25 minutes, until soft but still a bit firm at the center. Drain farro in a sieve placed over a heatproof bowl, reserving liquid. Place farro in a separate bowl and set aside.

**TWO:** While farro is cooking, toast nuts: Place a small heavy skillet over medium-high heat. When hot but not smoking, add nuts. Stirring constantly, toast until nicely browned, about 3 to 5 minutes. Transfer nuts to a plate and set aside to cool.

**THREE:** In a large sauté pan, heat oil over medium and swirl to coat pan. Add garlic, onion, carrot and celery and sauté, stirring frequently, until vegetables are soft but not brown, about 5 minutes. Add thyme, cranberries, apricots, salt and pepper. Sauté until softened slightly, 2 minutes longer. Add reserved farro and ⅔ cup reserved cooking liquid. Stir to combine, then stir in nuts. Remove mixture from heat, cover and set aside until ready to serve. Warm just before serving.

*Nutrients per ½-cup serving: Calories: 168, Total Fat: 9 g, Sat. Fat: 2 g, Monounsaturated Fat: 4 g, Polyunsaturated Fat: 3 g, Carbs: 20 g, Fiber: 3 g, Sugars: 7 g, Protein: 5 g, Sodium: 118 mg, Cholesterol: 0 mg*

**NUTRITIONAL BONUS:** Farro is an excellent source of complex carbohydrates and offers more than twice the amount of protein and fiber found in modern wheat. In addition, farro contains a special type of carbohydrate called cyanogenic glucosides, which helps strengthen the immune system and lower cholesterol.

# Steamed Broccolini

## WITH CARAMELIZED PEARL-ONION GARNISH

*Serves 12. **Hands-on time:** 20 minutes. **Total time:** 25 minutes.*

Broccolini, sometimes called baby broccoli, is a hybrid of broccoli and Chinese kale. It has a long, slender, juicy stem that is entirely edible and it is topped with small flowering buds. Its flavor is sweeter and more delicate than broccoli, so cook this baby variety briefly to retain its glorious green color and desired crispness.

### INGREDIENTS:

- 2 Tbsp olive oil
- 2 cups frozen pearl onions, thawed and halved lengthwise
- 1½ Tbsp raw honey
- ¼ tsp sea salt
- ½ tsp red pepper flakes (aka crushed red pepper)
- 1½ lb broccolini, bottom ends trimmed ⅛ inch

### INSTRUCTIONS:

**ONE:** Set a steamer basket in a large pot filled with 1 to 2 inches of water, making sure water is below the level of the basket. Cover pot with a tight-fitting lid and bring water to a boil. Turn heat to low and continue simmering.

**TWO:** In a medium sauté pan over medium-high heat, warm oil and swirl to coat pan. Add onions and sauté, until they begin to brown at edges, about 3 minutes. Add honey and salt. Continue to sauté, stirring constantly, until caramelized at edges, about 5 minutes. Add pepper flakes, stir and remove mixture from heat.

**THREE:** When onions are almost glazed and golden, arrange broccolini in steamer and steam for 3 minutes, until bright green and tender-crisp. Arrange broccolini on warm platter, scatter onions over top and serve immediately.

*Nutrients per 3-oz serving: Calories: 62, Total Fat: 2.5 g, Sat. Fat: 0.5 g, Carbs: 8 g, Fiber: 1.5 g, Sugars: 2 g, Protein: 3 g, Sodium: 57 mg, Cholesterol: 0 mg*

**NUTRITIONAL BONUS:** A member of the brassica family (relatives include Brussels sprouts, cauliflower, kale, bok choy and rutabagas), broccolini is packed with isothiocyanates, sulforaphane and indoles (aka indole-3-carbinol), phytochemicals studied for their reputed disease-fighting – especially anti-carcinogenic – properties. But such plant compounds may be diminished or lost in cooking water, so try eating your cruciferous vegetables raw or steamed (as shown here).

# 10 Common Cooking Mistakes
## ...and how to avoid them

Measuring, mixing, searing and seasoning. These are the everyday details of cooking, and with so much to consider – often simultaneously – mistakes are inevitable. To err is human, but to learn from your mistakes is divine. So, here we tell you how to avoid making the same mistake more than once.

### COOKING MISTAKE 1
### MAKING UNINFORMED SUBSTITUTIONS

Swapping one ingredient for another doesn't always work, though the ingredients may seem to be interchangeable. Subbing baking powder for baking soda, for example, can result in baked goods that don't rise properly.

**FIX:** Of course, some substitutions work well: You can swap skim milk for whole milk, arrowroot for flour, and raw honey for white sugar. But it's easy to make mistakes. So, to help make all of your substitutions smart ones, consult David Joachim's *The Food Substitutions Bible*, 2nd ed. (Robert Rose, 2010).

## COOKING MISTAKE 2
## NOT PREHEATING YOUR PAN

If you put cold food into cold oil in a cold pan, the food simply absorbs the fat before it gets hot enough to cook on top of the fat, making for heavy, oily foods.

**FIX:** Preheat your pan for at least a couple of minutes, add your oil and then wait until you can see it shimmer before adding room temperature food (you should hear it sizzle). Preheating also helps keep food from sticking. If your food still sticks, it simply means the food hasn't developed a crust yet – wait a bit longer and it should release easily.

## COOKING MISTAKE 3
## CROWDING THE PAN

When you want to speed up cooking, the temptation to pile too much food into a skillet is strong. "Resist the urge," advises Cheryl Sternman Rule, author of the forthcoming *Ripe: Satisfy Your Lust for Fruits and Vegetables with 75 Fresh Recipes and Hundreds of Simple Combinations* (Running Press).

**FIX:** "For best results, give your food room to breathe, and work in batches whenever necessary," says Rule. Why? Because food releases moisture as it cooks. If there's too much food in the pan, you'll end up steaming instead of searing, sacrificing flavor and texture.

## COOKING MISTAKE 4
## BEING AFRAID OF HEAT

If you cook on heat that's too low, your food might never brown, which means you'll miss out on the delicious flavors that browning adds. "Plus, a golden-brown sear helps keep foods juicy and tender," says Lucy Vaserfirer, author of *Seared to Perfection: The Simple Art of Sealing in Flavor* (Harvard Common Press, 2010).

**FIX:** Know when to use high heat, such as with roasts that are being seared before going into the oven, thinner foods like fish fillets, or foods that don't need to be cooked through, like a medium-rare steak. Use lower heat with thicker foods that need to be cooked throughout and cannot remain pink in the center.

## COOKING MISTAKE
# 5 NOT LETTING COOKED **MEAT REST**

Cutting into meat right after cooking discharges its juices. "As meat increases in temperature so does its kinetic energy, causing its fibers to vibrate, contract and expel their juices," says Adam Danforth, a professional butcher in New York City.

**FIX:** When you let meat rest after cooking – at least 10 minutes – it allows the muscle fibers to relax and reabsorb their juices. The result is "a lot more juice, and flavor, exploding into your mouth instead of onto your plate," observes Danforth.

## COOKING MISTAKE
# 6 BEING **AFRAID** OF SALT

"Most Americans eat far too much salt in the many processed foods they consume," notes Robin Asbell, a Minneapolis chef, culinary instructor and author of *The New Vegetarian* (Chronicle Books, 2009). But don't let that scare you into cutting it out completely. (If you practice clean eating, your daily sodium intake is probably at a safe and healthy level: 1,500 milligrams or less daily).

**FIX:** Wonder why recipes for baked goods call for salt? "It acts to even out the way yeast rises, so it doesn't all bloom at once," Asbell says. "It also strengthens the gluten strands in breads, giving them structure." Look for lesser-refined salts (think *CE*-approved sea salt) to use in baking and cooking. "Not only do they come loaded with beneficial trace minerals, but they also boast more flavor, so a little goes a longer way." Plus, as a flavoring agent, a bit of sea salt really can make food taste better. Asbell explains that "a pinch keeps foods from tasting flat. It brings out the sweetness that you would otherwise miss. In the kitchen, add a pinch while cooking and then a pinch at the end, so you get two levels of flavor."

## COOKING MISTAKE
# 7 **STORING OILS AND SPICES** ON OR ABOVE YOUR STOVE OR OVEN

You may love seeing your favorite ingredients on display, but the surrounding heat is conducive to rancidity and flavor loss. And keeping oil in the refrigerator is far from ideal, since the conditions are too humid for it.

**FIX:** Keep oils and spices in a cool, dark place – a cupboard away from the stove or oven is perfect.

## COOKING MISTAKE 8: SCOOPING TOO MUCH FLOUR

Many people scoop or pour flour, which can result in too much and ruin your baked goods, according to Jill O'Connor, author of *Sticky, Chewy, Messy, Gooey: Desserts for the Serious Sweet Tooth* (Chronicle Books, 2007).

**FIX:** To measure correctly, O'Connor says, "Stir the flour to lighten it, spoon it into your measuring cup until it overflows, then scrape off the excess with the back of a knife."

MISTAKE

FIX

## COOKING MISTAKE 9: FOLLOWING OLD WIVES' TALES WHEN COOKING PASTA

You put oil in the water before you cook your pasta; you rinse your noodles once they're cooked; you overcook your pasta. Find out how to avoid these gaffes from Janet Fletcher, author of *Four Seasons Pasta* (Chronicle Books, 2004).

**FIX: DON'T POUR OIL INTO THE WATER PRIOR TO COOKING.** "It makes pasta slick, while you want pasta to be rough so the sauce will cling," says Fletcher. Instead, to keep boiling pasta from clumping, use plenty of water to begin with, and stir every two or three minutes.

**DON'T RINSE YOUR PASTA AFTER IT'S COOKED.** "This cools pasta off, and pasta should be eaten hot," explains Fletcher. "Also, it rinses off the starch, and starch helps thicken the sauce."

**DON'T COOK BEYOND AL DENTE.** "Pasta loses all its charm if it doesn't have some bite. It shouldn't be chalky in the center, but it should have a pleasing firmness."

**213**

## COOKING MISTAKE 10: OVER-MIXING BATTERS

There's a reason that muffin, pancake and cake recipes say "stir until just combined" – if you overdo it, you'll develop the wheat's gluten, which can make your baked goods tough and chewy.

**FIX:** "While it's counter-intuitive, a few lumps are key to light and tender baked goods," notes Charmian Christie, a food writer and recipe developer from Guelph, Ontario. "So be lazy and 'stir until just combined.' Your muffins, pancakes and family will thank you."

# Apple Strudel
## WITH CINNAMON HONEY CREAM CHEESE SAUCE

*Serves* 12. **Hands-on time:** *45 minutes.* **Total time:** *1 hour, 30 minutes.*

**The trick to working with phyllo is to thaw it overnight in the refrigerator and then allow it to come to room temperature before using it, keeping it tightly sealed in its original packaging. This allows the phyllo to thaw slowly, which, in turn, prevents sticking and cracking.**

INGREDIENTS:

- 2½ lb Golden Delicious apples (about 5 large apples), peeled, cored and roughly chopped
- 1 cup unsweetened raisins
- 1 cup chopped unsalted walnuts, toasted
- 3 Tbsp raw honey
- 1 tsp pure vanilla extract
- 1 tsp ground cinnamon
- ¼ tsp ground nutmeg
- 12 sheets frozen whole-wheat or spelt phyllo, thawed
- 4 Tbsp olive oil
- ½ cup whole-wheat bread crumbs

INSTRUCTIONS:

ONE: Arrange rack in center of oven and preheat oven to 400°F. Line a large rimmed baking sheet with either parchment paper or a silicone baking mat.

TWO: In a large bowl, combine apples, raisins, walnuts, honey, vanilla, cinnamon and nutmeg; set aside.

THREE: Arrange 1 sheet of phyllo on a clean work surface, long edge parallel to the counter's edge. Using a pastry brush, brush a minimal amount of oil onto phyllo, then evenly scatter 2 tsp bread crumbs over top. Place another phyllo sheet directly on top. Again, brush with oil and scatter bread crumbs. Repeat layers for a total of 6 sheets of phyllo. Do not brush oil or scatter bread crumbs on top layer. Spread half of apple filling into a long log on top of phyllo sheets, leaving 1 inch at bottom and sides of phyllo. Snugly roll all phyllo layers over filling, jelly roll style, tucking in sides after first roll covers filling. Repeat steps to assemble and roll a second strudel with remaining 6 phyllo sheets and remaining half of apple filling. You should be left with 2 rolls, each measuring approximately 3 x 16 inches. Carefully transfer both rolls to baking sheet and brush rolls with oil.

FOUR: Bake strudels until deep golden brown and crisp, about 30 to 40 minutes. Transfer baking sheet to wire rack to cool. To serve, use a serrated knife to cut each roll crosswise into 6 portions. Serve warm or at room temperature with 1 Tbsp Cinnamon Honey Cream Cheese Sauce.

*Nutrients per serving (3 oz strudel and 1 Tbsp sauce): Calories: 294, Total Fat: 14 g, Sat. Fat: 2.5 g, Monounsaturated Fat: 5.5 g, Polyunsaturated Fat: 5 g, Carbs: 42 g, Fiber: 3.5 g, Sugars: 18 g, Protein: 4 g, Sodium: 150 mg, Cholesterol: 5 mg*

THE BEST OF CLEAN EATING 2

# How to Prep, Fill & Roll Your Apple Strudel

ONE: Arrange 1 sheet of phyllo on a clean work surface, long edge parallel to the counter's edge. Using a pastry brush, brush a minimal amount of oil onto phyllo, then evenly scatter 2 tsp bread crumbs over top.

TWO: Place another phyllo sheet directly on top. Again, brush with oil and scatter bread crumbs. Repeat layers for a total of 6 sheets of phyllo. Do not brush oil or scatter bread crumbs on top layer.

THREE: Spread half of apple filling into a long log on top of phyllo sheets, leaving 1 inch at bottom and sides of phyllo.

FOUR: Snugly roll all phyllo layers over filling, jelly roll style, tucking in sides after first roll covers filling. (NOTE: Tucking in sides to enclose filling will keep ends secure when phyllo is baked.)

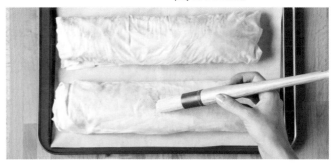

FIVE: Repeat steps to assemble and roll a second strudel with remaining 6 phyllo sheets and remaining half of apple filling. You should be left with 2 rolls, each measuring approximately 3 x 16 inches. Carefully transfer both rolls to a parchment-lined baking sheet and brush rolls with oil.

# Cinnamon Honey Cream Cheese Sauce

*Makes ²/₃ cup sauce. Total time: 5 minutes.*

**To maximize the flavor and consistency of this sweet sauce, remove it from the refrigerator about 30 minutes before serving.**

**INGREDIENTS:**

- ½ cup low-fat plain cream cheese (4 oz), at room temperature
- 2 Tbsp raw honey
- 2 Tbsp skim milk
- ¼ tsp ground cinnamon

**INSTRUCTIONS:**

In a small bowl, beat together all ingredients until evenly blended and smooth. Cover and refrigerate for at least 1 hour to allow flavors to meld.

# Southern Holiday Menu

Nothing beats celebrating the holidays surrounded by family and friends, good cheer and the savory smells of roasting turkey and pecan pie – except maybe spending them in the snow-free South! If heading South is not an option, at least you can get a little closer to down-home dining by preparing these lean and clean Southern holiday meals right at home. Yes, you read that right – low-fat and low-cal Southern cooking is possible! Best of all, we've preserved all the drool-inspiring flavor.

## ZLT Romaine Wedge Salad
### WITH *CE* RANCH DRESSING

*Serves 8.* **Hands-on time:** *15 minutes.* **Total time:** *1 hour, 15 minutes.*

**Each element of this salad may be prepared the day before for simple assembly at dinner.**

### INGREDIENTS:

- 1 cup cooked chickpeas (aka garbanzo beans; or BPA-free no-salt-added canned chickpeas, drained and rinsed)
- 4 tsp olive oil, divided
- 2 tsp fresh lemon juice
- ½ tsp chile powder
- Sea salt, to taste
- 2 cups grape tomatoes, halved lengthwise
- Fresh ground black pepper, to taste
- 2 medium zucchini, ends trimmed and sliced lengthwise ¼ inch thick
- 4 romaine hearts

**CE RANCH DRESSING**

- ¾ cup nonfat plain Greek yogurt
- ½ cup low-fat buttermilk
- 2 tsp fresh lemon juice
- 1 tsp Dijon mustard
- ½ tsp onion powder
- ¼ tsp garlic powder
- 2 Tbsp chopped fresh chives
- 1 Tbsp chopped fresh dill
- Sea salt and fresh ground black pepper, to taste

### INSTRUCTIONS:

**ONE:** Preheat oven to 400°F. Pat chickpeas dry. In a large bowl, toss chickpeas with 2 tsp oil, lemon juice, chile powder and salt. Transfer to a parchment-lined baking sheet and roast in oven for 35 to 45 minutes, until medium golden brown and crunchy. Allow to cool and set aside.

**TWO:** While chickpeas cool, in a medium bowl, toss tomatoes with 1 tsp oil and season with salt and pepper. Arrange tomatoes, cut side up, on a separate parchment-lined baking sheet and roast at 400°F for 15 to 20 minutes, until lightly browned. Set aside and allow to cool.

**THREE:** Meanwhile, brush zucchini with remaining 1 tsp oil and season with salt and pepper. Arrange on a parchment-lined baking sheet and roast at same time as tomatoes for 8 to 10 minutes, flipping once, until golden brown and softened. Set aside and allow to cool.

**FOUR:** Next, prepare *CE* Ranch Dressing: In a small bowl, whisk together yogurt, buttermilk, lemon juice, Dijon, onion powder, garlic powder, chives and dill until smooth and combined. Season with salt and pepper. Transfer to a sealable container, cover and refrigerate for a minimum of 1 hour or ideally overnight so flavors meld.

**FIVE:** Trim ends from romaine hearts, leaving leaves attached at the stem, and slice in half lengthwise. To assemble salad, arrange romaine pieces, cut side up, on a large platter. Top with zucchini strips. Drizzle with *CE* Ranch Dressing, garnish with tomatoes and crispy chickpeas and serve.

**Nutrients per 4-cup serving:** *Calories: 113, Total Fat: 3 g, Sat. Fat: 0.5 g, Carbs: 15 g, Fiber: 4 g, Sugars: 7 g, Protein: 7.5 g, Sodium: 90 mg, Cholesterol: 0.5 mg*

## Nutritional Bonus:

Buttermilk does not actually contain butter. It was originally the tangy leftover liquid from the butter-churning process. Most often, it is created by adding live active bacterial culture to milk. These active cultures fight bad bacteria and help stimulate the immune system. Also, people who are lactose-intolerant can cook with buttermilk because the cultures convert lactose into the more digestible lactic acid.

ZLT
Romaine
Wedge
Salad

**Creamed Greens Mac 'n' Cheese**

# Creamed Greens Mac 'n' Cheese

*Serves 8.* **Hands-on time:** *25 minutes.* **Total time:** *55 minutes.*

**Trying to get your family to eat dark leafy greens? This dish might just be the ticket. Here we've combined two Southern specialties into one fabulous, decadent dish.**

## INGREDIENTS:

- 2 cups each chopped collard greens, dandelion greens and spinach
- 2 tsp olive oil
- 1 medium yellow onion, diced
- 2 cloves garlic, minced
- 1 Tbsp chopped fresh thyme
- ¼ cup whole-wheat flour
- 3 cups skim milk
- 1 tsp Dijon mustard
- ½ cup low-fat plain cream cheese, softened
- ½ cup nonfat plain Greek yogurt
- 2 cups shredded low-fat cheddar cheese
- ¼ tsp sea salt, plus additional for pasta water
- ¼ tsp fresh ground black pepper
- Pinch each ground cayenne pepper and ground nutmeg
- 4 cups whole-wheat penne or elbow macaroni pasta (8 oz)
- Olive oil cooking spray
- ¾ cup whole-wheat panko bread crumbs
- ¼ cup fresh grated Parmesan cheese

## INSTRUCTIONS:

**ONE:** Preheat oven to 375°F.

**TWO:** Heat a large stockpot on medium-high. Add 3 Tbsp water and greens. Cook, stirring frequently, until just wilted, about 2 minutes. Transfer to a fine mesh strainer, let cool slightly and press to remove excess moisture. Set aside.

**THREE:** In a large saucepan, heat oil on medium-high. Add onion, garlic and thyme and cook, stirring frequently, for 2 to 3 minutes. Stir in flour and cook, stirring constantly, for 1 minute.

**FOUR:** Add milk and bring to a gentle simmer (not a rolling boil), reduce heat to medium and cook, stirring frequently, until thickened slightly, 4 to 6 minutes. Remove from heat and stir in mustard, cream cheese, yogurt, cheddar cheese, salt, pepper, cayenne and nutmeg. Set aside.

**FIVE:** While sauce is simmering, bring a large pot of salted water to a boil. Cook pasta according to package directions until al dente (the shortest cooking time noted on the suggested range). Drain well, reserving ½ cup pasta cooking liquid. Return pasta to pot and stir in cream cheese mixture, wilted greens and reserved pasta cooking liquid until combined. Coat a 9 x 13-inch casserole dish with cooking spray. Transfer pasta mixture to dish. In a small bowl, combine panko and Parmesan. Sprinkle mixture over top of pasta. Bake for about 25 minutes, until golden brown and bubbling.

*Nutrients per 1½-cup serving: Calories: 314, Total Fat: 9.5 g, Sat. Fat: 4 g, Monounsaturated Fat: 1 g, Polyunsaturated Fat: 0.5 g, Carbs: 41.5 g, Fiber: 5 g, Sugars: 7 g, Protein: 21 g, Sodium: 459 mg, Cholesterol: 19 mg*

# Watermelon Mint Sparkling Limeade

*Serves 10. Makes 6 cups.* **Hands-on time:** *15 minutes.* **Total time:** *15 minutes.*

## INGREDIENTS:

- 5 cups diced seedless watermelon, rind removed
- ⅓ cup fresh lime juice
- ⅓ cup fresh orange juice
- 3 Tbsp raw honey
- 1 cup torn fresh mint leaves
- Ice, as desired
- 2 limes, thinly sliced
- 1 cup sparkling water

## INSTRUCTIONS:

**ONE:** Working in batches, purée watermelon, lime juice, orange juice and honey in a blender until smooth. Transfer mixture to a large pitcher, add mint leaves and stir well. (Mixture may be prepared up to 24 hours in advance, covered and refrigerated.)

**TWO:** To serve, pour about ½ cup watermelon limeade into a glass over ice. Top with 2 to 3 lime slices and 2 Tbsp sparkling water.

*Nutrients per serving (½ cup limeade and 2 Tbsp sparkling water): Calories: 62, Total Fat: 0 g, Sat. Fat: 0 g, Carbs: 16 g, Fiber: 1 g, Sugars: 13 g, Protein: 1 g, Sodium: 5 mg, Cholesterol: 0 mg*

# Parmesan Panko Crusted Turkey
## WITH CORNBREAD & SAUSAGE STUFFING

*Serves 14. **Hands-on time:** 30 minutes. **Total time:** 5 hours, 35 minutes.*

Many people save turkey for a holiday meal, but a roast turkey is delicious at any time, and is especially good for leftovers to use throughout the week! Freshly roasted turkey meat is a much healthier alternative to processed deli turkey. You may not want to roast such a large bird, so for a smaller turkey just calculate the cooking time as 17 minutes for every pound the turkey weighs. When preparing a smaller bird, fill the cavity and freeze excess stuffing for future use.

## INGREDIENTS:

### STUFFING

- 1½ lb cornbread loaf, diced into ¾-inch pieces (about 8 cups)
- 2 tsp olive oil
- 3 raw natural turkey sausages, casings removed (3 oz each)
- 1 medium yellow onion, diced
- 3 cloves garlic, minced
- 2 ribs celery, diced
- 1 Tbsp each chopped fresh thyme and sage
- ⅓ cup toasted pumpkin seeds
- ½ cup dried unsweetened cranberries
- ½ cup low-sodium chicken broth
- ¼ cup chopped flat-leaf parsley
- 2 Tbsp fresh lemon juice
- Sea salt and fresh ground black pepper, to taste

### TURKEY SEASONING

- 2 cups whole-wheat panko bread crumbs
- ½ cup fresh grated Parmesan cheese
- 2 Tbsp each chopped fresh sage, flat-leaf parsley and thyme
- 2 Tbsp olive oil,
- 4 cloves garlic, minced
- 1 Tbsp lemon juice
- 1 tsp fresh ground black pepper

### TURKEY & GRAVY

- 2 medium yellow onions, chopped
- 2 medium carrots, peeled and chopped
- 2 ribs celery, chopped
- 4 cloves garlic, peeled
- 6 sprigs fresh thyme
- 4 cups low-sodium chicken broth, divided
- 1 whole turkey, skin removed (14 to 16 lb)
- ½ cup egg whites, whisked until just foamy
- ½ cup whole-wheat flour

## INSTRUCTIONS:

**ONE:** First, prepare stuffing. Preheat oven to 350°F. Divide cornbread among two parchment-lined baking sheets and bake in oven for 20 to 25 minutes, until toasted, stirring once halfway through cooking. Transfer to a large mixing bowl and set aside.

**TWO:** Heat oil in a large sauté pan on medium-high. Add sausages and cook, breaking up meat with a wooden spoon, until browned and no pink remains, about 3 to 4 minutes. Add onion, garlic, celery, thyme and sage to pan. Cook, stirring frequently, for 4 to 5 minutes or until onions are soft and translucent. Transfer mixture to bowl with cornbread.

**THREE:** Add pumpkin seeds, cranberries, broth, parsley and lemon juice to cornbread mixture. Season with salt and pepper. Let cool completely before stuffing turkey.

**FOUR:** Reduce oven temperature to 325°F.

**FIVE:** Prepare turkey seasoning: In a medium bowl, stir together panko, Parmesan, sage, parsley, thyme, oil, garlic, lemon juice and pepper; set aside.

**SIX:** Prepare turkey and gravy: In a large roasting pan fitted with a rack, arrange onions, carrots, celery, garlic, thyme and 3 cups broth below rack. Pat turkey dry with paper towel. Stuff turkey with stuffing, tie turkey legs together, up over cavity using butcher's twine, and cover cavity with aluminum foil.

**SEVEN:** Brush turkey with egg whites all over and sprinkle top and sides with turkey seasoning, lightly pressing into meat. Place turkey on rack and place roasting pan in oven. Roast for 30 minutes, uncovered, until crust starts to turn golden brown. Remove from oven, cover with roasting pan lid or aluminum foil and continue to cook until thermometer inserted into stuffing reads 160°F. Remove foil from whole turkey (leave foil on exposed stuffing) and roast for 20 to 30 minutes more to crisp crust, and until thermometer inserted into deepest part of thigh and stuffing reads 165°F. (**NOTE:** Be careful not to touch bone when testing temperature as bones conduct heat and will be hotter than meat.) Turkey will take about 17 minutes per pound to cook, or 3½ to 4½ hours total.

**EIGHT:** Remove turkey from oven, transfer rack with turkey to a cutting board, cover with foil and let rest for 20 to 30 minutes. Meanwhile, prepare gravy: In a small bowl, whisk flour with 1 cup remaining broth. Set aside. Strain vegetables in roasting pan through a fine mesh strainer over a medium saucepan, pressing gently to extract liquid; discard solids and skim excess fat from surface. Bring to a boil on high heat and add flour-broth mixture. Reduce heat to medium and simmer for 5 minutes, whisking frequently, until thickened.

**NINE:** Remove stuffing from turkey, carve turkey and serve with gravy on the side.

Nutrients per serving (5 oz white meat turkey, 1 cup stuffing, ⅓ cup gravy): Calories: 472, Total Fat: 13 g, Sat. Fat: 3 g, Monounsaturated Fat: 3 g, Polyunsaturated Fat: 1 g, Carbs: 36 g, Fiber: 3 g, Sugars: 11 g, Protein: 54 g, Sodium: 560 mg, Cholesterol: 135 mg

Parmesan
Panko
Crusted
Turkey

## Nutritional Bonus:

You are what you eat (and what your eats eat): Studies have proven that what a turkey eats makes a huge difference in its body composition. The amount of total fat and its composition, the amount of omega-3s and the protein content of turkey all closely depend upon the diet that the turkey has been fed.

# The Best Roasted Brussels Sprouts
## WITH SMOKED PAPRIKA & LEEKS

*Serves 8. Hands-on time: 20 minutes. Total time: 40 minutes.*

**These are not the mushy, stinky Brussels sprouts you may be afraid of! Cooking these little gems in a hot oven gives them a lovely golden brown color and brings out the natural sweetness of both the leeks and the sprouts. Smoked paprika gives the dish a slight bacon flavor, without costing you extra time on the treadmill.**

### INGREDIENTS:

- 2 lb Brussels sprouts
- 3 Tbsp olive oil, divided
- 1 tsp sweet smoked paprika
- ½ tsp ground cumin
- ¼ tsp ground cinnamon
- Sea salt and fresh ground black pepper, to taste
- 3 medium leeks, white and light green parts only, ends trimmed
- 2 Tbsp fresh lemon juice
- ¼ cup fresh grated Parmesan cheese, optional

### INSTRUCTIONS:

**ONE:** Preheat oven to 425°F. Ensure two oven racks are positioned in top and bottom thirds of oven.

**TWO:** Trim ¼ inch from end of each sprout and remove any yellow or blemished outer leaves. Cut sprouts in half through root and place into a large mixing bowl. Toss sprouts with 2 Tbsp oil, paprika, cumin and cinnamon until coated. Season with salt and pepper and transfer to a parchment-lined baking tray, cut sides of sprouts facing down.

**THREE:** Cut leeks in half lengthwise and rinse inside of leek thoroughly. Lightly brush cut sides with remaining 1 Tbsp oil. Season with salt and pepper. Arrange leeks on a second baking tray and place tray on bottom rack of oven. Place sprouts on top rack of oven. Roast for about 15 minutes, until sprouts are golden brown and tender and leeks are softened. Remove both from oven, chop leeks into 1-inch-wide pieces and toss in a large bowl with sprouts. (**NOTE:** For Holiday dinner preparation, prepare recipe to this point, cover and set aside until ready to serve. Warm in oven and proceed to Step Four.)

**FOUR:** Season with lemon juice, salt and pepper and toss until coated. Transfer to a serving platter and sprinkle with Parmesan, if desired.

*Nutrients per 1½-cup serving: Calories: 116, Total Fat: 6 g, Sat. Fat: 1 g, Monounsaturated Fat: 4 g, Polyunsaturated Fat: 1 g, Carbs: 15 g, Fiber: 5 g, Sugars: 4 g, Protein: 4 g, Sodium: 50 mg, Cholesterol: 0 mg*

**Nutritional Bonus:**
Don't turn up your nose at Brussels sprouts; these small but mighty greens contain three separate nutrients that help fight chronic inflammation. Glucosinolate and vitamin K help regulate the body's anti-inflammatory system, while omega-3 fatty acids, a somewhat surprising contributor, are important building blocks for your body's most effective anti-inflammatory molecules.

# Sweet Potato Pecan Pie

*Serves 10.* **Hands-on time:** *20 minutes.*
**Total time:** *1 hour, 40 minutes (plus 2 hours, chilling).*

Sweet Potato Pie is a dish similar to pumpkin pie, but creamier, and is traditionally made with whole milk, sugar, butter and eggs. Instead, we use silken tofu to achieve a creamy custard-like filling. We've also swapped a traditional pie crust for a much lighter oat-based crust.

## INGREDIENTS:

- 2 medium sweet potatoes, peeled and chopped (about 1½ lb or 5 cups)
- 1¼ cups rolled oats
- ¾ cup raw pecan halves, divided
- ⅓ cup white whole-wheat or whole-wheat flour
- ¾ cup Sucanat, divided
- 2 Tbsp plus 2 tsp olive oil, divided
- 1½ tsp pumpkin pie spice, divided
- ⅛ tsp plus ¼ tsp sea salt, divided
- 1 cup firm silken tofu, drained
- 1 tsp pure vanilla extract
- ½ cup unsweetened golden raisins
- 2 Tbsp pure maple syrup

## INSTRUCTIONS:

**ONE:** Place potatoes into a medium saucepan and add enough water to cover by 1 inch. Bring to a boil on high heat and cook until potatoes are tender when pierced with a knife, 12 to 15 minutes. Drain. Transfer potatoes to a food processor and purée until smooth. Transfer to fridge and chill completely, about 30 minutes.

**TWO:** Preheat oven to 350°F.

**THREE:** Prepare crust: In a food processor, purée oats and ¼ cup pecans into a fine powder. Add flour, ¼ cup Sucanat, 2 Tbsp oil, ½ tsp pumpkin pie spice, ⅛ tsp salt and 3 Tbsp water. Pulse until combined. Gently press mixture evenly into the bottom of a nonstick 9-inch springform pan. If mixture sticks to your fingers, dip fingertips in a bit of cold water, shake off excess water and continue to press crust gently. Place pan in oven and bake for 18 to 20 minutes or until crust is golden brown. Remove from oven and let cool completely at room temperature.

**FOUR:** Prepare filling: In food processor, purée tofu, remaining ½ cup Sucanat, vanilla, remaining 1 tsp pumpkin pie spice and remaining ¼ tsp salt until smooth. Add chilled potato purée and pulse until just combined and smooth. Pour into cooled pie crust and smooth top with an offset spatula. Bake pie in oven for 40 to 45 minutes, until filling is just firm in center, light golden on top and cracks begin to form in center of filling. Remove from oven and let cool completely on a wire rack, about 2 hours.

**FIVE:** While pie cools, prepare pecan topping: In a small saucepan on high, heat remaining ½ cup pecans, raisins, maple syrup, remaining 2 tsp oil and 2 Tbsp water until simmering. Reduce heat to medium and simmer, stirring frequently, for 5 minutes, until no liquid is left in pan. Transfer mixture to a bowl and let cool completely (do not handle with fingers or taste until cooled; sugar is extremely hot).

**SIX:** To serve, run a sharp paring knife around outside of pie to loosen from sides. Remove sides from springform pan. Sprinkle pecan topping over top of pie and slice into 10 servings.

**TIP: Dip your knife in water and dry with paper towel after each slice for cleaner cuts.**

Nutrients per 3-inch-wide serving: *Calories: 270, Total Fat: 11 g, Sat. Fat: 1 g, Monounsaturated Fat: 6 g, Polyunsaturated Fat: 2 g, Carbs: 39 g, Fiber: 3.5 g, Sugars: 24 g, Protein: 5 g, Sodium: 91.5 mg, Cholesterol: 0 mg*

# Using Your Holiday Leftovers

The aftermath of a holiday feast isn't always pretty, especially if you're stuck with a fridge full of leftovers. Groan! Yes, they're easy and economical, but how many turkey sandwiches can a person eat? You won't have that problem this year, though, because we've got the goods to breathe new life into what's left of your festive feast. Once you see how easy it is to create a clean and exciting new meal by just adding a few ingredients, you'll be cooking extra servings a lot more often.

## Brussels Sprout & Roasted Tomato Linguine

*Serves 4. **Hands-on time:** 15 minutes. **Total time:** 15 minutes.*

**Planned leftovers are a great time-saver for a busy week. Prepare two to four extra servings of your dinner, cover and refrigerate immediately. Raid your pantry the next day and mix up your leftovers to create new and exciting dishes! We've taken two simple roasted vegetable dishes and combined them into an easy pasta dish using ingredients you likely have in your kitchen.**

### INGREDIENTS:

- Sea salt, to taste
- 8 oz whole-wheat linguine (or your favorite whole-grain or brown rice pasta)
- 1 Tbsp olive oil, divided
- 3 cups leftover The Best Roasted Brussels Sprouts with Smoked Paprika & Leeks, thinly sliced (see recipe, p. 222)
- 2 cloves garlic, minced
- 1 cup leftover roasted grape tomatoes (from ZLT Romaine Wedge Salad; see recipe, p. 216)
- ¼ tsp red chile flakes
- 1 Tbsp fresh lemon juice
- Fresh ground black pepper, to taste
- 2 Tbsp coarsely chopped fresh basil
- 2 Tbsp fresh grated Parmesan cheese

### INSTRUCTIONS:

**ONE:** Bring a large pot of salted water to a boil on high heat. Cook linguine according to package directions. Reserve ¼ cup pasta cooking water and drain through a colander. Return to pot (off heat), toss with 1 tsp oil and keep warm.

**TWO:** Meanwhile, heat remaining 2 tsp oil in a large nonstick skillet on medium-high. Add Brussels sprouts and garlic and cook for 2 to 3 minutes, stirring frequently, until warm. Add ¼ cup water and scrape bottom of skillet with a wooden spoon to remove browned bits. Stir in tomatoes and chile flakes and cook, stirring frequently, until warm, about 2 minutes. Add vegetables to linguine, gently folding until thoroughly mixed. Add reserved pasta cooking water, 2 Tbsp at a time, as needed (it should coat noodles; there should be no water in bottom of pot). Add lemon juice, tossing gently. Season with salt and pepper and divide mixture among four bowls. Sprinkle each bowl with ½ Tbsp each basil and Parmesan. Serve immediately.

**TRY THIS: Substitute the Parmesan cheese with some toasted and crushed unsalted hazelnuts, almonds or walnuts for a little added protein and crunch.**

*Nutrients per 2-cup serving: Calories: 300, Total Fat: 9 g, Sat. Fat: 1.5 g, Monounsaturated Fat: 5 g, Polyunsaturated Fat: 1 g, Carbs: 52 g, Fiber: 9 g, Sugars: 4 g, Protein: 10 g, Sodium: 150 mg, Cholesterol: 2.5 mg*

**Nutritional Bonus:**
Reserving some of the water that the pasta was cooked in is the perfect way to add a rich, luscious feel to any pasta dish without adding additional oils or cream. By using pasta cooking water instead of more olive oil in the latter stages of this dish, you cut a whopping 7 g of fat per serving.

**Brussels Sprout & Roasted Tomato Linguine**

Porcini & Garlic Mashed Potatoes

Butternut Squash Bread Pudding

# Porcini & Garlic Mashed Potatoes

*Serves 6. **Hands-on time:** 20 minutes. **Total time:** 45 minutes.*

Porcini are wild mushrooms with a meaty texture and rich flavor, making them a natural pairing for full-flavored turkey broth. While it's rare to find fresh porcini in the US, they're readily available dried at your local supermarket. Pair this creamy side with virtually any main dish for an add-on that really hits the spot.

## INGREDIENTS:

- 2 lb Russet potatoes, peeled and cut into 1½-inch chunks
- 8 cloves garlic
- ⅔ cup 1% low-fat milk
- ⅔ cup homemade or low-sodium turkey broth (or chicken broth)
- 2 Tbsp chopped dried porcini mushrooms
- 1 Tbsp chopped fresh thyme leaves
- ¼ tsp fine sea salt
- ¼ tsp fresh ground black pepper

## INSTRUCTIONS:

ONE: Place potatoes and garlic in a large saucepan or small stockpot, cover with cool water by 1 inch and bring to a boil over high heat. Cook until potatoes and garlic are very tender, 15 to 18 minutes.

TWO: Meanwhile, in a small saucepan, combine milk, broth and mushrooms. Bring to a simmer over medium heat, cover and set aside.

THREE: Drain potatoes and garlic and return mixture to pot. Add milk-mushroom mixture, thyme, salt and pepper and mash with a potato masher to desired consistency. Garnish with additional thyme leaves, if desired.

Nutrients per ¾-cup serving: *Calories: 149, Total Fat: 0.5 g, Sat. Fat: 0.25 g, Carbs: 32 g, Fiber: 2.5 g, Sugars: 2.5 g, Protein: 5 g, Sodium: 104 mg, Cholesterol: 1.5 mg*

# Butternut Squash Bread Pudding
## WITH FALL HERBS

*Serves 6. **Hands-on time:** 35 minutes. **Total time:** 1 hour, 30 minutes.*

This dish is a deliciously rich, satisfying and versatile way to enjoy your Thanksgiving leftovers: Try it as a light entrée paired with a green salad or as a hearty side dish. Looking for something a bit more substantial tonight at mealtime? You can add up to two cups of shredded cooked turkey to fill out this savory autumn recipe.

## INGREDIENTS:

- 1¼ cups homemade or low-sodium turkey broth (or chicken broth)
- 1¼ cups 1% low-fat milk
- 1½ tsp chopped fresh rosemary leaves
- 1 tsp chopped fresh thyme leaves
- 1 tsp chopped fresh sage leaves
- ¼ tsp fresh ground black pepper
- 1 tsp olive oil
- 1 lb butternut squash, seeded, peeled and cut into ½-inch dice (about 2½ cups)
- 7 large egg whites
- 10 oz crusty artisan whole-wheat bread, crusts left intact, cut or torn into ¾-inch pieces (about 10 cups)
- 3 oz Gruyère cheese, shredded (about 1 cup)
- Olive oil cooking spray

## INSTRUCTIONS:

ONE: In a medium saucepan, combine broth, milk, rosemary, thyme, sage and pepper. Bring to a simmer over medium heat, then remove from heat and set aside to cool slightly.

TWO: Meanwhile, in a large nonstick skillet, warm oil over medium heat. Add squash and cook, stirring occasionally, until tender, 6 to 8 minutes. Remove from heat and set aside.

THREE: In a large bowl, whisk egg whites. Whisk in cooled broth mixture, then add bread, cheese and squash, stirring until well combined. Set aside for 15 minutes to allow bread to absorb liquid, gently stirring occasionally.

FOUR: Meanwhile, preheat oven to 375°F. Coat a 2-qt casserole dish or six ramekins (1¼ to 1½ cups each) with cooking spray. If using ramekins, arrange them on a rimmed baking sheet. Pour mixture into prepared casserole dish or ramekins and bake until browned and set, 30 to 35 minutes. Garnish with additional herbs, if desired.

Nutrients per 1¼-cup serving: *Calories: 251, Total Fat: 7 g, Sat. Fat: 3 g, Monounsaturated Fat: 3 g, Polyunsaturated Fat: 1 g, Carbs: 29 g, Fiber: 4.5 g, Sugars: 7 g, Protein: 17 g, Sodium: 356 mg, Cholesterol: 17 mg*

# Turkey Pasta Casserole

Serves 6. *Hands-on time:* 30 minutes. **Total time:** 1 hour, 5 minutes.

This colorful pasta bake combines leftover turkey with a light cheese sauce and tons of fresh vegetables. If you're short on turkey, omit it or substitute cooked ground turkey instead. And, if time isn't on your side – and you're willing to give up the browned top and slightly richer texture – skip the baking and serve this dish straight out of the pot, sprinkled with toasted almonds.

### INGREDIENTS:

- 1 cup 1% low-fat milk
- 1½ tsp arrowroot
- 6 oz shredded low-fat cheddar cheese (about 2 cups)
- ½ cup low-fat plain yogurt
- ½ tsp fine sea salt
- Olive oil cooking spray
- 8 oz whole-wheat rotini pasta
- 2 carrots, peeled and cut on a diagonal into ¼-inch slices
- ½ red onion, cut into ¾-inch dice
- 1½ cups bite-size broccoli florets
- 1½ cups bite-size cauliflower florets
- 8 oz cooked skinless turkey breast, cut into ¾-inch dice (about 2 cups)
- ¼ cup chopped flat-leaf parsley leaves
- ⅓ cup sliced unsalted raw almonds

### INSTRUCTIONS:

ONE: In a medium saucepan, whisk together milk and arrowroot. Place over medium heat and cook, stirring, until mixture comes to a simmer and thickens, about 3 minutes. Remove from heat and add cheese, whisking until melted. Whisk in yogurt and salt, cover and set aside.

TWO: Preheat oven to 375°F. Coat a 2-qt casserole dish with cooking spray.

THREE: In a large pot of boiling water, cook pasta according to package directions. Three minutes before pasta is done, stir in carrots and onion. Two minutes before pasta is done, stir in broccoli and cauliflower.

FOUR: Drain pasta and vegetables and return mixture to pot. Stir in cheese sauce, turkey and parsley. Transfer to prepared casserole dish, sprinkle with almonds and bake until almonds are toasted and casserole is heated through, about 20 minutes.

**NUTRITIONAL BONUS:** Topping your casserole with almonds adds taste, texture and a healthy dose of vitamin E. As an antioxidant, the vitamin helps reduce the oxidative stress that can lead to cell damage.

**Nutrients per 1⅓-cup serving:** *Calories: 319, Total Fat: 7.5 g, Sat. Fat: 2 g, Monounsaturated Fat: 2 g, Polyunsaturated Fat: 1 g, Carbs: 35 g, Fiber: 8 g, Sugars: 7 g, Protein: 29 g, Sodium: 420 mg, Cholesterol: 40 mg*

**NEW!**

# Creamy Turkey Potato Salad

Serves 4. *Hands-on time:* 10 minutes. **Total time:** 30 minutes (plus 1 hour of chilling).

Roast turkey is a perfect leftover that can be added to just about any dish. This simple potato salad is a great no-fuss meal with a bowl of soup or with a big handful of mixed greens tossed with a little lemon juice.

### INGREDIENTS:

- 1 lb mini Yukon gold potatoes
- ½ cup leftover CE Ranch Dressing (see recipe, p. 216)
- 8 oz leftover Parmesan Panko Crusted Turkey, white meat, shredded (see recipe, p. 220)
- 4 leftover roasted zucchini strips, chopped (from ZLT Romaine Wedge Salad; see recipe, p. 216)
- 1 rib celery, diced
- 1 Tbsp each finely chopped fresh chives and dill
- Sea salt and fresh ground black pepper, to taste

### INSTRUCTIONS:

ONE: Place potatoes in a medium saucepan and add enough water to cover by 2 inches. Bring to a boil on high heat, reduce heat to medium-high and simmer for about 15 minutes or until potatoes are tender when pierced with a knife. Drain in a colander and let cool to room temperature. Cut potatoes in half and transfer to a large mixing bowl.

TWO: Add *CE* Ranch Dressing, turkey, zucchini, celery, chives and dill to potatoes and gently stir until combined. Season with salt and pepper. Transfer to a sealable container and refrigerate for a minimum of 1 hour or up to 24 hours to allow flavors to meld.

**Nutrients per 1¼-cup serving:** *Calories: 175, Total Fat: 2 g, Sat. Fat: 0.5 g, Carbs: 24 g, Fiber: 2 g, Sugars: 2 g, Protein: 15 g, Sodium: 160 mg, Cholesterol: 27 mg*

## Nutritional Bonus:

**Need a vitamin C boost? Eat a potato! Sailors in the 19th century ate potatoes to help fend off scurvy, a symptom of vitamin C deficiency. One medium potato with skin provides about 42 mg of vitamin C, 70% of your recommended daily intake!**

Creamy Turkey Potato Salad

# Transform Your Turkey-Day Sides

Turkey may not be the only thing you're left with after the holidays. Here are a few ways to turn the green beans, cranberry sauce and stuffing into all-new recipes for your family of four.

Stuffing
LEFTOVERS

## STUFFING RIBOLLITA

Arrange ¾ cup warm leftover stuffing in each of 4 shallow bowls. Top each with ½ cup finely shredded cabbage, ½ cup diced tomatoes and 2 Tbsp shredded or shaved Parmesan cheese. Pour ¾ cup hot low-sodium chicken broth into each bowl.

— NEW —
Stuffing
Ribollita

**DID YOU KNOW?**
Literally meaning "reboiled" in Italian, ribollita is a traditional Tuscan soup using leftover stale bread. Our riff on the European classic may not include the traditional beans, but its colorful produce and flavorful stuffing will not disappoint.

## GREEN BEAN SUCCOTASH

Sauté ½ diced red onion over medium-high heat until tender. Add 1 cup halved or chopped leftover green beans, ¾ cup thawed-from-frozen corn kernels, ¾ cup thawed-from-frozen lima beans and ⅓ cup low-sodium chicken or vegetable broth, stirring occasionally until heated through, 1 to 2 minutes. Stir in ¼ cup sliced scallions.

Green Beans LEFTOVERS

— NEW —
Green Bean Succotash

**FROM SCRATCH:** If you don't have leftover green beans on hand, cooking them will only take about 10 more minutes. Add 1 inch of water to a large saucepan. Place a steaming basket in saucepan, cover and bring water to a boil over high heat. Put about ½ lb French-style green beans in steamer and reduce heat to low. Cook, covered, until beans are tender, about 6 minutes. Transfer beans to a serving bowl or chop and add to Green Bean Succotash recipe.

## CRANBERRY YOGURT PARFAITS

Combine 1 cup leftover cranberry sauce with 1 cup low-fat plain yogurt. Dice 4 pears. Layer pears and cranberry mixture in 4 parfait glasses or tall tumblers. Top each with 2 Tbsp homemade or all-natural granola (*CE* pick: Bear Naked 100% Pure & Natural Granola).

Cranberry Sauce LEFTOVERS

— NEW —
Cranberry Yogurt Parfaits

## Storing, Freezing & Thawing

When working with leftovers, your first priority is proper storage. Perishable fare should be sealed and refrigerated or popped into the freezer within two hours of cooking. Cooked turkey can be kept refrigerated for two to three days, while turkey broth will last for one to two days. As for freezing, foods will keep indefinitely. But, for best quality, use frozen cooked turkey within about four months and frozen broth in two to three months.

When you're ready to use your leftovers, transfer the frozen foods to your refrigerator to thaw. (Thawing time will depend on the size and thickness of the food.) Then, dig in to our redux recipes.

# Clean Desserts

Fig Tartlets, p. 250

Contrary to popular belief, desserts are an excellent way to squeeze a few more healthy ingredients into your day. In fact, some of our sweetest recipes are made with the most nutrient-dense seasonal selections. Get the nutrition of an apple in our Amazing Baked Apples, the antioxidant power of berries in our Double Berry Peach Pie and don't miss the reenergizing power of bananas in our Chocolate Banana Freezer Pie. Is your mouth watering yet? These recipes are doable, delicious and downright good for you.

# Chai "Crème" Brûlée

**Serves** 6. **Hands-on time:** *15 minutes.* **Total time:** *40 minutes.*

A tea- and spice-infused crème brûlée, complete with caramel-like coating, all for three grams of fat and fewer than 130 calories? Yes, with *Clean Eating* it is possible.

INGREDIENTS:

- 1 cup 1% milk
- 3 chai tea bags
- 3 whole cloves
- 1 cinnamon stick, broken into pieces
- 2 cardamom pods
- 8 oz firm tofu, drained of all water
- 1 egg
- 2 egg whites
- ⅓ cup plus 2 Tbsp organic evaporated cane juice, divided

INSTRUCTIONS:

ONE: Preheat oven to 325°F.

TWO: In a small saucepan, heat milk to a simmer over medium. Remove from heat and add tea bags, cloves, cinnamon and cardamom. Cover and let stand for at least 5 minutes.

THREE: Meanwhile, in a food processor fitted with a metal blade, combine tofu, egg, egg whites and ⅓ cup cane juice; process until very smooth.

FOUR: Remove tea bags and spices from milk. With food processor running, slowly pour milk through feed tube until combined. Divide mixture equally among six ramekins. Place ramekins in a baking dish and fill dish with hot water until it reaches halfway up the sides of the ramekins.

FIVE: Bake in oven for 18 to 22 minutes, until set. Remove from oven and chill until serving. To serve, top each crème with 1 tsp cane juice and place under preheated broiler until crystals melt and become browned.

Nutrients per individual crème brûlée: *Calories: 126, Total Fat: 3 g, Sat. Fat: 1 g, Carbs: 18 g, Fiber: 0 g, Sugars: 16 g, Protein: 7 g, Sodium: 63 mg, Cholesterol: 38 mg*

Chocolate
Banana
Freezer Pie

# Chocolate Banana Freezer Pie

**Serves** 8. **Hands-on time:** 15 minutes. **Total time:** 5 hours (includes freezing time).

This pie is reminiscent of the chocolate peanut novelty cones doled out by ice cream trucks every summer and those chilly, chocolate-robed frozen bananas of childhood. Sweetened only by the bananas themselves, the thick custard-like filling sits in a peanutty crust for a cold indulgence on a hot night.

## INGREDIENTS:

- 5 small ripe bananas (about 1 lb), peeled and broken or cut into small pieces
- ¼ cup unsweetened cocoa powder
- 1 cup light coconut milk
- 1 tsp pure vanilla extract
- 1 baked Extra-Easy Whole-Grain Pie Crust (see recipe, p. 238), using nut variation with peanuts
- 2 Tbsp unsalted dry roasted peanuts, chopped
- 1 oz dark chocolate (70% or greater), finely chopped

## INSTRUCTIONS:

ONE: Combine bananas, cocoa, coconut milk and vanilla in the jar of a blender. Blend until very smooth (like thin cake batter), stopping to scrape down sides of jar and stir mixture 2 or 3 times (to ensure all banana is puréed).

TWO: Pour banana purée into baked pie crust. Sprinkle peanuts and chocolate across surface of pie. Cover very tightly with plastic wrap and freeze for a minimum of 4 hours, or overnight.

THREE: To serve, remove plastic wrap and set at room temperature for about 30 minutes (longer if pie was frozen for more than 4 hours), until pie is just soft enough to yield to the cut of a knife. Slice and serve.

*Nutrients per serving (⅛ of pie): Calories: 237, Total Fat: 9 g, Sat. Fat: 3 g, Monounsaturated Fat: 3 g, Polyunsaturated Fat: 1.5 g, Carbs: 35 g, Fiber: 6 g, Sugars: 10 g, Protein: 6 g, Sodium: 73 mg, Cholesterol: 27 mg*

# Double Berry Peach Pie
## WITH LEMON CREAM & ALMOND CRUST

**Serves** 8. **Hands-on time:** 45 minutes. **Total time:** 3 hours (includes chilling time).

Beneath a creamy swirl of lemony topping is a strikingly vibrant, sweet and tart, jam-like fruit filling. The natural sugars in the peaches and berries, the fiber-rich whole-grain crust and thick calcium- and protein-rich yogurt actually make a slice of this *CE* pie as reasonable a breakfast choice as a clean granola parfait. Its lovely lightness, though, earns it a nomination as the perfect dessert for a summer-time dinner.

## INGREDIENTS:

- 4 medium peaches (about 1 lb), pitted and cut into large chunks (For more peachy info, see p. 252.), or 1 lb frozen sliced peaches
- 1 cup raspberries, divided
- 1 cup blackberries, divided
- 2 Tbsp Sucanat
- 1 Tbsp fresh lemon juice
- 3 Tbsp arrowroot
- 1 baked Extra-Easy Whole-Grain Pie Crust (see recipe, p. 238), using nut variation with almonds
- 1 tsp lemon zest
- 1 cup nonfat plain Greek yogurt

## INSTRUCTIONS:

ONE: In a medium saucepan on medium-high heat, combine peaches, ½ cup raspberries, ½ cup blackberries, ⅓ cup water, Sucanat and lemon juice. Bring liquid to a boil and cover pan. Reduce heat to medium-low and simmer fruit for 15 minutes, until peaches are very tender and berries have broken apart into the liquid.

TWO: Meanwhile, in a small mixing bowl, whisk together arrowroot and ⅓ cup water. Whisk well to eliminate any lumps. Once fruit has simmered for 15 minutes, pour arrowroot mixture into pan and stir to combine. Increase heat to high and bring liquid to a boil. Let boil for 2 minutes, until liquid thickens.

THREE: Transfer fruit-arrowroot mixture to a large glass bowl and let cool slightly, about 15 minutes. Gently stir in remaining ½ cup raspberries and ½ cup blackberries. Pour mixture into baked pie crust. Cover tightly with plastic wrap and refrigerate until cold and firmly set, a minimum of 2 hours, or overnight.

FOUR: In a small bowl, combine lemon zest and yogurt. Drop mixture by heaping spoonfuls all over surface of pie. Spread across, leaving about a 1-inch border, exposing fruit filling below. Slice and serve.

*Nutrients per serving (⅛ of pie): Calories: 199, Total Fat: 4 g, Sat. Fat: 1 g, Carbs: 36 g, Fiber: 6 g, Sugars: 11 g, Protein: 7 g, Sodium: 80 mg, Cholesterol: 26 mg*

# Extra-Easy Whole-Grain Pie Crust

***Makes*** *1 9-inch pie crust.* ***Hands-on time:*** *15 minutes.*
***Total time:*** *40 minutes (plus cooling time).*

**With all of the debate among purists, finding the perfect pie crust can be a daunting task. Seek no further, pilgrim, for our labor is your reward: a *Clean Eating* crust that's versatile enough for all sorts of fillings while remaining wholesome and uncomplicated.**

### INGREDIENTS:

- 1½ cups whole-wheat pastry flour, plus additional for work surface
- 1 tsp Sucanat
- ¼ tsp sea salt
- ½ tsp baking powder
- ⅓ cup low-fat milk
- 1 egg yolk
- 1 Tbsp safflower oil
- 1 Tbsp apple cider vinegar

### EQUIPMENT:

- Rolling pin
- 9-inch glass or ceramic pie dish

### INSTRUCTIONS:

ONE: Preheat oven to 375°F. In the bowl of a food processor, combine flour, Sucanat, salt and baking powder. Pulse dry ingredients several times to mix thoroughly.

TWO: In a spouted measuring cup, whisk together milk, egg yolk, oil and vinegar. With the processor running, slowly pour liquid through the food chute into dry ingredients. Process just enough to combine ingredients. (The mixture will be partially crumbly, but will stick together when squeezed.)

THREE: Dump dough out onto a well-floured surface. Squeeze dough together into a singular mound and pat it down into a disc, about ½ inch thick. Using a rolling pin, roll dough out until 12 inches in diameter. Set rolling pin at bottom edge of dough and gently roll dough onto pin, so that dough drapes over pin. Transfer dough to pie dish. Gently press dough into the edges of the dish and up the sides. Fold excess dough under and pinch, creating a roughly ½-inch rim. Using your fingers, or with the tines of a fork, crimp entire rim. Poke dough all over with a fork to create steam holes.

FOUR: Transfer to oven and bake for 20 minutes, until edges and center are just golden. Remove from oven and cool completely before using.

*Nutrients per serving (⅛ of crust): Calories: 112, Total Fat: 3 g, Sat. Fat: 0.25 g, Carbs: 19 g, Fiber: 3 g, Sugars: 1 g, Protein: 3 g, Sodium: 67 mg, Cholesterol: 26 mg*

**IF YOU DON'T HAVE A FOOD PROCESSOR: Simply whisk dry ingredients together very well in a large mixing bowl. Whisk wet ingredients in a spouted measuring cup. Then pour wet ingredients across the surface of the dry ingredients. Using clean hands or a wooden spoon, gently toss all ingredients together to combine thoroughly. Squeeze dough together into a singular mound and then pat down into a disc, about ½-inch thick. Continue with pie crust recipe as instructed.**

**NUT VARIATIONS: Go nuts with our basic pie crust! Substitute ¼ cup whole-wheat pastry flour with ¼ cup unsalted nuts of your choice, finely chopped or ground. Add them to the food processor in Step One, along with the Sucanat and sea salt (no flour or baking powder just yet). Pulse 10 or more times, until nuts are finely chopped. Then add 1¼ cups flour and baking powder and proceed with the recipe as instructed.**

# Preparing Your Pie Crust

ONE: Squeeze dough together into a singular mound and pat it down into a disc, about ½-inch thick. Using a rolling pin, roll dough out until 12 inches in diameter.

TWO: Set rolling pin at bottom edge of dough and gently roll dough onto pin, so that dough drapes over pin. Transfer dough to pie dish. Gently press dough into the edges of the dish and up the sides.

THREE: Fold excess dough under and pinch, creating a roughly ½-inch rim.

FOUR: Using your fingers, or with the tines of a fork, crimp entire rim. Poke dough all over with a fork to create steam holes.

Double
Berry
Peach Pie
p. 237

Strawberry Rhubarb Crisp

# Strawberry Rhubarb Crisp

*Serves 8. **Hands-on time:** 7 minutes. **Total time:** 40 minutes.*

**The sweetness of strawberries balances out tart rhubarb in this low-cal dessert, resulting in a succulent summery crisp.**

INGREDIENTS:

- 2 stalks rhubarb, sliced (1½ cups)
- 18 to 21 medium strawberries, sliced (3 cups)
- 1 tsp ground cinnamon
- 3 Tbsp organic evaporated cane juice
- Juice ½ lemon
- 3 Tbsp spelt flour

INGREDIENTS (TOPPING):

- 1 cup old-fashioned rolled oats
- ¼ cup Sucanat
- ¼ cup coconut oil
- 2 Tbsp spelt flour
- 2 tsp ground flaxseeds
- 1 tsp ground cinnamon

INSTRUCTIONS:

ONE: Preheat oven to 350°F.

TWO: In an 8 x 8-inch baking pan, combine rhubarb, strawberries, 1 tsp cinnamon, evaporated cane juice and lemon juice. Sprinkle with 3 Tbsp flour and gently toss to coat.

THREE: Prepare topping: In a medium bowl, add all topping ingredients. Using a pastry blender or your hands, mix until well combined, then spread over fruit mixture in baking pan.

FOUR: Place pan in oven and bake for 25 to 35 minutes, until topping is golden brown. Serve warm or at room temperature.

Nutrients per serving (about ⅔ cup): Calories: 193, Total Fat: 8 g, Sat. Fat: 6 g, Carbs: 27 g, Fiber: 4 g, Sugars: 13 g, Protein: 3 g, Sodium: 8 mg, Cholesterol: 0 mg

# Coconut Cream Cups

*Serves 6. **Hands-on time:** 7 minutes. **Total time:** 1 hour, 30 minutes (includes chilling time).*

**With its exhilarating contrast of smooth coconut cream and a crispy toasted garnish, this easy-to-make dessert is guaranteed to take your taste buds on an exotic tropical adventure – all for only 100 calories!**

INGREDIENTS:

- 1 lb plain silken firm tofu (454 g)
- 1 cup coconut water
- ¼ cup organic evaporated cane juice
- 1 whole egg plus 2 egg whites
- 1 tsp pure vanilla extract
- 1 tsp organic coconut extract
- 2 Tbsp unsweetened coconut, shredded and toasted, for garnish

INSTRUCTIONS:

ONE: Preheat oven to 350°F.

TWO: Drain tofu in a colander, cover with two sheets of paper towel and press down gently to squeeze out majority of water.

THREE: In the bowl of a food processor fitted with a steel blade, combine drained tofu, coconut water, cane juice, egg and egg whites, vanilla and coconut extract. Process until very smooth, about 5 minutes.

FOUR: Divide mixture evenly between six 4-oz ramekins. Place ramekins into a large (9 x 13 inch) baking pan and place on center oven rack.* Fill pan with about 4 cups very hot tap water, until water level reaches halfway up ramekins, being careful not to get water inside any of the ramekins.

FIVE: Bake until coconut cups are set, about 40 to 45 minutes. (They will still jiggle a bit in the center.)

SIX: Carefully remove baking pan from oven and remove ramekins from their water bath. Allow them to cool slightly, then chill in refrigerator for at least 30 minutes. Garnish each with 1 tsp shredded coconut prior to serving.

**\*CAUTION: When placing the baking pan with ramekins into the preheated oven, first extend the oven rack, set down the pan and carefully and quickly fill it with hot water before gently sliding the rack back into the oven. Or, you can also fill an empty baking pan with hot water before placing it into a cold oven; then heat the oven and carefully place the ramekins in the water bath once the oven reaches the desired temperature.**

Nutrients per ½-cup serving: Calories: 100, Total Fat: 4 g, Sat. Fat: 1.5 g, Carbs: 11 g, Fiber: 1 g, Sugars: 9 g, Protein: 6 g, Sodium: 75 mg, Cholesterol: 30 mg

# Amazing Baked Apples
## WITH VANILLA-HONEY YOGURT

*Serves 4.* **Hands-on time:** *15 minutes.* **Total time:** *55 to 60 minutes.*

**As this simple dessert bakes in your oven, the spicy aroma of cinnamon and apples will swirl through your home, setting appetites on fire.**

INGREDIENTS:

- 1 medium lemon
- 4 large, firm apples, cored and hollowed, leaving bottoms intact (Best picks: Macintosh, Empire or Ida Red)
- 2 Tbsp unsalted roasted almond butter (or any unsalted natural nut butter of your choice)
- 1 Tbsp unsweetened dried apricots, chopped
- 1 Tbsp dried, pitted prunes, chopped
- 1 Tbsp unsweetened raisins
- 2 Tbsp toasted shaved hazelnuts, divided
- 2 tsp raw organic honey
- ⅛ tsp cinnamon, ground

**VANILLA-HONEY YOGURT**

- 1 cup low-fat plain yogurt
- ½ tsp pure vanilla extract
- 2 tsp raw organic honey

INSTRUCTIONS:

ONE: Preheat oven to 375°F. Juice lemon, yielding about 2 Tbsp juice. Then split open lemon and rub inside flesh over outside of each apple. Drizzle about ⅛ tsp lemon juice inside cavity of each apple, reserving remaining juice. In a bowl, combine almond butter, apricots, prunes, raisins, hazelnuts (reserving 1 tsp for garnish), honey and cinnamon. Stuff each cavity with filling, dividing evenly among 4 apples. Press stuffing down firmly and place apples, cavity side up, in a shallow baking dish. Mix together remaining lemon juice and ¼ cup water and pour around apples. Place dish in oven for 40 to 45 minutes or until firm but tender.

TWO: Prepare Vanilla-Honey Yogurt: Place yogurt in a wire strainer lined with paper towel and set strainer over a bowl. Let sit in refrigerator for no less than 1 hour, or until thick. Pour off liquid, place thickened yogurt in a bowl and stir in vanilla and honey. Spoon 1 Tbsp yogurt over each warm baked apple and sprinkle with remaining hazelnuts.

*Nutrients per apple (about 4 oz) and 1 Tbsp yogurt: Calories: 188, Total Fat: 9.5 g, Sat. Fat: 1 g, Carbs: 25.5 g, Fiber: 4 g, Sugars: 16 g, Protein: 3.5 g, Sodium: 12 mg, Cholesterol: 1 mg*

# Lemon Meringue Cupcakes

**Makes** *12 cupcakes.* **Hands-on time:** *30 minutes.* **Total time:** *50 minutes.*

**We borrowed the soft, light topping of a classic pie, cleaned it up and popped it into a moist lemony cupcake for a lovely single-serving dessert.**

INGREDIENTS:

CUPCAKES

- 1½ cups light spelt flour
- 2 tsp baking powder
- ½ tsp fine sea salt
- ½ cup organic evaporated cane juice
- ¼ cup safflower oil
- 1 egg
- 2 egg whites
- ½ cup fresh lemon juice
- Zest 1 lemon
- ¾ cup skim milk

TOPPING

- 4 egg whites
- ½ tsp cream of tartar
- ⅓ cup organic evaporated cane juice
- Zest 1 lemon, finely grated

INSTRUCTIONS:

ONE: Preheat oven to 350°F.

TWO: Prepare cupcakes: Line a 12-cup muffin pan with cupcake liners. In a small bowl, combine flour, baking powder and salt. In a large mixing bowl, beat together cane juice, oil, egg, egg whites, lemon juice and zest until pale yellow in color. Add milk and stir to combine. Add dry ingredients and stir until just combined. Divide batter between 12 muffin cups and bake for 15 to 18 minutes, until a toothpick inserted into the middle of a cupcake comes out clean. Remove from oven and let cool. Transfer cupcakes to a baking sheet.

THREE: Prepare topping: In a large mixing bowl, beat egg whites and cream of tartar with an electric beater until soft peaks begin to form. Slowly add cane juice and continue beating until stiff peaks form. Gently fold in lemon zest with a rubber spatula.

FOUR: Ensure that oven rack is in center position in oven and preheat broiler. Add topping mixture to a pastry bag (or, alternately, a zip-top plastic bag with 1 corner cut off) and pipe topping onto cupcakes, dividing evenly. Place baking sheet with cupcakes under broiler until lightly browned, about 1 to 2 minutes. Garnish with additional lemon zest, if desired.

*Nutrients per cupcake: Calories: 160, Total Fat: 5 g, Sat. Fat: 0.25 g, Carbs: 25 g, Fiber: 1 g, Sugars: 14 g, Protein: 5 g, Sodium: 129 mg, Cholesterol: 0.25 mg*

Lemon
Meringue
Cupcakes

**Nutritional Bonus:**
One serving of regular chocolate cake can tally over 50 g of fat and 800 calories! While our version is still an indulgence, you can have a piece and safely keep within your daily nutritional requirements.

Chocolate Chip Cookie Dough Chocolate Cake

# Chocolate Chip Cookie Dough Chocolate Cake

*Serves* 12. *Hands-on time:* 30 minutes.
*Total time:* 1 hour, 10 minutes (plus 2 hours for chilling).

**Cookie dough fanatics will adore this moist, fudge-like cake! We've lightened up a typical fatty calorie bomb with yogurt, apple-sauce, cocoa powder and a drizzle of chocolate on top instead of a slather of icing.**

## INGREDIENTS:

### CHOCOLATE CAKE

- 2½ cups white whole-wheat flour or whole-wheat flour
- 1 cup unsweetened cocoa powder
- 1 tsp each baking powder and baking soda
- ¼ tsp sea salt
- 1¼ cups unsweetened applesauce
- 1 cup low-fat plain yogurt
- ½ cup pitted dates
- ⅓ cup raw honey
- ¼ cup olive oil
- 2 tsp pure vanilla extract
- 12 egg whites
- ¼ cup dark chocolate chips (70% cocoa or greater)
- 3 Tbsp skim milk

### CHOCOLATE CHIP COOKIE DOUGH

- 2 Tbsp natural buttery spread (TRY: Earth Balance Buttery Spread with Olive Oil)
- ¼ cup Sucanat
- ¼ tsp pure vanilla extract
- ⅔ cup white whole-wheat flour
- ¼ tsp baking powder
- Pinch sea salt
- ½ cup dark chocolate chips (70% cocoa or greater)

## INSTRUCTIONS:

ONE: Preheat oven to 375°F.

TWO: Prepare cookie dough: In a medium bowl, combine buttery spread and Sucanat, 3 Tbsp water and vanilla until smooth. Stir in flour, baking powder and salt until just incorporated. If mixture is dry, add water, 1 Tbsp at a time, until mixture comes together in a ball. Add chocolate chips and stir until combined. Roll mixture into 18 balls, about 1 Tbsp each, and place onto a small baking sheet. Loosely cover and place baking sheet into freezer for 10 minutes to chill.

THREE: Prepare chocolate cake: In a medium bowl, whisk together flour, cocoa powder, baking powder, baking soda and salt; set aside. In the bowl of a food processor, combine applesauce, yogurt, dates, honey, oil and vanilla. Pulse until smooth.

FOUR: Gradually mix wet ingredients into dry ingredients, until just combined (do not over mix). In a separate dry bowl, beat egg whites into soft peaks with an electric beater on high speed. Using a rubber spatula, fold egg whites into batter. (Batter should seem a little lumpy; do not over mix.)

FIVE: Pour batter into a 10-inch nonstick springform pan. Remove cookie dough from freezer and gently drop balls into cake batter, spreading balls evenly over cake and gently pressing to submerge. Bake for about 45 minutes or until top of cake cracks and a toothpick inserted in center comes out almost clean. Transfer to a wire rack to cool for 1 hour.

SIX: Once cake is cooling, set a small bowl over a pot of barely simmering water. Add chocolate and heat until just melted, stirring occasionally. Stir in milk until smooth. Drizzle mixture over top of cake and let cool.

Nutrients per 2 ½-inch wedge: *Calories: 389, Total Fat: 13 g, Sat. Fat: 6 g, Monounsaturated Fat: 4 g, Polyunsaturated Fat: 1 g, Carbs: 60 g, Fiber: 10 g, Sugars: 26 g, Protein: 12 g, Sodium: 232 mg, Cholesterol: 2 mg*

# Chocolate Walnut Brownie Cookies

*Makes 24 cookies.* *Hands-on time:* 15 minutes. *Total time:* 35 to 39 minutes.

**It's a brownie... it's a cookie... it's a flourless chocolate treat that'll delight, thanks to its sinful flavor and angelic calorie count.**

## INGREDIENTS:

- 6 egg whites
- Pinch sea salt
- ¾ cup organic evaporated cane juice
- ¾ cup unsweetened cocoa powder
- 1 tsp instant espresso powder (TIP: Make sure to opt for instant; standard espresso will be too gritty)
- ½ tsp pure vanilla extract
- 1 oz dark chocolate (70% cocoa or greater), chopped
- ½ cup chopped unsalted walnuts

## INSTRUCTIONS:

ONE: Line 2 cookie sheets with parchment paper. Preheat oven to 350°F.

TWO: In a large bowl, beat egg whites with salt using an electric beater until soft peaks form. Gradually add cane juice and continue beating until stiff peaks form. Add cocoa powder, espresso, vanilla, chocolate and walnuts and mix until combined (no need to fold; mixture will lose some volume).

THREE: Drop batter by rounded tablespoon onto prepared cookie sheets, dividing evenly. Bake one cookie sheet at a time on oven's middle rack for 10 to 12 minutes per sheet, until cookies are no longer shiny.

Nutrients per cookie: *Calories: 56, Total Fat: 2.5 g, Sat. Fat: 1 g, Carbs: 8 g, Fiber: 1 g, Sugars: 6 g, Protein: 2 g, Sodium: 23 mg, Cholesterol: 0 mg*

# Roasted Pear & Ginger Shortcakes

*Serves 6. **Hands-on time:** 40 minutes. **Total time:** 1 hour, 20 minutes.*

**For great low-fat shortcakes, the dough should be handled as little as possible. Quickly forming rustic "drop biscuits" with your hands instead of rolling them out makes it easy and cuts down on fuss. The pears may be roasted ahead of time, but the biscuits are best right after they are made.**

## INGREDIENTS:

- 4 pears, peeled, halved and cored
- 1 navel orange
- 6 Tbsp Sucanat, divided
- 1½ cups whole-wheat pastry flour
- 1½ tsp ground ginger
- 1½ tsp baking powder
- ½ tsp baking soda
- ½ tsp sea salt
- 3 Tbsp safflower oil
- ½ cup plus 2 Tbsp low-fat buttermilk, divided
- ¾ cup nonfat plain Greek yogurt
- 2 Tbsp pure maple syrup

## INSTRUCTIONS:

ONE: Preheat oven to 425°F. Cut each pear half into six equal slices and place in a large baking dish. Remove peel from orange in thick strips with a vegetable peeler; use a paring knife to scrape off any remaining white pith and add peel to baking dish. Juice orange and add to pears, then sprinkle with 2 Tbsp Sucanat. Roast for 40 minutes, turning pears with spatula twice during cooking. Pears are done when a paring knife meets little resistance when inserted and juices have thickened. Remove from oven, cover with aluminum foil and set aside. (Pear mixture may be refrigerated for up to 2 days.)

TWO: In a large bowl, whisk together 3 Tbsp Sucanat, flour, ginger, baking powder, baking soda and salt. Add oil and stir to combine. Add ½ cup plus 1 Tbsp buttermilk and stir just until moistened; do not over mix. Turn dough out onto a lightly floured surface, dust hands with flour and quickly shape dough into a thick circle. Divide dough into six equal mounds, about 2 inches wide and ¾ inch high. Place mounds on a parchment-lined baking sheet and brush tops with remaining 1 Tbsp buttermilk, dividing evenly. Sprinkle with remaining 1 Tbsp Sucanat. Bake for 13 to 15 minutes or until bottoms are lightly browned and a toothpick comes out clean when inserted in center. Transfer biscuits to a rack and cool for 5 minutes.

THREE: In a small bowl, combine yogurt and maple syrup. Reheat pears, if necessary. Split biscuits and divide pears and yogurt mixture evenly between pieces. Or, layer two biscuit pieces, pears and yogurt mixture as you choose for one layered shortcake. Serve immediately.

*Nutrients per serving (1 whole biscuit, ⅓ of pears, 2 Tbsp yogurt mixture):*
*Calories: 349, Total Fat: 8 g, Sat. Fat: 1 g, Monounsaturated Fat: 5.5 g, Polyunsaturated Fat: 1 g, Carbs: 64 g, Fiber: 8 g, Sugars: 30 g, Protein: 8 g, Sodium: 315 mg, Cholesterol: 1.5 mg*

# How to Make Shortcakes

SAVORY OPTION: **Turn our dessert biscuits into dinnertime rolls simply by removing the ginger and adding a bit of low-fat cheddar cheese to the mixture. And instead of sprinkling the tops with additional Sucanat before baking, why not add a sprinkling of Parmesan?**

ONE: Turn dough out onto a lightly floured surface, dust hands with flour and quickly shape dough into a thick circle.

TWO: Divide dough into six equal mounds, about 2 inches wide and ¾ inch high. Place mounds on a parchment-lined baking sheet.

THREE: Brush tops of dough with 1 Tbsp buttermilk and sprinkle with 1 Tbsp Sucanat. Bake.

FOUR: Transfer biscuits to a rack and cool for 5 minutes.

FIVE: Split biscuits and divide pears and yogurt mixture evenly between pieces. Or, layer two biscuit pieces, pears and yogurt mixture as you choose for one layered shortcake.

Roasted
Pear &
Ginger
Shortcakes

Roasted
Apples

**Nutritional Bonus:**
A, B, C and E – pumpkins
offer all of these vitamins
and more! Pumpkin flesh is
also a good source of fiber,
potassium, copper and iron,
while the squash's seeds serve
up protein and vitamin K.

# Roasted Apples
## WITH PUMPKIN-MAPLE TOPPING

**Serves** 4. **Hands-on time:** 10 minutes. **Total time:** 55 minutes.

**Save money and pass up on canned pumpkin by easily roasting your own. Every pound of pumpkin will yield about one cup of purée to be used immediately or conveniently frozen. Alternatively, you can cut the raw pumpkin flesh into cubes and simmer them until tender, then mash them into a purée or freeze them.**

### INGREDIENTS:

- 1 fresh pumpkin (1 to 1½ lb)
- 2 crisp apples (Braeburn, Fuji or Pink Lady)
- ½ cup whole-milk Greek yogurt
- 2 Tbsp pure maple syrup
- ⅛ tsp ground cloves
- ¼ tsp ground nutmeg

### INSTRUCTIONS:

ONE: Preheat oven to 375°F. Using a large, heavy chef's knife, cut pumpkin in half, scoop out seeds and place pumpkin, cut side up, on a baking sheet.

TWO: Place apples in a loaf pan and fill pan with 1 inch of water. Cover pan tightly with foil.

THREE: Place pumpkin and apples in oven and bake for 30 minutes. Uncover apples and keep baking both apples and pumpkin for another 10 minutes. Remove apples from oven and test tenderness of pumpkin by seeing how easily a sharp knife slides into the flesh. If pumpkin still seems hard, continue baking for another 10 minutes and check doneness again. (TIP: Steps One through Three can be completed the night before.)

FOUR: When pumpkin is cool enough to handle, scoop out ½ cup flesh and place in a medium glass bowl. (Freeze or refrigerate leftover pumpkin flesh for later use.) Carefully spoon yogurt out of its container without stirring the whey (the liquid) back into it (yogurt should be as thick as possible) and add to bowl with pumpkin. Stir in syrup and spices.

FIVE: Cut cooked apples in half and scoop out seeds and stems. Plate halves, then top each with ¼ cup pumpkin mixture. Serve at room temperature. Leftovers can be covered and refrigerated for up to 3 days. Garnish with additional nutmeg, if desired.

*Nutrients per serving (½ apple and ¼ cup topping): Calories: 123, Total Fat: 1 g, Sat. Fat: 0.5 g, Carbs: 28 g, Fiber: 3 g, Sugars: 17 g, Protein: 4 g, Sodium: 14 mg, Cholesterol: 0 mg*

# Upside-Down Banana Cream Pie
## WITH COCONUT CRUST

**Serves** 18. **Hands-on time:** 30 minutes.
**Total time:** 30 minutes (plus 3 hours or overnight to set).

**For an interesting twist on a comfort-food classic, we took Banana Cream Pie and flipped it over into a baking pan – bananas on the bottom and crust on top! Vegans or those who are lactose intolerant don't have to shy away from this dessert: You can make the recipe dairy free simply by using silken tofu in place of the strained yogurt.**

### INGREDIENTS:

#### FILLING

- 8 semi-ripe bananas, peeled, divided
- 1 Tbsp fresh lemon juice
- 1 tsp pure vanilla extract
- 1 cup unsalted raw macadamia nuts, soaked in warm water for 30 minutes to 1 hour
- 6 unsweetened dried pitted dates (Medjool or Noor)
- ⅛ tsp cinnamon, ground
- Pinch nutmeg, ground
- ½ cup low-fat plain yogurt, strained, or nonfat plain Greek yogurt

#### CRUST

- 1 cup unsweetened shredded coconut
- 2 cups rolled oats
- 2 Tbsp coconut butter
- 2 Tbsp raw honey
- 2 Tbsp water

### INSTRUCTIONS:

ONE: Prepare crust: In a food processor, combine all crust ingredients. Pulse until combined and crumbly. Scrape out into a small bowl, cover with plastic wrap and refrigerate until ready to use. (Crust mixture may be prepared 1 day ahead, covered and refrigerated.)

TWO: Prepare filling: Place 5 bananas, lemon juice and vanilla into a clean food processor and pulse until puréed and smooth. Scrape banana purée into a medium mixing bowl and set aside. Do not wash food processor bowl. Place macadamia nuts and dates into food processor and purée until a smooth, sticky paste forms. Add banana purée back into food processor bowl and purée until smooth, stopping processor occasionally to scrape down the sides and bottom of the bowl. Add cinnamon, nutmeg and yogurt to banana mixture and pulse until combined.

THREE: Thinly slice remaining 3 bananas and arrange them on the bottom of a rectangular baking pan (9 x 11 x 2 inches) in a single layer. Pour banana mixture over sliced bananas and smooth top of filling with a spatula. Cover with plastic wrap and refrigerate for a minimum of 2 hours or overnight to set. After pie has set, crumble crust mixture over top of pie. Slice into 18 squares and serve immediately.

*Nutrients per 2-inch square: Calories: 193, Total Fat: 10.5 g, Sat. Fat: 5 g, Carbs: 26 g, Fiber: 4 g, Sugars: 13 g, Protein: 4 g, Sodium: 5 mg, Cholesterol: 0 mg*

# Salted Caramel Hazelnut Coffee Cake

*Serves 16. **Hands-on time:** 30 minutes. **Total time:** 1 hour, 10 minutes.*

**Coffee cake is a dense, sugary cake that is meant to be served – surprise! – with coffee. Drinking decaf? No worries, our coffee cake will definitely perk you up – in part because of the mouthwatering salted caramel sauce, but also thanks to mood-boosting folate found in the hazelnuts.**

## INGREDIENTS:

### SALTED CARAMEL SAUCE

- 2 Tbsp natural buttery spread (TRY: Earth Balance Buttery Spread with Olive Oil)
- ¼ cup raw honey
- ¼ cup Sucanat
- 1 tsp baking soda
- ¼ tsp sea salt

### HAZELNUT CRUMBLE

- 1 cup whole unsalted hazelnuts
- ½ cup rolled oats
- 1 Tbsp whole-wheat flour
- 3 tsp Sucanat
- ¼ cup unsweetened apple butter
- 1 Tbsp natural buttery spread

### BATTER

- Olive oil cooking spray
- 2 cups white whole-wheat flour
- 1 tsp baking soda
- ½ tsp ground cinnamon
- ¼ tsp sea salt
- ½ cup Sucanat
- 3 Tbsp natural buttery spread
- 2 tsp ground flaxseeds
- 1 tsp pure vanilla extract
- 1¼ cup low-fat plain yogurt

## INSTRUCTIONS:

**ONE:** Preheat oven to 350°F.

**TWO:** Prepare salted caramel sauce: In a medium saucepan on medium heat, combine buttery spread, honey and Sucanat and cook, whisking frequently, until simmering. Once simmering, remove from heat and whisk in baking soda and salt. Mixture will bubble and fizz. Continue to stir until no large bubbles remain. Set aside and let cool completely.

**THREE:** Prepare hazelnut crumble: Place hazelnuts on a baking sheet and toast in oven for 6 to 8 minutes, until fragrant. Remove from oven and let cool slightly. (Leave oven on at same temperature). Rub hazelnuts in between a clean dry tea towel to remove most of brown skin. Let cool, coarsely chop and transfer to a medium bowl. Add oats, flour, Sucanat, apple butter and buttery spread and stir until combined. Set aside.

**FOUR:** Mist an 8-inch square cake pan with cooking spray and line bottom with parchment paper, allowing parchment to hang over 2 parallel sides (this will provide handles to make it easy to lift cake from pan).

**FIVE:** Prepare batter: In a bowl, whisk flour, baking soda, cinnamon and salt. In a separate bowl, use a spatula to beat together Sucanat, buttery spread, flaxseeds, vanilla and 6 Tbsp water. Stir in yogurt until combined. Fold buttery mixture into flour mixture until just combined.

**SIX:** Pour three-quarters of batter into pan. Top with half of hazelnut crumble and drizzle with half of salted caramel sauce. Pour remaining batter into pan and smooth out. Top with remaining hazelnut mixture. Bake for about 30 minutes at 350°F until toothpick inserted into center comes out clean. Remove from oven and let cool for 5 minutes. Remove cake from pan and let cool completely on a baking rack. Cut cake into 2-inch squares and serve, drizzled with remaining salted caramel sauce.

*Nutrients per 2-inch square: Calories: 232, Total Fat: 10 g, Sat. Fat: 2 g, Monounsaturated Fat: 5 g, Polyunsaturated Fat: 2 g, Carbs: 32 g, Fiber: 3 g, Sugars: 17 g, Protein: 5 g, Sodium: 195 mg, Cholesterol: 1 mg*

# Fig Tartlets

*Serves 10. **Hands-on time:** 10 minutes. **Total time:** 37 minutes.*

**These two-person tartlets echo a popular trend on restaurant menus: sharing. But with this hard-to-resist crumbly crust similar to short-bread, tender figs and crunchy walnuts, we take no responsibility for arguments over who gets the larger half!**

## INGREDIENTS:

- 1 tsp olive oil
- 1 cup spelt flour
- ¾ cup ground unsalted hazelnuts
- 4 Tbsp safflower oil
- 4 Tbsp raw honey, divided
- 8 fresh figs, sliced
- 2 Tbsp unsalted walnut pieces

## EQUIPMENT:

- 5 tart pans (4 inches each) with removable bottoms

## INSTRUCTIONS:

**ONE:** Preheat oven to 375°F. Lightly brush tart pans with olive oil.

**TWO:** In a food processor fitted with a steel blade, pulse flour, hazelnuts, safflower oil and 3 Tbsp honey until crumbly. Divide mixture evenly among prepared pans and press into bottoms and sides. Place pans on 1 cookie sheet.

**THREE:** Bake crusts until they begin to brown, about 10 to 12 minutes.

**FOUR:** Remove crusts from oven and reduce heat to 350°F.

**FIVE:** Arrange figs in crusts, sprinkle with walnuts and drizzle remaining 1 Tbsp honey over top, dividing all ingredients evenly among 5 tarts.

**SIX:** Return tarts to oven and bake until figs are softened, about 10 to 12 minutes. Serve warm or at room temperature.

*Nutrients per ½ tart: Calories: 194, Total Fat: 11 g, Sat. Fat: 1 g, Monounsaturated Fat: 7 g, Polyunsaturated Fat: 2 g, Carbs: 24 g, Fiber: 3 g, Sugars: 10 g, Protein: 3 g, Sodium: 0.5 mg, Cholesterol: 0 mg*

**For a photo of this recipe, see page 232.**

Salted
Caramel
Hazelnut
Coffee
Cake

# Peaches

Prized for their sharp floral aromas and creamy flesh, peaches are perfect for canning, baking or eating fresh on a hot summer day. We'll show you which types are best for each task, as well as how to store, slice and pit this fuzzy fruit.

The downy "pinch-ripe" peach could easily get an XXX-rating for the suggestive prominent curvy cleft dividing the fruit into two plump cheeky halves. Notoriously finicky, fuzzy peaches and their cousins, smooth nectarines, must be harvested by hand by experienced pickers. With more than 2,000 peach varieties worldwide, the most important attributes to look for in a peach are wooly, mealy, tree-ripened and juicy.

With a short precious lifespan of just three weeks after picking, the best peaches are found at fruit stands and farmers' markets. In season from July to September, local peaches are often still wearing their protective coat of natural fuzz. A day or two after being picked, their heady fragrance develops and they become juicy enough to drip down your chin when bitten into.

## What You'll Need:

- Cutting board
- Bowl of ice water
- Pot of boiling water
- Paring knife
- Slotted spoon

## Types of peaches

Peaches are classified by name according to how firmly their flesh attaches to the stone. Clingstones have firm flesh that stubbornly resists coming away from the stone (hence their clever name), which can be maddening for slicing but a boon to canners because their flesh holds its shape and texture. Therefore, much of the crop ends up in cans in the grocery store. (Remember to select only BPA-free cans when going this route.) Larger than clingstones, freestones come into season later and their flesh tends to pull away easily from the pit. With a fine balance of sweetness and acidity, freestones are ideal for eating out-of-hand and perfect for cooking and baking. Semi-freestones are newer hybrids and work well for eating fresh as well as for canning. Clingstones are the first to market, followed by semi-freestones and, finally, freestones – for which peach lovers wait impatiently.

As a peach ripens, its green chlorophyll fades and its underlying warm reddish-gold hues develop with deeper hues close to the pit. Its legendary fragrance flourishes, its flesh ripening into juicy succulence from the shoulders down. A peach contains only the amount of sugar it has when picked but will taste sweeter as it ripens and its acid content decreases. Its texture gets softer and juicier as the pectin that glues the cells together breaks down. If you've ever placed a bowl of peaches in your kitchen, you've likely noticed how the aroma fills the room.

## Choosing, ripening and cooking peaches

Choose peaches without "green shoulders," a telltale sign that this oh-so-tender fruit is unlikely to ripen properly. A fully mature peach will have plump, rounded shoulders – the top of the peach surrounding the stem end – and a full bulging line that runs from top to bottom alongside the cleft. Avoid peaches that display tan spots, which are an early sign of decay.

To ripen peaches, store them in a single layer in a brown paper bag at room temperature. If you leave these delicate fruits in the open, they tend to shrivel because their skin doesn't contain natural protective oils. White-fleshed fruits ripen almost twice as fast as those with yellow flesh, such as nectarines.

Store fully ripened peaches in a paper bag in the refrigerator for up to five days.

# Pitting and Slicing a Peach

**ONE:** Start with firm but ripe freestone or semi-freestone fruits. Use a sharp paring knife and, starting at the stem end, cut through the natural cleft and then all the way around the peach, rotating your hand with the peach and ending back at the stem end, making sure to cut all the way through to the stone.

**TWO:** Firmly grasp the two halves and twist them in opposite directions. One half will pop off, leaving the second half attached to the stone. If the peach resists, repeat, scraping at the stone to make sure you have cut all the way through.

**THREE:** Insert the tip of the paring knife between the edge of the pit and peach and pry the pit free. If the pit resists, see Step 4.

**FOUR:** If the pit resists, cut the pitted half in half again, cutting through to the stone again. Twist off the first wedge. The remaining wedge will be attached to the stone and will be easy to twist off.

**FIVE:** To cut into slices, cut each section of the peach into three or four slices from the flesh side toward the skin. (The riper the peach, the easier it will bruise, so it's important to use a sharp knife.)

# Peeling a Peach

Peaches don't require peeling for baking because their nutrient-rich skins add color and flavor, but for those who prefer their peaches peeled, here's how:

**ONE:** With a paring knife, cut an "x" on the bottom end of the peach.

**TWO:** Bring a pot of water to a boil and prepare a bowl of ice water. Gently drop ripe peaches into the pot. Leave peaches in hot water for 1 minute. With a slotted spoon, scoop the peaches out and place in ice water until ready to peel.

**THREE:** Starting at the "x" cut, slowly peel back skin using the paring knife to loosen the tip and get you started. Continue on all sides until completely peeled.

# Label Savvy

## Read a Nutrition Label Like a Pro

You don't need a PhD to read a nutrition facts panel. Here's your quick guide to deciphering the little box on all food packaging.

**Calories:** The number of calories is calculated based on a single serving. So, be sure to multiply the number of calories based on the number of servings you actually consume. As well, multiply all other nutrition data similarly, especially fats and sodium numbers.

**TIP:** Use the "Calories From Fat" section on your food labels to help you meal plan for the day. Balance out foods with a high number of calories from fat, such as heart-healthy olive oil, with foods that have a lower number, such as salad greens.

## Nutrition Facts

Serving Size 3 oz. (85g)

| Amount Per Serving | As Served |
|---|---|
| **Calories** 38 | **Calories from Fat** 0 |

| | % Daily Value |
|---|---|
| **Total Fat** 0g | 0% |
| **Saturated Fat** 0g | 0% |
| **Cholesterol** 0g | 0% |
| **Sodium** 0g | 2% |
| **Total Carbohydrate** 0g | 3% |
| Dietary Fiber 0g | 8% |
| Sugars 0g | |
| **Protein** 0g | |

| | | | |
|---|---|---|---|
| **Vitamin A** 270% | • | **Vitamin C** 10% | |
| **Calcium** 2% | • | **Iron** 0% | |

Percent Daily Values are based on a 2,000 calorie diet. Your daily values may be higher or lower depending on your calorie needs:

| | | Calories | 2,000 | 2,500 |
|---|---|---|---|---|
| Total Fat | Less than | | 65g | 80g |
| Sat Fat | Less than | | 20g | 80g |
| Cholesterol | Less than | | 300mg | 300mg |
| Sodium | Less than | | 2,400mg | 2,400mg |
| Total Carbohydrate | | | 300g | 375g |
| Dietary Fiber | | | 25g | 30g |

**Serving size:** "All of the information on the label relates to this number," explains Joan Salge Blake, MS, RD, spokesperson for the American Dietetic Association. It's important to know how a single serving measures up.

**% DV:** Denotes "percent of daily value" of certain nutrients. A %DV greater than 20 means the food is high in that nutrient; a value lower than five means the food is low in that nutrient.

# Ingredients to Watch Out For

Even foods that seem wholesome may contain additives you might consider avoiding. Keep an eye out for these three:

## Oxidation inhibitors

Dried fruits and seafoods are often laced with sulfites to prevent discoloration. These inhibitors have been shown to trigger severe allergic reactions, such as quickened heartbeat, rashes, wheezing, upset stomach, dizziness or fainting in some, even if you don't have a history of sulfite sensitivity. Luckily, the FDA banned the use of sulfites on raw fruits and vegetables.

## Flavor enhancers

Yeast extract, autolyzed yeast and hydrolyzed vegetable protein are used to add flavor to processed foods (even those employing natural ingredients), from mock meat products and veggie burgers to chicken broth and organic macaroni and cheese. Trouble is, nearly all of them contain free glutamate, the substance in MSG that may cause headaches and nervousness in some people.

## Preservatives

Sodium benzoate is ubiquitous in processed foods, from fruit juices to pickles to hummus. Researchers believe it may cause cell damage when combined with ascorbic acid (vitamin C) because the pairing creates the chemical benzene, a known carcinogen.

# Label Lingo

Labels, starbursts, banners and the like on food packages often make big promises that persuade you to buy, but what do they really mean? Here's the lowdown.

## "Zero trans fats"

Trans fats – which increase "bad" LDL cholesterol and decrease beneficial HDL cholesterol – are created when hydrogens are added to liquid vegetable oils. The "zero trans fats" label means the food in question contains less than 0.5 grams of trans fats per serving.

## "Fat free"

A product labeled "fat free" must contain less than 0.5 grams of fat per serving. *Note: Because removal of fat often causes foods to lose flavor, the products displaying this notification often contain artificial sweeteners or added sugars as enhancers of taste. Be careful.*

## "Organic"

To be eligible for this rating, produce has to have been grown without pesticides or synthetic fertilizer; if an animal product is to carry this rating, the animals must have been raised free from antibiotics and growth hormones. A product labeled "organic" consists of a minimum of 95 percent organically produced ingredients.

## "Free range"

Animals that are "free range" have access to outdoor grazing areas and are not confined to cages. *Note: Some farmers, however, still limit the space their animals can roam (a practice called yarding when referring to poultry).*

# Beverages

Everybody's Favorite, p. 266

The Alkalizer, p. 266

Red, She Said, p. 267

Sweet Morning Eye-Opener, p. 267

Let's Go Green!, p. 267

Drink your way to good health with our collection of carefully chosen clean beverages. These selections are fast, flavorful and brimming with vitamins and minerals. Kick-start a busy day with a Mango Shake or unwind with a Cocoa Spiced Latte while sitting by the fire. You'll love our kid-friendly options too – the Candy Cane Hot Chocolate Mix is a must-try. With these yummy beverages, you'll definitely feel the goodness of nutrition in a glass.

# Blood Orange Pomegranate Spritzer

*Serves* 4. ***Hands-on time:*** *10 minutes.* ***Total time:*** *10 minutes.*

**This fresh and fizzy drink is definitely a multitasker! It will stylishly quench your thirst while boosting your immune system.**

## INGREDIENTS:

- 24 fresh spearmint leaves
- Ice (enough to fill 4 glasses)
- ¾ cup fresh-squeezed blood orange juice, strained
- ½ cup bottled 100% pomegranate juice
- 2 packets powdered stevia
- 2 cups sparkling water

## INSTRUCTIONS:

ONE: Divide mint leaves among 4 glasses. Using a spoon, lightly bruise leaves in bottom of each glass. Fill glasses with ice.

TWO: In a pitcher, stir together orange juice, pomegranate juice and stevia. Add sparking water and stir gently to combine. Divide spritzer mixture evenly among 4 glasses. Serve immediately.

*Nutrients per 6½-oz serving: Calories: 41, Total Fat: 0.25 g, Sat. Fat: 0 g, Carbs: 9 g, Fiber: 0.5 g, Sugars: 7 g, Protein: 0.5 g, Sodium: 5 mg, Cholesterol: 0 mg*

.................................................................................

# Mango Shakes

*Serves* 4. ***Hands-on time:*** *10 minutes.* ***Total time:*** *40 minutes.*

**This cool and refreshing skim-milk shake gets its yellow color from ripe mango and sweet-sour pineapple, and a welcome kick from crystallized ginger.**

## INGREDIENTS:

- 1 mango, peeled and sliced (2 cups)
- ½ fresh medium pineapple, cored, peeled and chopped (about 1 cup)
- 1 tsp organic crystallized ginger, chopped
- 1 cup skim milk
- 1 Tbsp raw honey
- 4 to 6 ice cubes
- Fresh mint, chopped, optional

## INSTRUCTIONS:

ONE: Place mango and pineapple on a large baking sheet and freeze for 30 minutes.

TWO: Process frozen mango and pineapple along with ginger, milk, honey and ice in a blender until smooth, stopping occasionally to scrape down sides of blender jar. (Add more liquid or let mixture settle for a few minutes if you prefer a thinner consistency.)

*Nutrients per 1-cup serving: Calories: 104, Total Fat: 0.25 g, Sat. Fat: 0 g, Carbs: 26 g, Fiber: 2 g, Sugars: 21 g, Protein: 3 g, Sodium: 34 mg, Cholesterol: 1 mg*

**Nutritional Bonus:**
Famous for its stores of immune-boosting, free-radical-fighting vitamin C, the orange is also a good source of thiamine, folic acid and vitamin B6, which keep nerve cells healthy, repair assorted cells and help create the feel-good chemical serotonin, respectively. Plus, both oranges and pomegranates are rich in potassium, an essential mineral needed to regulate water balance, blood pressure and muscle and nerve cell function.

Blood-Orange Pomegranate Spritzer

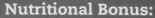

**Nutritional Bonus:** Sweetening this family favorite with natural ingredients such as Sucanat, instead of traditional white sugar, allows this holiday hit to become a lower-glycemic liquid treat.

Candy Cane Hot Chocolate Mix

# Candy Cane Hot Chocolate Mix

*Serves 14. **Hands-on time:** 5 minutes. **Total time:** 5 minutes.*

**Instead of adding chunks of sugar-filled candy cane to this classic, we've given it a healthy twist with no compromise on taste. Look for high-quality organic peppermint loose-leaf tea to ensure you get the most authentic flavor with some additional antioxidant benefits to boot. HINT: Our mix makes perfect stocking-stuffers for pennies a bag!**

## INGREDIENTS:

- 2 cups skim milk powder
- ½ cup Sucanat
- ½ cup unsweetened cocoa powder
- 2 Tbsp peppermint tea leaves, crumbled
- 1 cup dark chocolate (70% cocoa or greater), chopped
- Cinnamon sticks, for garnish, optional

## INSTRUCTIONS:

In a bowl, stir together skim milk powder, Sucanat, cocoa powder, tea leaves and dark chocolate. Spoon into an airtight container, seal and store at room temperature for up to 1 month.

**TO BREW:** Stir ¼ cup hot chocolate mix into 1 cup very hot skim milk until mix is dissolved and well blended. Garnish with cinnamon stick, if desired.

*Nutrients per ¼-cup mix: Calories: 170, Total Fat: 5 g, Sat. Fat: 3.5 g, Carbs: 28 g, Fiber: 2 g, Sugars: 20 g, Protein: 7 g, Sodium 380 mg, Cholesterol: 0 mg*

# Gingered Hot Chocolate

*Serves 4. **Hands-on time:** 5 minutes. **Total time:** 5 minutes.*

**Opting for dark chocolate squares rather than cocoa powder for this traditional wintertime beverage may take an extra minute or two, but the creamy, rich results are well worth a few swirls of the whisk.**

## INGREDIENTS:

- 3.5 oz dark chocolate (85% cocoa), broken into squares
- 2 cups skim milk
- 2 cups water
- 2 tsp ground ginger
- 2 Tbsp plus 2 tsp honey

## INSTRUCTIONS:

Combine all ingredients in a 2½-qt saucepan and place over lowest heat setting on stovetop. As chocolate slowly melts, whisk often to prevent chocolate from clumping and burning, about 3 minutes. When chocolate is fully melted, whisk one last time before pouring mixture into four mugs, dividing evenly. Serve hot.

*Nutrients per 8-oz serving: Calories: 214, Total Fat: 9 g, Sat. Fat: 6 g, Monounsaturated Fat: 0 g, Polyunsaturated Fat: 0 g, Carbs: 27 g, Fiber: 3 g, Sugars: 22 g, Protein: 7 g, Sodium: 65 mg, Cholesterol: 2 mg*

# Cocoa Spiced Lattes

*Serves 6. **Hands-on time:** 10 minutes. **Total time:** 15 minutes.*

**Lattes are traditionally made with espresso, so we recommend either using an espresso-style coffee in this homemade treat (TRY: Bustelo and Pilon) or simply increasing the strength of your regular brew. And, if you're not a fan of caffeine, decaf may always be substituted.**

## INGREDIENTS:

- 3 cups low-fat milk
- 2½ Tbsp unsweetened natural cocoa powder (not Dutch-process)
- 1½ tsp pure vanilla extract
- ¼ scant tsp ground cardamom
- 3 cups strong brewed coffee (24 oz)
- CE-approved sweetener, such as stevia, optional

## INSTRUCTIONS:

**ONE:** In a medium saucepan, combine milk, cocoa, vanilla and cardamom and place on medium-high heat. Keep a close eye on milk to avoid scorching and whisk frequently until steam begins to form, 5 to 10 minutes. Reduce heat to medium-low and whisk constantly until cocoa is dissolved and milk is hot and frothy; avoid boiling.

**TWO:** Fill six mugs halfway with coffee (about ½ cup each). Add about ½ cup hot milk mixture to each mug and serve with sweetener, as desired.

*Nutrients per 8-oz serving: Calories: 64, Total Fat: 2 g, Sat. Fat: 1 g, Carbs: 8 g, Fiber: 1 g, Sugars: 6 g, Protein: 5 g, Sodium: 68 mg, Cholesterol: 8 mg*

**For a photo of this recipe see page 21.**

# Homemade Orange-Ginger Soda

*Serves 4. **Hands-on time:** 5 minutes. **Total time:** 5 minutes.*

Making your own soda is almost too easy to be true: Start with unflavored sparkling water and then add your own fresh juices, herbs or extracts (vanilla and almond are surefire crowd pleasers!) and finish with a bit of honey.

## INGREDIENTS:

- 2 oranges, cut into halves
- 1 2-inch piece ginger, peeled and cut into 4 lengths (about ½ inch each)
- 2 tsp raw honey
- 32 oz plain sparkling water
- Ice cubes, optional

## INSTRUCTIONS:

Working one glass at a time, squeeze juice from one orange half into glass. Pass one piece of ginger through a garlic press and add ginger juice to glass, discarding remaining fibers. Add ½ tsp honey and 8 oz sparkling water to each glass. Stir or whisk thoroughly to combine. Serve with ice cubes, if desired.

**Nutrients per 8-oz serving:** *Calories: 44, Total Fat: 0 g, Sat. Fat: 0 g, Carbs: 11 g, Fiber: 0 g, Sugars: 9 g, Protein: 0.5 g, Sodium: 0.5 mg, Cholesterol: 0 mg*

## Nutritional Bonus:

Ground ginger is good, but fresh ginger is better: It alleviates motion sickness, provides relief for arthritis and migraines, and lowers cholesterol levels. Try adding ginger juice to beverages and dressings or making teas with freshly sliced ginger root.

# Cranberry-Orange Wassail

*Serves 4. **Hands-on time:** 10 minutes. **Total time:** 35 minutes.*

This modern-day twist on a classic European beverage uses cranberries and honey in place of traditional apples and white sugar. (We left out the brandy to make this a kid-friendly option!) Feel free to tone down the spices to suit your tastes – experiment with half the amount of nutmeg and cloves and leave out the cardamom.

## INGREDIENTS:

- 2 cinnamon sticks or 2 tsp ground cinnamon
- 10 whole cloves or ½ tsp ground cloves
- 8 whole allspice berries or 1½ tsp ground allspice
- 3 cardamom pods or ½ tsp ground cardamom, optional
- 1 piece ginger root (½ inch long), peeled
- Juice and zest 1 orange
- 1½ cups cranberries, fresh or frozen
- 4½ cups water
- ¼ cup raw honey
- ¾ tsp ground nutmeg

## EQUIPMENT:

- Cheesecloth

## INSTRUCTIONS:

**ONE:** Place cinnamon sticks, cloves, allspice and cardamom, if desired, on a 6 x 6-inch square of cheesecloth; smash them slightly to break them up. Add ginger and orange zest, then pull corners of cheesecloth together and twist to form a secure bag. Tie bag shut with a clean 12-inch-long piece of cotton string and tie a loop at the end to make the bag easy to retrieve later on. (If you're using ground spices, simply tie ginger and zest inside of cheesecloth pouch.)

**TWO:** Place pouch and remaining ingredients into a 2½-qt saucepan, whisk to combine and bring to a boil. Immediately reduce heat to low and let simmer for 15 minutes.

**THREE:** Mash simmering cranberries with a potato masher. Let mixture simmer for an additional 10 minutes. Remove spice pouch.

**FOUR:** Strain mixture into a bowl or pitcher, using the back of a spoon to press the juice out of the cranberry skins. Discard skins and all other solids in strainer. Divide wassail into four mugs. Serve hot.

**Nutrients per 6-oz serving:** *Calories: 103, Total Fat: 0.25 g, Sat. Fat: 0 g, Carbs: 27 g, Fiber: 3 g, Sugars: 22 g, Protein: 0.5 g, Sodium: 2 mg, Cholesterol: 0 mg*

Cranberry-
Orange
Wassail

## Nutritional Bonus:
Thanks to this brew's spices, you can expect not only fresh breath but also a boost to your body's anti-inflammatory responses. A serving of wassail also offers almost a quarter of your day's vitamin C in a single 6-oz glass!

# Mulled Pomegranate Orange Sipper

*Serves 4. **Hands-on time:** 5 minutes. **Total time:** 25 minutes.*

When the cold winter winds begin to blow, what could be better than curling up with a warm mulled beverage? How about curling up with a warm mulled beverage *Clean Eating*-style? We've omitted the alcohol and sugar, kept the spices and thrown in some all-powerful pomegranate. Cheers!

## INGREDIENTS:

- 2 cups unsweetened pomegranate juice
- Peel 1 orange
- ½ cup fresh orange juice (from about 2 oranges)
- ½ cup water
- 2 cinnamon sticks
- 6 cloves, whole
- 2 tsp raw organic honey

## INSTRUCTIONS:

**ONE:** Combine all ingredients in a medium saucepot over medium heat. Cover pot and simmer for at least 20 minutes.

**TWO:** Strain cinnamon sticks and cloves from liquid and divide mulled juice into mugs.

**THREE:** Serve with or without orange peel pieces in beverage, as garnish.

*Nutrients per 6-oz serving: Calories: 100, Total Fat: 0 g, Sat. Fat: 0 g, Carbs: 24 g, Fiber: 0 g, Sugars: 15 g, Protein: 1 g, Sodium: 15 mg, Cholesterol: 0 mg*

## Nutritional Bonus:

Rich in flavonoids (namely catechins and kaempferols), green tea's antioxidant and anti-carcinogenic properties have now become famous. But numerous studies have shown that the tea may also help reduce your risk of diabetes, promote mental alertness and lower stress hormone levels.

# Green Tea Pomegranate Lemonade

*Serves 8. **Hands-on time:** 5 minutes. **Total time:** 37 minutes (includes chilling time).*

The popular tea boasts a smorgasbord of health benefits, and, thanks to *Clean Eating*, a bevy of flavors as well. The sweet side of pomegranate balances the tartness of the lemon juice.

## INGREDIENTS:

- 7 green tea bags
- 7 cups hot water
- ¾ cup Sucanat
- ¾ to 1 cup fresh lemon juice
- ¼ cup 100% pomegranate juice
- Ice cubes, as required
- Lemon slices and fresh mint for garnish (optional)

**TIP: If you like your lemonade a bit less tart, use only ¾ cup lemon juice in your brew.**

## INSTRUCTIONS:

In a large bowl or pitcher, combine tea bags and water, steeping bags for 5 minutes. Add Sucanat, then lemon and pomegranate juices, stirring until Sucanat is dissolved. Chill for at least 30 minutes. Discard bags, add ice and pour into glasses. Serve garnished with a lemon slice and mint, if desired.

*Nutrients per 4-oz serving: Calories: 81, Total Fat: 0 g, Sat. Fat: 0 g, Carbs: 21 g, Fiber: 0 g, Sugars: 18 g, Protein: 0 g, Sodium: 21 mg, Cholesterol: 0 mg*

**NUTRITIONAL BONUS: Pomegranate is an excellent source of potassium, an essential mineral that supports kidney function, and is also an energy-supplying electrolyte.**

# Juicer Juices

Juicing is one of the easiest and most delicious ways to maximize your health. With a few of your favorite seasonal fruits and veggies and the press of a button, you can easily transform a wide variety of healthful ingredients into a delicious beverage that's full of the vitamins and minerals you need to stay at your best. In this mini-section, you'll find a number of our tastiest (and most intriguingly titled) selections.

## Everybody's Favorite

*Serves* 1.

INGREDIENTS:

- 3 cups spinach
- 2 to 3 carrots
- 1 apple
- 1 beet
- 1-inch square peeled chunk fresh ginger (or more if you like it hot)

INSTRUCTIONS:

ONE: Wash spinach and apple and scrub carrots and beet but do not peel.

TWO: Peel ginger.

THREE: Juice everything, stir gently and enjoy.

Nutrients per serving: *Calories: 212, Total Fat: 0.75 g, Sat. Fat: 0 g, Carbs: 53 g, Fiber: 14 g, Sugars: 30 g, Protein: 5 g, Sodium: 266 mg, Cholesterol: 0 mg*

NUTRITIONAL BONUS: **The spinach provides lutein and zeaxanthin, two important carotenoids for eye health.**

## The Alkalizer

*Serves* 1.

INGREDIENTS:

- ½ cucumber
- 1 carrot
- ½ cup packed parsley
- 3 stalks celery
- ¼ lime

INSTRUCTIONS:

ONE: Wash vegetables and parsley very well and shake to dry.

TWO: Slice cucumber portion in half lengthwise so it will fit easily into the juicer's feeder.

THREE: Juice cucumber and carrot. Juice parsley, and then finish with celery.

FOUR: Squeeze lime into juice, stir gently and enjoy.

Nutrients per serving: *Calories: 80, Total Fat: 0.5 g, Sat. Fat: 0 g, Carbs: 17 g, Fiber: 6 g, Sugars: 8 g, Protein: 4 g, Sodium: 155 mg, Cholesterol: 0 mg*

NUTRITIONAL BONUS: **Parsley is one of the world's most popular herbs and it's known for its detoxifying properties. The National Cancer Institute found that umbelliferous vegetables (of which parsley is one, along with others like carrots and parsnips) are among a select group of foods with the highest anti-cancer activity.**

# Red, She Said

*Serves 1.*

INGREDIENTS:

- 1 red bell pepper, quartered, seeds removed
- 1 apple
- 2 radishes
- 1 tomato
- ½ cup fresh or frozen cranberries

INSTRUCTIONS:

ONE: Wash pepper, apple, radishes and tomato, but don't peel.

TWO: Juice everything, stir gently and enjoy.

*Nutrients per serving: Calories: 177, Total Fat: 1 g, Sat. Fat: 0 g, Carbs: 43 g, Fiber: 10.5 g, Sugars: 29 g, Protein: 3 g, Sodium: 17 mg, Cholesterol: 0 mg*

**NUTRITIONAL BONUS: The red bell pepper found in this homemade juice recipe is an ideal immunity booster. One medium pepper offers a jaw-dropping 253% of your daily vitamin C fix, a well-known immune system supporter. The sweet veggie also offers over 17% of your daily need of vitamin B6, a multitasker that helps in the synthesis of disease-fighting immune system antibodies.**

# Let's Go Green!

*Serves 1.*

INGREDIENTS:

- 1 pear
- 4 stalks celery
- 1 parsnip
- 1 cucumber
- 1 stalk broccoli, stem and florets, optional

INSTRUCTIONS:

ONE: Wash everything. Don't peel parsnip or cucumber.

TWO: Juice everything, stir and enjoy.

*Nutrients per serving: Calories: 249, Total Fat: 0.5 g, Sat. Fat: 0 g, Carbs: 62 g, Fiber: 18 g, Sugars: 30 g, Protein: 5 g, Sodium: 243 mg, Cholesterol: 0 mg*

**NUTRITIONAL BONUS: Celery is a great source of silicon, a little-known trace mineral that figures in strong bones, joints, skin, hair and nails. Sulforaphane, a phytonutrient abundant in broccoli and often touted for its anti-cancer properties, may also help eliminate the stomach bacteria Helicobacter pylori (H. pylori).**

# Sweet Morning Eye-Opener

*Serves 1.*

INGREDIENTS:

- 2 carrots
- 1 red apple (try Delicious, Fuji or Pink Lady)
- 1-inch square peeled chunk of fresh ginger (or more if you like it hot)

INSTRUCTIONS:

ONE: Scrub carrots and apple; wash but do not peel.

TWO: Peel ginger.

THREE: Juice everything, stir gently and enjoy.

*Nutrients per serving: Calories: 149, Total Fat: 0.65 g, Sat. Fat: 0 g, Carbs: 38 g, Fiber: 8 g, Sugars: 25 g, Protein: 2 g, Sodium: 07 mg, Cholesterol: 0 mg*

For photos of all five of these recipes, see pages 256-257.

**Nutritional Bonus:**
Apples are a great source of boron, a mineral that supports strong bones. They also contain quercetin, a potent anti-inflammatory. But make sure to juice the skin since that's where most of the helpful compound is concentrated.

# Credits

## Contributors:

Peter Agostinelli, Robin Asbell, Susan Bentley, Anna Lee Boschetto, Jonny Bowden, PHD, CNS, Paula Bowman, Sandy Cordeiro, Tara Mataraza Desmond, Jason Gaskins, Pamela Graver, Aliza Green, Nicole Hamaker, Jessica Goldbogen Harlan, Tiffany Haugen, Jill Silverman Hough, Lisa Howard, Nancy S. Hughes, Jeanette Hurt, Jennifer Iserloh, Dianne Jacob, Scot Jones, Alison Lewis, Joanne Lusted, Christina Machamer, Jennifer MacKenzie, Allison Makowski, Linda Melone, Nancy Midwicki, Robin Miller, Diane Morgan, Julie O'Hara, Tosca Reno, Alicia Rewega, Victoria Abbott Riccardi, Claire Robinson, Amy Rosen, Jessie Shafer, Nicole Springle, RD, Lisa Turner, Diane Welland, MS, RD, Marianne Wren, Allison Young, Nicole Young

*All new recipes created by Joanne Lusted*

## Photographers:

Buceta, Paul: 118

Chou, Peter: 75-76, 232-233, 240

Duivenvoorden, Yvonne: 12, 14, 17-18, 21-22, 25, 38, 42, 53, 106-107, 117, 120-121, 135, 149, 157, 166, 177-178, 192, 196, 235-236, 239

Griffith, Donna: 45, 95-96, 114, 124, 130, 140, 146, 153, 161-162, 181, 187-188, 216, 218-219, 221-223, 225, 229, 244, 251, 256-257

Pond, Edward: 10-11, 28-29, 31, 36, 57, 61-62, 78-79, 81, 84-85, 88, 92, 98, 123, 127-128, 132, 137, 139, 145, 154, 158, 165, 169-170, 184, 191, 194, 200, 202-203, 205, 208, 210-213, 215, 243, 247, 259-260

Pudge, Jodi: 13, 26, 32, 35, 41, 46, 50-51, 65-66, 69, 91, 104, 111-112, 143, 174, 183, 199, 226, 230-231, 248, 263, 100-101

Reynolds, Bradley: 211 (scallops in pan)

Tsakos, Joanne: 47, 49, 54, 58-59, 64, 70-71, 82, 87, 103, 108-109, 133, 138, 150-151, 167, 172-173, 207, 214, 238, 246, 253, 264

iStock: 39, 48, 71 (bottom right), 99, 206, 211 (frying pan), 212 (bowl of salt), 252, 254-255, 267

**Cover Photography by Donna Griffith**

**Back Cover Photography:** Jodi Pudge (Pita Paninis with Tuna, Sprouts, Zucchini and Avocado Cream, p. 175), **Yvonne Duivenvoorden** (French Toast with Dark Cherry-Citrus Topping, p. 16), **Donna Griffith** (Spatchcock Chicken with Porcini Bread Crumbs & Garlic Rapini, p. 163; Creole Manhattan Clam Chowder, p. 97; Quinoa-Stuffed Collard Green Rolls, p. 189; Parmesan Panko Crusted Turkey with Cornbread & Sausage Stuffing, p. 220; Chocolate Chip Cookie Dough Chocolate Cake, p. 245), **Edward Pond** (Spaghetti & Meatball Casserole, p. 138)

## Food Stylists:

Ashley Denton: 17-18, 25, 31, 35-36, 38, 41-42, 46, 76, 88, 106-107, 120-121, 127, 132, 149, 154, 157, 178, 191-192, 196, 200

Adele Hagan: 26, 32, 69, 75, 117, 123, 135, 143, 145, 169, 174, 199, 202-203, 205, 208, 215

Lucie Richard: 28-29, 57, 92, 137, 165, 194, 232-233, 240, 243

Claire Stubbs: 12-14, 22, 45, 50-51, 53, 65-66, 78-79, 84-85, 87, 91, 95, 96, 114, 124, 130, 140, 146, 153, 161-162, 173, 181, 184, 187-188, 216, 218-219, 221-223, 225, 229, 236, 239, 244, 251, 260

SugarTart: 47, 49, 54, 58-59, 64, 70, 71, 82, 108-109, 172, 238

Marianne Wren: 103-104, 111-112, 133, 138, 150-151, 158, 166-167, 177, 183, 207, 210-214, 235, 246, 253, 256-257, 264

Nicole Young: 10-11, 21, 61-62, 81, 98, 100-101, 128, 139, 170, 226, 230-231, 247-248, 259, 263

## Prop Stylists:

Martine Blackhurst, Laura Branson, Catherine Doherty, Lynda Felton, Madeleine Johari, Jay Junnila, Carolyn Souch, Genevieve Wiseman

## Models:

Pamela Graver (hands), Virginia Kingston, Jennifer MacKenzie (hands), Tosca Reno

## Hair & Make-up:

Franca Tarullo (Tosca Reno)

# Index

THE BEST OF CLEAN EATING 2